THE POLITICS
OF MARGINALITY

Race, the Radical Right and Minorities
in Twentieth Century Britain

Edited by
TONY KUSHNER and **KENNETH LUNN**

FRANK CASS

First published 1990 in Great Britain by
FRANK CASS & CO. LTD
Gainsborough House, 11 Gainsborough Road,
London E11 1RS, England

and in the United States of America by
FRANK CASS
c/o Rowman & Littlefield Publishers Inc.
8705 Bollman Place, Savage MD 20763, USA

British Library Cataloguing in Publication Data

The politics of marginality: race, the Radical Right and
minorities in twentieth century Britain.
1. Great Britain. Racism, history   2. Great Britain.
Facism. Political aspects, history
I. Kushner, Tony   II. Lunn, Kenneth   III. Immigrants and
minorities
305.8′00941

ISBN 0-7146-3391-7

Library of Congress Cataloging in Publication Data

The Politics of marginality : race, the radical right, and minorities
in twentieth century Britain / edited by Tony Kushner and Kenneth
Lunn.
   p.   cm.
   "Immigrants and minorities special issue 8.1."
   ISBN 0-7146-3391-7 : £19.50
   1. Minorities—Great Britain—History—20th century.   2. Great
Britain—Politics and government—20th century.   3. Great Britain-
-Race relations.   4. Conservatism—Great Britain—History —20th
century.   5. Radicalism—Great Britain—History—20th century.
6. Racism—Great Britain—History—20th century.   I. Kushner, Tony
(Antony Robin Jeremy)   II. Lunn, Kenneth.
DA 125.A1P65   1989   89-25202
305.8′00941—dc20   CIP

This group of studies first appeared in a Special Issue: 'The Politics of Marginality: Race, the Radical Right and Minorities in Twentieth Century Britain' of *Immigrants and Minorities,* Vol. 8, No. 1, published by Frank Cass & Co. Ltd.

Typeset by Selectmove Ltd. London
Printed in Great Britain by
Antony Rowe Ltd, Chippenham

Contents

Notes on Contributors

David Cesarani is Director of Studies at the Wiener Library and Institute of Contemporary History. He is currently writing a history of English Zionism in the inter-war period and has edited a forthcoming collection of essays on Anglo-Jewish history for Blackwell.

Bryan Cheyette is British Academy Fellow in the School of English at the University of Leeds. He is literary editor of the Jewish Quarterly and is currently writing a study of *Jewish Representations in English Literature and Society, 1875–1925: A Study in Semitism.*

Martin Durham is a Lecturer in Politics at Wolverhampton Polytechnic and is researching aspects of right-wing politics in Britain. He has published on the Thatcher government and the 'moral right' and is presently completing a book on the subject. He is also about to publish an essay on women and the National Front.

Tony Kushner is Parkes Fellow in the Department of History, University of Southampton. He is author of *The Persistence of Prejudice: Antisemitism in British Society During the Second World War* (Manchester, 1989) and with Kenneth Lunn, *Traditions of Intolerance: Historical perspectives on fascism and race discourse in Britain* (Manchester, 1989).

Kenneth Lunn is Principal Lecturer in the School of Social and Historical Studies, Portsmouth Polytechnic. He is an editor of *Immigrants and Minorities* and has published articles on the history of British anti-Semitism and on the British labour movement's attitudes to immigration and race. He is currently writing a social history of British labour since 1870.

David Mayall is Senior Lecturer in Social History, Sheffield City Polytechnic. He is the author of *Gypsy-travellers in Nineteenth-century Society* (Cambridge, 1988) and co-editor (with John Burnett and David Vincent) of *The Autobiography of the Working Class: A Critical Annotated Bibliography, Vol.1, 1790–1900* (Brighton, 1984) and *Vol. 2, 1900–1945* (Brighton, 1987).

Mark Mitchell is Head of the School of Social and Historical Studies at Portsmouth Polytechnic. His previous publications include articles on social theory and he has written several pieces with Dave Russell on racism and current politics in South Africa and Britain. His current research interests include the development of anti-racist professional practice in Britain.

Panikos Panayi is lecturer in History at the University of Keele. He is author of *The Enemy in our Midst: Germans in Britain During the First World War*, to be published in Summer 1990.

Dave Russell is Senior Lecturer in the School of Social and Historical Studies, Portsmouth Polytechnic. He has written articles in collaboration with Mark Mitchell on race and politics in Britain and South Africa.

Henry Srebrnik obtained a PhD at Birmingham University for a thesis on Jewish politics in the East End of London. He has worked as a journalist on the *Washington Jewish Post* and is currently teaching history at Gettysburg College, Pennsylvania.

Julie Wheelwright is a freelance writer and the author of *Amazons and Military Maids: Women who Dressed as Men in Pursuit of Life, Liberty and Happiness* (Pandora Press, 1989). She lives in London and is currently writing a biography of traveller, Rosita Forbes.

Stella Yarrow has studied history and Italian at the University of Sussex and has written a study of Germans in Britain during the First World War. She is currently working as a researcher for *Which* magazine in London.

Preface

'Schools need more English history, more kings and bishops. . .The non-existent history of ethnic entities and women leads to incoherent syllabuses.'
Sir Geoffrey Elton at the Historical Association lobby,
House of Lords, 13 January 1986

The aim of this collection of essays is, above all, to try to produce work which will help challenge the oft-stated need for more British history, 'British' (or 'English') being defined as 'Anglo-Saxon' and unwilling to acknowledge racism, conflict, intolerance and ethnicity as part of mainstream society. Such writing and research is still not recognised as significant in widening the scope of British history; indeed, some of the contributors to this volume have been unable to find permanent academic employment in Britain, an indication of the marginalization still of the subject material. Our thanks go, therefore, to Frank Cass for his commitment to this project and to Lydia Linford at Frank Cass and Company for her tolerance and support. Sybil Lunn prepared the index.

TONY KUSHNER
KENNETH LUNN

Editors' Introduction

Immigration to Britain has rarely achieved the levels experienced by the United States. Yet, despite the smaller numbers, it is nevertheless true of all periods of British history that 'immigrants, refugees and soujourners have been continually present'.[1] That few historians have acknowledged this fact is, perhaps, a measure of the scope and tenacity of British xenophobia. The irony that insularity has led to a failure to recognize the ethnic diversity of the British is compounded by an equal reluctance to identify a parallel tradition of intolerance towards the ethnic, racial and religious minorities of 'John Bull's Island'.[2] Unlike America, the study of immigration, minority groups and racism has not concerned the 'mainstream' of historians of Britain.[3] If, therefore, those brave enough to examine this uncharted and disdained area of study have been consigned to ghettos, the fault lies not with the immigrant and minority specialist but in the narrowness of vision of the general historical profession in Britain.[4] This apportioning of blame may lead the specialist into a position of self-satisfaction and complacency. The loneliness of the route and the enormity of the task of covering so neglected an area are, however, no excuses for historians of immigrants and minorities. Their failure to engage in dialogue with one another (for example, those interested in Anglo-Jewish and black minorities have paid little attention to each others' work), or indeed with the generalist by putting their work in a broader context, is marked. The purpose of this volume is to open up further discussion of this new area of history.

The first products of what might be called the 'Sheffield school' for the historical study of immigration, minorities, racism and Fascism in Britain have been important for breaking new ground.[5] *Immigrants and Minorities*, launched in 1982, is one particular representation of this approach. However, there is now a need for more intensive debate. In this field, sociologists of race and race relations in Britain have a head start — they have already formulated a theoretical basis for their work. One can sympathize with Paul Rich's comment that 'the main task that confronts researchers in (race relations) is less one of intellectual pyrotechnics and endless debates over sociological theorising and nomenclature, but hard and detailed empirical research into an area that is rich in sources'.[6] Nevertheless, this is no reason for the historian not to emulate the sociologists and to develop not only empirical research but also more theoretical and analytical frameworks as a consequence of debate with each other. While we may have the beginnings of a history of immigration, ethnicity and race in Britain, there is a lack of historiographical awareness in the subjects. The essays in this collection, ranging from specific case studies to broad themes, are thus an attempt to provide a basis for future discussion.

The first section of the collection deals with the previously neglected or trivialized area of gender and Fascism. Discussions on women and Fascism have begun to make some impact on the general theme of Fascism but the bulk of the work has concentrated on continental Europe, particularly Germany and Italy. By comparison, consideration of the British dimension has been almost non-existent. Several themes have been identified in the recent literature: for example, Lesley Caldwell's essay on women and the family in Fascist Italy[7] has drawn attention to the similarities between Fascist policy and that of the 'democracies' in the inter-war years. However, it is clearly the context within which such measures were introduced which determines the reactionary implications for women and Caldwell is careful to identify the 'lived forms of a culture',[8] the ways in which individuals and groups respond to and initiate attitudes within any particular situation, which define the exact nature of the impact of such policies. Claudia Koonz has, in her major survey on women and the family in Nazi politics,[9] produced perhaps an even more challenging thesis in that she appears to identify women's role in Nazism as an essential safe haven from which the perpetrators of the Holocaust could seek refuge from the enormity of their crimes. As Jane Caplan has written: 'Her provocative conclusion is that German women were so eager to cultivate their separate sphere that they not only welcomed the Nazi promise of masculine protection, but actively, if perhaps unwittingly, facilitated the very worst of that evil regime's crimes.'[10] Caplan and others have pointed out the risky nature of such a consideration and the dangers of confusing 'what is done to women with what they do themselves'.[11] They are, however, generally supportive of an analysis which argues about the real meaning and effects of women's beliefs and actions.

More generally, writing in this field has concentrated on two areas. The first is a concern over the kind of support and involvement which women gave to Fascist movements and regimes. This is usually discussed in terms of membership of organizations, voting patterns and more general notions of 'consensus', the extent to which there was active and/or passive support for Fascist policy and ideology, particularly in states where Fascism came to power. The second area of consideration has been a particular focus on women in Fascist ideology and policy. Here, the major debates have centred on the 'separate spheres' concept of gender which has appeared dominant in Fascist ideology and the extent to which this was sustained in practice. To date, most work has again concentrated on Germany and Italy, but the essays presented in this volume now begin to develop a British dimension to the general discussion.

Martin Durham's study of the British Union of Fascists' policies and attitudes to women produces some challenging views with regard to the 'progressive' nature of some features of the ideology.[12] While he identifies quite clearly a movement led by males and a style of 'macho' politics, one which insists on the separate spheres perspective, Durham also notes some variation from that dominant pattern. For example, he notes a certain emphasis on the equality of the sexes and on a sometimes uneasy dichotomy between the concept of women as mothers and women as citizens. Looking at women active within British Fascism, he notes support which came from those previously involved in labour politics and in the suffrage campaigns and suggests the importance of these backgrounds in shaping the rather more ambiguous views on women and the family which he detects. Just as Koonz has identified the links between some members of the German feminist movement and Nazism, so too Durham appears to be uncovering a British model. This is not to argue that feminism leads to Fascism; just as it would be absurd to equate socialism with Fascism, so too with feminism, but it is a recognition of the contribution and adaptation of aspects of those ideologies for those who were to become Fascists.

David Mayall's assessment of the case of Nellie Driver, women's district leader of the Nelson branch of the BUF, offers an explanation of why one woman found a role within a Fascist organisation. Using her autobiography, Mayall attempts to analyse the motives for her involvement with the BUF. While Mayall stresses the attempts of the Mosleyites to take advantage of the effects of the Depression in Lancashire cotton towns such as Nelson, what comes across from this particular source is the deeply personal and psychological drives which led Nellie Driver to Fascism. Less well defined or discussed within the autobiography is any sense of why it was Fascism and a Fascist organization which fulfilled such a function or how this related to issues of gender. However, as an exploration of one person's involvement with the BUF, and for the context within which the organization gained local impetus, Driver's autobiography offers some valuable insights into the support of such a movement. Few other sources give any indication of motivation for involvement. Usually, explanations are not sought. Thus, Arthur Harding could talk of the Blackshirts' 'strong mob in Hoxton. They had women and all belonging to it, lots of women and girls used to march with the band'[13] but provide no clues as to why this should be. As with Luisa Passerini's work on Italy, it is the gaps and silences which are just as significant.[14]

On the personal/psychological level, but again one that must be seen in a broader social, economic and political context, 'Colonel Barker' offers further evidence of the particular attractions and the contradictions of Fascism in the dimensions of gender. Julie Wheelwright's exploration of how one woman came to symbolize a rejection of a limiting domestic ideology focuses on the involvement of Valerie Arkell-Smith with the National Fascisti in the 1920s. Dressing as a man initially to escape her husband, she found herself a degree of security by joining an organization which fervently articulated women's place in the home. In certain ways, Arkell-Smith found an identity in her new role from the very assertion of such a masculine dominance. Ultimately, of course, it brought no long-term change in the dominant ideology, but it is a timely reminder of the complexities of gender roles and debates in those inter–war years and brings the discussion of such issues much closer to the themes emerging in work published on other countries.

As Stuart Rawnsley has argued, 'the BUF, like other fascist organizations, attracted all sorts of people who joined for a variety of reasons'.[15] The contributions of Mayall and Wheelwright rightly emphasize the importance of personal factors in this process. The final essay in 'Women and Fascism' stresses the more general theme of class considerations. Kushner's article on domestic service illustrates the attempt of Fascist ideology to appeal to women of all class backgrounds. Nevertheless, it indicates how, in practice, class conflict within the BUF limited its potential support from both the mistress and the maid. The issue of domestic service revealed both the radical and reactionary tendencies within the movement and also the ability of women, including previously-ignored working-class women, to influence BUF policy. By also focusing on the experience of Jewish refugee women who became domestic servants in Britain, and the reactions of the British Fascists as well as the general public to them, Kushner draws connections with Nazi Europe. In Britain, as in Germany, the Fascists (both male and female) did not differentiate on grounds of gender when considering the Jewish minority.

The second section of this volume confronts the vital subject of war and its impact on minorities. Nowhere is the marginality of ethnic and racial groups so exposed as in times of conflict. One need think only of the Armenian genocide in the First World War, the Jewish and Gypsy holocaust in the Second, or, more recently, the persecution of the Kurds in the Iran–Iraq conflict, to see the destructive potential of war for vulnerable minorities.[16] Yet this negative reaction is only part of a complex series of simultaneous equations which determine the treatment of minorities during conflict.[17] It is also the case that marginal groups in society, such as women and the disabled, as well as immigrant, racial and ethnic minorities, can find, through the demands of total war, economic and social opportunities previously denied them in society. It was because of both world wars, it must be remembered, that a substantial Afro-Caribbean community was established in Britain — in the ports in the 1914–18 conflict and more widely between 1939 and 1945. There was a certain relaxation of the colour bars in employment, if not elsewhere, as black workers helped Britain meet the demands of war economies.[18]

David Cesarani's contribution indicates a similar process of economic mobility operating among working-class Jews in Britain during the First World War. He also, however, indicates how such progress actually emphasized the marginality of all Jews in British society and thus 'exposes the delicate fabric of the Anglo-Jewish identity'. Through distortion caused by a tradition of anti-Jewish antipathy and the tensions of war society, Jews were accused of profiteering, job-snatching and of panicking in the shelters. The 'otherness' of the Jews was stressed, forming the economic and social background of the 1917 anti-Semitic riots, disturbances which were ignited by the more blatant issue of alien Jews and military service.[19] It is significant that a similar reaction against black 'progress' in the war was one element behind a series of riots against Britain's black population two years later.[20]

Henry Srebrnik's contribution here indicates that similar accusations and processes occurred in the Second World War. Cesarani points out that Anglo-Jewish communal organizations were unable, for fear of appearing disloyal, to defend their foreign Jewish brethren over issues such as internment. Srebrnik suggests a similar pattern for the 1939–45 conflict. Organizations such as the Board of Deputies of British Jews were silent on the internment of Jewish refugees, accusations of Jewish black-marketeering and the release from prison in 1943 of the British Fascist leader, Sir Oswald Mosley. In the absence of leadership amongst Anglo-Jewry, the British Communist Party engaged in a campaign specifically designed to attract Jewish support. It resulted in the formation of a National Jewish Committee of the Communist Party in 1943 and the election of a Jewish Communist MP and several councillors immediately after the War.

The Communist Party, in rejecting assimilationist solutions to the 'Jewish question' and in stressing a new-found pride in Jewish ethnic identity, was also able to make use of the pro-Soviet euphoria in Britain during the latter stages of the War. The Soviet Union was portrayed as a country which had destroyed anti-Semitism and was encouraging Jewish cultural expression. In the First World War, the Anglo-Jewish relationship with Russia was much more problematic. Russian Jews in Britain were understandably reluctant to fight on the same side as their former country, given its record of intense anti-Semitism. As Cesarani illustrates, this led to the various stages of the Aliens Military Service issue. For Germans and Austrians (Jewish and non-Jewish), the situation between 1914 and 1918 was even more critical. This leads us to consider the other major determinant of the well-being of a minority group in war — its relationship to the enemy. Two chapters in this collection, by Panikos Panayi and Stella Yarrow, indicate how important this factor could be.

Anti-German sentiment in British society during the First World War was so intense that anything which was even perceived as German in origin became a legitimate target. Individual and mass violence, as well as a state policy of harsh internment, deportation and confiscation of property, combined to make German life in Britain untenable. Yarrow shows how all these elements of intolerance actually affected the German minority. Indeed, her essay is a useful corrective to those who study racism and xenophobia without considering its impact on the group under attack. She also indicates that persecuted minorities are rarely the passive recipients of hostility but organize themselves in their own defence. Panayi's contribution reveals how this vicious xenophobic atmosphere was exploited and fanned by a radical anti-German and anti-socialist organization, the British Empire Union. Its influence, whether on a popular level in inciting hatred of the 'Hun' or in pushing the Government into ever more draconian internment of enemy aliens, was an indication of the power of the radical right in Britain during a period of crisis. Too often, uncritical statements are made about the decency and gentleness of British society.[21] Yarrow and Panayi act as a corrective against such glib assumptions. As the latter concludes, between 1914 and 1918 'intolerance became the dominant ethos'.

The final section of this volume, 'Racism and Revision', covers the whole period of twentieth century history. The four essays deal with both black and white minorities, reactions and responses to those actually in Britain as well as to those who, it was feared, might descend on the country. They are united not necessarily in specific subject matter but more in questioning the validity of previous scholarship, whether in its theoretical basis or the limitations of its research. The study of British anti-Semitism has been hindered on both accounts. It is an area that has received little attention, partly due to a conviction that Britain could not possibly have an anti-Semitic tradition or traditions. Kushner's article argues that this reluctance to accept the existence of anti-Semitism has created a barrier to the understanding of many issues concerning Britain and the Jews. In the 1930s, he suggests, the apparent contradictions and inconsistencies of British reactions to the Nazi persecution of Jews can be explained by a mixture of humanitarian sympathy restrained by anti-Semitism of a liberal (assimilationist) and conservative (exclusionist) nature. British anti-Semitism, he concludes, was able to shape both Jewish refugee policy in the 1930s as well as the treatment of refugees actually in Britain.

Not surprisingly, given the undeveloped historiography, we are still a long way from a theoretical understanding of British anti-Semitism. Bryan Cheyette's contribution is an attempt to begin to rectify this shortcoming, or at least to identify methodological weaknesses of previous work on this area. If there is a dominant tendency in recent literature, it is towards an 'interactionist' or 'convergence' explanation of anti-Semitism. This theory suggests that the role of the minority in society needs to be considered in the understanding of a conflict situation. At worst, the interactionist model, in the hands of a Fascist such as Mosley, can degenerate into a 'well-earned' theory of prejudice — simply blaming the victim, because of his behaviour, for his own misfortune. Some scholars, however, such as Colin Holmes, have used it in a more subtle form, emphasizing the need to place the ethnic and racial conflict in its economic, social and political context. In the process, they have exposed some of the possible weaknesses of the scapegoat model of prejudice — why is it, for example, that certain minorities are singled out for persecution?[22]

Cheyette's essay in this volume suggests that, even in a sophisticated form, the interactionist model of anti-Semitism tends, by concentrating on the immediate issues involved in a conflict situation, to minimize antipathetical cultural traditions. The latter can be brought into play at times of crisis, as with the Marconi Scandal in Britain before the First World War. Cheyette emphasizes not the Jewish role in finance capital at the time, but the tenacity of hostile racial representations (and specifically here the fear of alien Jewish power) which could allow anti-Semites such as Hilaire Belloc and the Chestertons to exploit a favourable political situation to their own advantage. Cheyette, Kushner and Cesarani's contributions on anti-Semitism all indicate that, in terms of British racism, 'the problematic exists not at the level of specific instances of conflict, at the level of "interaction" between social groups, but in the realms of ideology'.

The paucity of theory in the study of British anti-Semitism is matched by that on British racism. Although much has been written on the subject, it is clear that we are still far from an adequate sociology of race relations in Britain.[23] This is, in some measure, due to the lack of historical work on black history and black–white relations in Britain, despite the immense general and academic interest in the subject. The lack of detailed information has resulted in a substantial literature which is marred by unjustified generalizations. Ken Lunn's essay on the *Empire Windrush,* the first ship carrying a sizeable West Indian migrant contingent in the post-war years, acts as a corrective to earlier approaches to the subject. He moves away from the deceptively simple model of British government responses based solely on Cabinet records. Instead, Lunn carries out a detailed examination of the responses of the Ministry of Labour (the government department most directly involved in this immigration procedure). He suggests that Britain was not so unprepared for New Commonwealth immigration as is so often assumed. This was reflected in detailed national and local strategy to accommodate the new arrivals, a policy that was intended above all to avoid the embarrassing problem of racism.

It is evident that more research and, of equal importance, more sophisticated analytical frameworks are needed before, as Colin Holmes suggests, 'a serious discussion on immigration becomes possible, and polemic is put in its proper place'.[24] Too readily, academics and commentators have been prepared to label individuals, organizations, policies, even countries, as 'racist' without realising the complexity and diverse nature of the subject. The issue of racism and the 'New Right' is no exception. The blanket denials of racism from those in the 'New Right' are not necessarily convincing or helpful, but neither are the imprecise accusations of racial prejudice or even Fascism levelled against them by some on the left. In the final essay in this collection, Mitchell and Russell attempt a sober analysis of the subject. They argue that there are too many contradictions within the 'New Right' and its ideology for it to have a consistent line on the issue of race. Furthermore, they suggest that, although elements of the 'New Right' have emphasized 'anti-anti-racism' in an effective way, racism and questions of race have not been a major feature of government policy since Margaret Thatcher became Prime Minister in 1979. By concentrating on what they perceive as the gap between 'New Right' rhetoric and Conservative government practice, Mitchell and Russell indicate the complexity of assessing the significance of racism at state and public level. They conclude that only a more sophisticated analysis of racism will enable a more successful anti-racist initiative in Britain.

The 12 essays presented here, although diverse in character, achieve cohesion through their desire to challenge previous scholarship and to inject interest in neglected, but important, issues in modern British history. They hope to stimulate further research, but also to help create new theoretical frameworks for their subject matter. Ultimately, this volume seeks to make it clear to the general historian that subjects such as race, immigration, ethnicity and gender can be excluded from consideration only at the continuing cost of producing narrow, elitist, chauvinistic and incomplete histories of Britain.

TONY KUSHNER
Southampton University
KENNETH LUNN
Portsmouth Polytechnic

NOTES

1. C. Holmes, *John Bull's Island: Immigration and British Society, 1871–1971* (London, 1988) p.276.
2. See, however, T. Kushner and K. Lunn (eds.), *Traditions of Intolerance: Historical Perspectives on Fascism and Race Discourse in British Society* (Manchester, 1989).
3. Thus, general synthetic histories of America by British historians such as H. Brogan's *The Pelican History of the United States* (London, 1987) especially pp.403–17 and M. Jones, *The Limits of Liberty: American History 1607–1980* (Oxford, 1983) passim, or similar American attempts such as S. Morison et al., *A Concise History of the American Republic* (New York, 1983) and C. Dollar et al., *America: Changing Times* (Cambridge, 1986) deal adequately with matters of immigration and race, while volumes in series such as *The Oxford History of England* or the *Pelican Social History of Britain* rarely touch these subjects.
4. For hostility to 'ethnic history', see Sir Geoffrey Elton's comment to the Historical Association in the House of Lords, 13 Jan. 1986, about 'the non-existent history of ethnic entities', quoted in *The Times Educational Supplement*, 17 Jan. 1986. David Katz has referred, with regard to the writing of Jewish history, to the 'self-ghettoization of its practioners' in *English Historical Review*, vol.CII (Apr. 1987) p.425. See T. Kushner, 'Beyond the Ghetto?', *Jewish Quarterly*, vol.35, no.3 (Autumn 1988) pp.62–3 for critical comment on this statement.
5. The phrase 'Sheffield school' refers to the fact that Colin Holmes and Richard Thurlow were based in the University of Sheffield Department of Economic and Social History and that the Department had several postgraduate students, including the present authors, who have since published in the field of minorities, racism and Fascism.
6. P. Rich, *Race and Empire in British Politics* (Cambridge, 1986) p.xi.
7. L. Caldwell, 'Reproducers of the Nation: Women and the Family in Fascist Policy', in D Forgacs (ed.), *Rethinking Italian Fascism* (London, 1986).
8. Ibid., p.135.
9. C. Koonz, *Mothers in the Fatherland: Women, the Family and Nazi Politics* (London, 1987).
10. J. Caplan, 'Hitler's women's movement', *The Guardian*, 15 May 1987.

11. Ibid.
12. In this respect, Durham is enlarging upon the somewhat limited analysis of more recent writers. For example, Stephen Cullen has noted the '"revolutionary" nature of the role of Blackshirt women in the movement' (S. Cullen, 'The Development of the Ideas and Policy of the British Union of Fascists, 1932–40', *Journal of Contemporary History*, vol.22, no.1 (Jan. 1987) p.133) and stressed the 'decidedly modern' role which they played in the movement. D.S. Lewis challenges this perspective by talking of the 'bankruptcy' of the equality argument (D.S. Lewis, *Illusions of Grandeur: Mosley, Fascism and British Society, 1931–81* (Manchester, 1987) p.79), although noting the roles assigned to, and played by, women during the 1930s. The linkages between suffrage campaigners and their subsequent involvement with Fascism have been identified by Thurlow (R. Thurlow, *Fascism in Britain: A History, 1918–1985* (Oxford, 1987) p.70). Discussions on the relationship between women and Fascism after 1945 have been even scarcer in the standard literature and lack any consistency of purpose. Most settle for the simple comment about the middle-class status of women activists (see, for example, N. Fielding, *The National Front* (London, 1981) p.51), although the honourable exception to this is Christopher Husbands' work on National Front support, which deals with gender dimensions, particularly in relation to other variables such as unemployment (see C. Husbands, *Racial Exclusionism and the City: The Urban Support of the National Front* (London, 1983) pp.100–102, 133, 140–1). A series of articles has appeared in various feminist journals but the significance of the topic has largely passed by the attention of 'mainstream' sociologists and historians.
13. R. Samuel, *East End Underworld: Chapters in the Life of Arthur Harding* (London, 1981), p.275.
14. See L. Passerini, 'Work Ideology and Consensus under Italian Fascism', *History Workshop*, vol.8 (1979) pp.82–108 and her recently published *Fascism in Popular Memory: the cultural experience of the Turin working class* (Cambridge, 1987).
15. S. Rawnsley, 'The Membership of the British Union of Fascists', in K. Lunn and R. Thurlow (eds.), *British Fascism* (London, 1980) p.164.
16. See, for example, the section 'Holocaust and Genocide Comparisons' in the collection of conference papers *Remembering for the Future: Jews and Christians During and After the Holocaust* (Oxford, 1988).
17. A. Smith, 'War and Ethnicity', *Ethnic and Racial Studies*, vol.4, no.4 (Oct. 1981), pp.375–97 is a useful introduction to the subject.
18. P. Fryer, *Staying Power: The History of Black People in Britain* (London, 1984) pp. 295–7, 332–9.
19. For details, see Cesarani's contribution in this volume.
20. See Fryer, op. cit., pp.298–321; N. Evans, 'The South Wales Race Riots of 1919', *Llafur*, vol.3 (1980) pp.5–29.
21. See Kushner and Lunn's introduction in *Traditions of Intolerance* and Holmes, op. cit., pp.294–5 for an alternative interpretation of the nature of British society.
22. T. Kushner, *The Persistence of Prejudice: Antisemitism in British Society During the Second World War* (Manchester, 1989) pp.5–7 has critical comments on both the interactionist and scapegoat models.
23. S. Zubaida indicates the lack of theory in this subject in the introduction to his *Race and Racialism* (London, 1970) p.1. R. Miles, 'Marxism versus the Sociology of "race relations"', *Ethnic and Racial Studies*, vol.7 no.2 (Apr. 1984), pp.217–37 is scathing about liberal and Marxist 'sociology of race relations'.
24. Holmes, op. cit. p.317.

I WOMEN AND FASCISM

Women and the British Union of Fascists, 1932–1940

While much has been written on the British Union of Fascists, very little attention has been given to the role of women both in the movement and in its ideology. Yet the BUF put a great deal of effort into recruiting women and developed policies that were disconcertingly different from our usual picture of Fascism. In the Corporate State of the future, its propagandists claimed, women would not be confined to the home but would achieve full equality. Closer examination suggests a more ambiguous attitude, especially towards married women, and the movement remained very much male-led. But women played an important part in BUF activity including, surprisingly, campaigning against war, and the article concludes by exploring the different factors that drew women to the movement.

In 1932 the former Labour Minister, Sir Oswald Mosley, formed the British Union of Fascists (BUF). The organization enjoyed a rapid growth, reaching perhaps 40,000 in the first half of 1934. This, however, was short-lived and the extensive publicity given to the violence of Blackshirt stewards at Mosley's Olympia meeting in early June, followed by the murder of political opponents in Nazi Germany in the Night of the Long Knives at the end of the month, led to the loss of much of the movement's support. For several years the BUF was reduced to a third or less of its 1934 peak, and many of the recruits it did gain were concentrated in London's East End, where the movement's anti-Semitism gained it support in such areas as Limehouse and Bethnal Green. If anti-Jewish feeling was one basis of the movement's propaganda, another was its opposition to Britain's entanglement in European politics and, against a backdrop of appeasement and fears of war, the BUF (which in the late thirties became simply British Union) appears to have experienced renewed growth in the final years of the decade.[1] Ultimately, in 1940, shortly after the outbreak of war, Mosley and other Fascists were interned and the organization banned.

The BUF, Britain's largest Fascist organization, has been the subject of a considerable amount of research. Much, however, remains to be uncovered and this essay focuses on an area that has been almost completely neglected — women and the BUF. In recent years, with the rise of feminism and of women's history, a number of writers have turned their attention to the subject of Fascist policies towards women. In particular, they have focused on German Nazism, both before and after its coming to power; but work has also been carried out on Italian Fascism, the British National Front and other extreme right movements.[2] Surprisingly, almost no attention has been paid to women and the BUF, and, in part, this essay is intended to repair that deficiency. It would be unnecessarily restrictive, however, to limit a discussion of women and Fascism simply to matters of policy. There is a second aspect of the subject which writers have tended to pass over or even ignore — the involvement of women in Fascist movements — and in this essay I will examine the role that women played in the BUF and their possible reasons for joining.[3]

In exploring these areas, I want to argue against two common ways of seeing Fascism's relationship to women. When we think of Fascism, often we see it not just as led by men but as something more, as a movement saturated with and defined by a belligerent masculinity. Yet in country after country such movements, although disproportionately male in their electoral support, have appealed to female voters and, although overwhelmingly male in composition, have been successful in recruiting women members.[4] This is especially true in the British case: the BUF very much wanted women to join, made a special effort to recruit them and developed structures and policies in an attempt to make Fascism attractive to women.

If we usually see Fascist movements as essentially male in a way that far surpassed the other male-led political movements of the time, we also have a particular understanding of the kinds of policies that Fascists espouse. Along with its nationalism, its anti-Communism, its corporatism, we expect Fascism to be blatantly patriarchal. When it speaks of relationships between the sexes, it would be in terms of men occupying the public sphere while women stay in the home; when it discusses unemployment, it would denounce women working while men are without jobs; when it speaks of war, it calls on men to become warriors and women to produce the large numbers of children needed for victory.[5] Such views, as we will see, were certainly present in the BUF's propaganda. But alongside support for a 'separate spheres' view of gender and a pronatalist (and to some degree eugenic) population policy there were other elements of British Fascist discourse that conform far less to our usual understanding of Fascism.

In *The Greater Britain*, published in 1932 at the very inception of the BUF, Mosley spent a little over two pages discussing 'Women's Work'. While this partly concerned the role of women in the movement, which will be discussed later, its main focus was on the future Corporate State. In such a state, he argued, professional and industrially-employed women would be represented within their occupations but more important was the representation of 'the great majority of women who seek the important career of motherhood'. On such women, he wrote, depended 'the future of the race' and, where now they were represented by women politicians whose '[o]ne idea is to escape from the normal sphere of women and to translate themselves into men', in a Corporate State mothers would be organized as such to express their views on housing, health, education and other matters. As guardian of the future, the Fascist State would care for mother and child and 'the normal woman' would be seen as 'one of the main pillars of the State'.[6]

Although presented as an expansion of women's role in the state, Mosley's argument domesticated that contribution, taking women out of the private sphere into a public arena predominantly identified with an extension of maternal responsibilities. By concentrating on housing, education and health, by contrasting 'normal' women with 'abnormal' women politicians, the argument defined women by 'the home' even when they ventured outside it. But, although less emphasized, in Mosley's Corporate State of the future, women could still be found earning wages and salaries and having a say, not only in housing or health, but in 'matters of still wider political and social significance'. In this hazily-drawn picture lay a tension between women's role in the home and their place in economy and polity that British Union writers would grapple with again and again during the decade but could never finally resolve.

A very different tone from *The Greater Britain* can be seen in a BUF publication which appeared three years later. Written by the BUF's Woman Propaganda Officer, Anne Brock Griggs, *Women and Fascism* declared on its cover 'You have the Vote — Yet are still powerless'. In the Corporate State, Griggs argued, women would be represented as workers, as consumers and as home-makers. Fascism would give women equal status to men, encourage them to enter the profession of their choice and introduce equal pay for equal work. There would be no marriage bar on any career, working conditions for women would be improved and sex discrimination ended. The pamphlet also expounded policy proposals concerning improvements in health, housing, education and the provision of food. Least surprisingly, substantial attention was given to maternal and child welfare and Griggs urged the importance of reducing the maternal mortality and morbidity rates through an increase in clinics and maternity beds, improved training and education and '[m]ore women doctors, who may be preferred by the patient'. But it was the promises about women's representation, equality and access to employment, not women's home responsibilities and infant welfare, that were given priority in the pamphlet's argument; and within the discussion of maternity provision, no reference was made to the birth-rate, let alone to eugenics. The promises of a better future for women were not all that they seemed — women's freedom to pursue any career was qualified at one point by the demands of 'national need' and the argument for equal pay, as we will discuss, was at least as troubled by men being undercut and deprived of employment as it was by discrimination against women. But what was striking about the pamphlet was its emphasis on equality and its concentration on women as citizens and workers far more than as mothers and wives. Even more disconcertingly, where the pamphlet did refer to motherhood, its proposals bore a marked resemblance to socialist and feminist writings of the period.[7]

If Griggs's pamphlet is one indication of a more 'progressive' intonation in the BUF's appeal to women than we would expect, another is to be found in the evolution of the organization's conception of a future Corporate State. Writing in the *British Union Quarterly* in early 1937, a reviewer of a new book on the subject by the movement's leading theoretician, Alexander Raven Thomson, drew attention to an important change in his argument compared with an earlier work. One of the corporations, it was noted, was no longer described as the 'Married Women's Corporation' but the 'Domestic Corporation'. This, the reviewer continued, was 'certainly an improvement. Since male servants will presumably be included, it disposes of the contention that Fascism is anti-Feminist'. Considering Fascist policies towards women in Germany and Italy, let alone aspects of the BUF's own argument, this, to say the least, was somewhat optimistic. Yet, however half-heartedly, Thomson had discarded a formulation that appeared to suggest that married women were a separate category and would not be found in any occupational corporation. In addition, unlike his earlier work, the new book now included a pledge of equal pay for women and opposition to the marriage bar. Even Mosley himself, by the latter part of the thirties, had shifted the balance in his argument in his new book *Tomorrow We Live*. He argued that, while women should not be forced into the labour market by economic pressures, Fascism would not seek to 'drive women from industry' and would ensure working and professional women were represented within occupational corporations. Women would not be confined to the home in the Corporate State, he declared, and the movement had already presented 'a larger proportion of women candidates to the electorate than any other party'.[8]

How far-reaching was this apparent acceptance of women's equality? Did it merely represent an attempt to win newly enfranchized women as supporters and voters, or was something more substantial at work? Here strong reservations need to be noted. On women's employment, in particular, the movement was highly ambiguous about where it stood. In *Women and Fascism* Griggs had commented that the employment of poorly paid women caused men's loss of jobs, sent 'married women into industry to support their husbands who had been displaced' and was both damaging to future mothers and a cause of immorality among girls unable to survive on such wages. Similarly, her criticism of the marriage bar had been followed by the assurance that under Fascism 'married women will not be forced by economic reasons to work to maintain the home'. But she also criticized unequal pay on grounds of 'injustice to women', supported the principle that jobs should go 'to the best worker — man or woman' and used as evidence a trade union leader's speech calling on young women not to undercut men 'or their own sister workers'.[9]

If Griggs's pamphlet was in some ways ambiguous about women's place in the labour market, some BUF writers openly argued that the introduction of equal pay for women might well result in their widespread dismissal, to the benefit of the nation. Thus, in an early issue of the Mosleyite paper, a discussion of equal pay took the form of an imaginary member's reply to an enquiry on the subject. 'There probably would be a lot of women displaced from situations of work', he declared,

> but in the long run this could cancel itself out, because through greater employment of men at a *wage that is equitable and ample*, these men will be encouraged to marry, and the need for women to 'go out to work' would be removed. No married women should find it necessary to work, any more than any man desires it to-day. We must face this problem without fear — women's birthright is to be a wife and a mother, not a breadwinner.

If women ignored their destiny, he continued, then the state would face terrible problems. 'Fewer marriages mean declining birth-rate; fewer children must ultimately mean the Suicide of a Race . . . The end of home-life, the moral decadency that must follow such a lunatic state of affairs as now exist, these problems must be met by a sane and benevolent Government.'[10]

In a later article, 'The Problem of the Woman Worker. National Socialism Will Solve It', another writer, identified only by initials, reiterates this view. Women, it was argued, had the right to work — but at what? Under the present system, they were 'flocking to the factories', not because they wanted to but because the husband's or father's income was too small for the family and because industrialists wanted cheap labour. Under National Socialism, women would enter occupations suited to their 'natural abilities and qualities' and would be able 'if she so desires, to exercise her natural vocation of wifehood and motherhood'. By introducing equal pay, it would be ensured that women were no longer attractive to employers solely on grounds of cheapness, and, as a result of raising wages generally, they would no longer need to work to supplement family incomes. Women would still be allowed to work, the article concluded, but the family would be restored to centrality, larger families would encouraged by the state and there would be an emphasis on women's 'peculiar contribution to society in the sphere of the home, leaving gainful occupation and the support of the family to her man'.[11]

It is not possible here to explore fully the question of the relationship between gender and differences among BUF members over the role of women. Tensions between men and women were very evident in some of the material published, perhaps most distinctly in an article published in 1937, 'A Young Man Looks at Marriage', in which the writer bewails a system that paid women as much or more than him, rather than paying a family wage that would make marriage economically vital for young women.[12] But to explain the traditionalist elements of BUF propaganda solely by the patriarchal impulses of its male members would obscure the differences that existed among women members themselves. Thus, for the woman author of a 1935 article, 'Fascism will Mean Real Equality for Women', Fascism was compatible with feminism, not contradictory. This stood for a very different future from that portrayed three months earlier by the author of 'Fascist Women Do Not Want Equal Rights With Men', with her call for the restoration of traditional relationships between the chivalrous male and what she called 'the weaker sex'.[13] Some of the tensions within the movement will be considered later in this discussion. What is already evident, however, is the ambiguity of demands such as equal pay — what for some members could secure greater equality, for others could ensure a restoration of male privilege.

If BUF views on women's role in economic production were not always what might be expected, what did it have to say about women's role in reproduction? In *Women and Fascism*, Griggs had raised issues of maternal welfare but said nothing about population or birth control, so often the subjects of Fascist strictures in other contexts. How typical was this of British Union writing? In a number of articles, BUF writers discussed the falling birth-rate in Britain and advanced arguments as to how, by economic expansion, family allowances and other measures, it could be reversed.[14] As has often been noted, questions of population were an important aspect of rightist thought of the time, and Mosley himself declared in one of the movement's publications that Fascism would 'secure the production of children by the fit . . . At present birth control is known and practised by the relatively well-off. It is largely unknown and less practised by the very poor. The result is exactly the reverse of the national interest'.[15] Yet the movement gave less attention to eugenic arguments about population 'quality' than might have been expected. Why this was so is unclear. Such views, no doubt, could have proved somewhat unpopular among the poor of the BUF's East End heartland, and this may have been one reason for its relative absence from the movement's propaganda. In addition, it has been suggested that the BUF's corporatism and anti-Communism made it attractive to some Catholics. Sustaining such support would not have been helped by the championing of eugenics, which was condemned by the Church, and Mosley was strongly criticized when he defended the sterilization of 'the unfit' in an interview with the *Catholic Herald* in the late thirties.[16]

If eugenics was little emphasized by the BUF, it also seems to have had problems dealing with birth control. In correspondence with the League of National Life, which campaigned against contraception between the wars, Alexander Raven Thomson declared in 1934 that it could 'rest assured that the question of race suicide has been given our earnest attention' and that the Union was 'definitely opposed to any restriction of population'. The following year, however, the League's journal noted that the BUF's Director of Policy had told the press that birth control and sterilization were 'not matters in which the Fascist movement is prepared to be dogmatic, but they will be submitted after we come to power to the full consideration of medical and moral authorities'. Such a policy, *National Life* commented, would not do.[17] But while the official policy was reticent about birth control, some British Union writers certainly opposed it. Thus, in *Action* in 1940 an article in support of the State Endowment of Motherhood declared that it would encourage childbearing and end the situation where financial pressures forced prospective parents to resort to birth control, 'that policy of despair'. Likewise, a review in 1937 of the French Socialist Leon Blum's book on marriage made the classic anti-Semite argument that 'the destruction of the family by the use of contraceptives' should, like the spread of psychoanalysis, Marxism and 'Hollywood sex-filled entertainment', be seen as the work of the Jews.[18] Yet, despite such hostility, the BUF, unlike the League of National Life, did not campaign for the banning of birth control. Its propagandists, when they considered the issue, interpreted the falling birth-rate as an expression of lack of confidence in the system, incapable either of solving its economic problems or averting the danger of war. National Socialism, they believed, would restore confidence in the future. To call for legislation to restrict contraception, although it might attract some potential supporters, not only risked alienating others but might have seemed to suggest that a BUF government would be incapable of inspiring Britons to increase their birth-rate.

As we have seen, if the BUF sometimes addressed women as workers and citizens, it was also concerned with them as mothers, and this was particularly the case in one surprising respect. In the customary view of the nature of Fascism, along with its masculinity we also see it as bellicose, a movement that despises pacifism and glorifies violence and war. Yet the BUF spent much of its energies in the thirties campaigning *against* war, invoking images of women not as the heroic mothers of soldiers but as the natural protectors of life.

To Norah Elam, writing in 1935 on 'Fascism, Women and Democracy', women's achievement of the vote had not only been unable to prevent mass unemployment or improve housing conditions, but had not stopped 'the alleged National Government' from pursuing alliances with 'the avowed enemies of this country' while at the same time leaving the country defenceless. The Corporate State, she claimed, would gain equal status and equal pay for women, and 'most important of all Fascism comes to lay forever the haunting spectre of war, by removing the fundamental causes' — the power of international finance.[19] Underpinned by this analysis, the BUF time and time again, especially in its later years, polemicized against war, frequently drawing on the argument that women as mothers had a natural attachment to peace. Thus in 1938, in 'Women! You Can Stop This War', Olive Hawks, another leading BUF woman, argued that 'Women, as the givers of life, must hate the insensate destruction of warfare' and 'must be prepared to devote tireless energy to the prevention of war in the future'. It was up to them, she argued, to make children realise that Britons should only fight if their country was attacked. Women should boycott 'war-mongering' papers, condemn the 'mischief-making of the Labour Party' whose 'repeated insults to foreign countries' increased the risk of conflict and use 'the women's vote' to protect home and country against the threat of war.[20] The dangers of war to women was emphasized by Mosley in a speech the following year:

> There are thousands of women living here in East London today with their husbands, their brothers, their children who may be doomed by this war conspiracy to the bitterest tears that a woman can shed. What good does it do to such a woman to know that German women, too, are doomed by us striking back at a foreign city? . . . Is that going to bring the broken body of a child back to life? War is a crime against the people of all lands.[21]

The reference to Germany, of course, is crucial to understanding the BUF's peace campaign. The British Union drew on a widespread fear of a repetition of the First World War; after the 1939–45 war had broken out, *Action* predicted that it would become 'a war of mothers against this foul system of democracy that calls upon them every twenty years to sacrifice their sons'.[22] But while BUF propagandists emphasized war's devasting consequences for women, their families and homes, it was a particular war they were campaigning against, one in which the British 'Financial Democracy' they loathed allied with the even more detested France and the Soviet Union against National Socialist Germany, the country which the movement admired and sought to emulate. When one woman writer urged that women 'can stop this war', her argument was not limited to the fears that 'It is *our* children who will be bombed, *our* homes that will be destroyed, *our* husbands and fathers they will take from us'. It is 'we women who bear the children they would lead to the slaughter', she wrote. But who were the 'they' she spoke of? Her answer is evident in her claim that 'the big guns of Jewish propaganda' were trying to drag the country into war.[23] When she spoke of the horrors that war visited upon women, she was seeking to persuade them to oppose a war against Nazism. Where women peace campaigners of the left argued that it was 'women's work to be the keepers of the young life in this country' and marched under banners proclaiming 'Mothers of England. Shall Youth be Slaughtered', they were campaigning against war and Fascism.[24] Where BUF women drew on the same vocabulary, they were campaigning against war and *for* Fascism.

We have seen, then, that the BUF had a great deal to say about women's place in society and that it was more complex than we might have thought. But if the BUF said much about women, what role did women play in its ranks? Richard Thurlow has suggested that women probably made up over 20 per cent of its membership:[25] why did they join, and what did they expect of Fascism, both as a movement and as a future ordering of society?

Writing in *The Greater Britain* in 1932, Mosley noted that it had 'been suggested that hitherto, in our organisation, too little attention has been paid to the position of women'. This, he claimed, was not because the movement under-rated women but because physical clashes with opponents made it necessary in the early stages to concentrate 'on the organisation of men'. 'The part of women in our future organisation will be important', Mosley assured his readers, but it would be 'different from that of the men; *we want men who are men and women who are women*'.[26]

These phrases, resonant with notions of 'separate spheres' and male chivalry, encapsulate the traditional understanding of women's wholly secondary role in Fascist movements. As we will see, however, as the movement developed, while it remained defined by its male leadership, some women were able to play an important role within its ranks.

The Women's Section of the BUF was formed in March 1933, six months after the movement's creation. If the early appointment of Lady Maud Mosley, 'the Leader's Mother',[27] to head the section suggests that it may initially have been seen as an auxiliary, then the British Union's subsequent choice of a women's organizer suggests a different interpretation. In Mary Richardson, the BUF found a woman whose political record included being imprisoned for her activities in the pre-war suffragette agitation and standing as a Prospective Parliamentary Candidate for the Labour Party.[28] Richardson had been a member of the New Party, the organization Mosley had formed after splitting from Labour and, the BUF proudly announced in late 1933, had in the past opposed Fascism. She now, however, saw it as the 'only path to "a Greater Britain" . . . And having regard to my previous political experience, I feel certain that women will play a large part in establishing Fascism in this country'.[29]

An article in June 1934 noted that when the Women's Section had been formed it had only been 17 strong. Now there were women's sections throughout the country, women were engaged in Study Circles to develop their understanding of the movement's policy and some were training to speak at public meetings. Women were also attending classes in First Aid, fencing and other skills, it went on, and above all they were being prepared for '*their* work for the Movement — that of canvassing'. Streets and blocks of streets were assigned to women to visit and distribute literature to its occupants. Some women were being trained in ju-jitsu in order to hold public meetings in hostile conditions without male assistance while others were wanted as 'canteen helpers', to paint posters, entertain or run children's clubs. 'Whatever your talent', the article promised, 'there is a place for you in the Fascist Movement!'[30]

While women speakers, stewards and others were important for the BUF, it was as canvassers that women were seen as particularly vital for the organization. Mosley, speaking at a Cabaret Ball in 1934 'held in aid of the Women's Section' made this clear when he told those present that 'We are now entering into a phase in our work when the activities of the women are vital. That phase is the building up of an electoral machine, and when it comes to electoral work . . . I think we men have to give first place to the women'.[31]

What exactly happened in this period is far from clear. Crucially, no copies are known to have survived of the *Woman Fascist*, a fortnightly publication started in early 1934 and referred to several times in the BUF press.[32] But in September 1934 in 'A Message to the Women Blackshirts', Lady Mosley announced that it had been decided to terminate the *Woman Fascist* and take up an offer of space in the *Blackshirt*. It was vital, she argued, for men's and women's sections to work as a team and a 'women's corner' of the paper was much to be preferred to 'any publication that might even suggest a separate existence'. For 'all thinking members', she continued, it was becoming evident that there was no place for any but 'the friendliest "rivalry"'; the leader had emphasized the importance of women's co-operation in the movement and therefore all should lay aside individual likes and dislikes and devote themselves to the British Union.[33] For the moment articles by Mary Richardson continued to appear in the paper but the following month it reported that, due to a car accident, she would be unable to carry out speaking engagements or deal with correspondence for a fortnight, and when the fortnight elapsed it stated that she was progressing but it was not possible to say when she would resume her work. Richardson returned to work at Women's Headquarters but soon after disappeared from the pages of BUF publications and, seemingly, from the organization itself.[34] Two years later, in a profile of Anne Brock Griggs, appointed in 1935 as Woman Propaganda Officer and subsequently put in charge of women's activities in the South, reference was made to 'the many differences which arise in running the women's section of the Movement' and how valuable her advice had been in 'smoothing out friction on many occasions'.[35] But of the nature of these tensions, and what disagreements existed about the role of women in Fascism, we know almost nothing.[36]

While the British Union did not, in the event, run candidates in the 1935 General Election, it did propose to do so in the contest expected at the end of the decade (an election which would turn out to be aborted by the outbreak of war). It chose 80 prospective candidates, 11 of whom were women, and also ran Anne Brock Griggs as one of its six candidates in the 1937 LCC elections in east London.[37] Throughout the period the emphasis on women as canvassers continued. Thus in 1937 Griggs, writing on 'the next stage in women's organisation', concentrated on the creation of women's teams to canvass particular areas. 'Closely allied with this door-step propaganda', she added, would be the organisation of street and afternoon meetings, the latter 'being more important for the women's side'.[38] But as the thirties wore on, another aspect of women's work — as campaigners against war — became important.

British Union of Fascists women had played a part in the movement's campaign against British intervention when Mussolini invaded Abyssinia in the mid-thirties[39] but they took on a greater importance later in the decade as the possibility of war with Nazi Germany began to threaten British homes directly. In late 1938 the movement organized peace poster parades and sales drives of its paper in the West End of London, with *Action* drawing special attention to the 'strenuous work put in by women members'. All over Britain, Griggs claimed, women were demonstrating against going to war over Czechoslovakia. British mothers, she wrote, wanted to fight, but for their children and for a government that would bring work not war.[40] Chamberlain's return from Munich and Britain's abandonment of the Czechs temporarily postponed the war the British Union feared but the following year international tension rose again and BUF women marched against war in the East End.

'British Mothers Unite for Peace', *Action* declared, and when war none the less broke out Griggs called on women members to stand firm and work for 'our children, the new generation' to win peace.[41] The call-up of men for the war effort made women's role in the movement of crucial importance, and at the beginning of 1940 *Action* announced that, in order to give them the experience to 'shoulder the sternest tasks of District organisation and propaganda' and to 'take the message of Peace to the women of the country, a Women's Peace Campaign is being prepared'. An indoor meeting in London at the end of February opened the campaign, and London and provincial meetings took place throughout March. The campaign finally culminated on 13 April with a mass meeting in London addressed by Mosley and three prominent women members, although a London 'Women's Peace Meeting' was reported the following month in one of the last accounts of British Union women's activity before the internment of leading activists of both sexes.[42]

There were many forms of activity for Fascist women. The BUF press contains numerous reports of women public speakers, accounts of women's propaganda marches and even a Women's Drum Corps, just as there were classes in fencing and ju-jitsu.[43] (Indeed, observers' accounts of Blackshirt brutality towards hecklers at the 1934 Olympia rally included references to the violence of women Fascists.[44]) But there were also less public, more traditional roles for women Fascists — as one appeal for women members declared, some would sell papers on the street, others check the Parliamentary register or make goods for sale or be responsible for 'the keeping clean and in order of District Headquarters Premises'.[45] What remains unclear, however, is the distribution of women members to the different roles the movement offered — how many spoke or marched, how many canvassed or were involved in bazaars or merely remained what the movement called 'non-active members'. But however active women members might be, there were barriers to their advancement beyond a certain point. Wider expectations and assumptions within society meshed with male prejudice within the movement to ensure that those women who did show leadership abilities exercised them over women, not over men.

As Mandle's study of the BUF national leadership makes all too clear, it was very much a male leadership, while at local level, although Nellie Driver, the subject of David Mayall's essay in this collection, was the dynamic force behind the Nelson branch, she was denied the position of District Leader and was restricted to the rank of Women's District Leader.[46]

What made women join the movement? Here, more research is called for, but we have two sources of particular interest — articles in the BUF press in which women explained their reasons for joining and interviews with former members conducted in recent years. There are problems with both sources — in the accounts of the time, it is sometimes difficult to be sure if the articles are authentic and not the journalistic creation of figures emblematic of the movement's appeal. In the case of recent interviews (and occasionally memoirs), not only will there be vagaries of memory but some former members are likely to be hesitant in explaining why they joined an organization which from early on was inextricably associated with anti-Semitism and political violence. But while there are problems with such sources, they can give important indications as to the appeal of Fascism to women.

Four pseudonymous women, writing in successive weeks in 1939 on 'Why I Joined Mosley', gave their different reasons. For one, it was because as a working-class mother she wanted to end unemployment, exploitation and the risk of an unwinnable war; for another, a secretary in the City, it was revulsion against Stock Exchange corruption; for a third, a journalist, it was in protest against the pressures advertisers put on the press. The fourth, a cabaret dancer, had joined in protest against the number of foreign acts in her profession. Cabaret, she claimed, was 'controlled by the Jews'.[47]

Five years earlier, in a similar set of profiles, 'Five Fascist Women' explained why they had joined the movement. 'The woman of twenty-five . . . the young mother . . . the business woman of thirty-seven . . . the mother of working children . . . the grandmother', all, declared the *Blackshirt*, had found 'in Fascism the answer to their problems and the fulfilment of their hopes'. For the young mother peace and prosperity for her children was what Fascism seemed to promise; for the businesswoman life seemed empty, in part because her chances of marriage had faded in the face of the losses of so many men in 'the fields of Flanders'; for the grandmother, the parliamentary machine had failed and only Fascism, modern and patriotic, could take the nation forward.[48]

The profiles of women candidates published in the BUF press may well be more reliable than the kind of account considered above in that they at least refer to identifiable members, although here we need to be cautious about regarding leading members as typical of the movement's rank and file women membership. For Muriel Whinfield, Prospective Parliamentary Candidate for Petersfield, five years as Chairman of the local Women's Unionist Association had led to dissatisfaction with the Conservative Party, just as for Mercedes Barrington, Prospective Parliamentary Candidate for West Fulham, involvement with Conservatism had resulted in disgust with its 'ineffectuality', an impression deepened by her study of 'conditions in some of the distressed areas'. As for Doreen Bell, the candidate for Accrington, it was the combination of social policy and patriotism in Mosley's *The Greater Britain* which had won her from her 'Socialist sympathies'.[49]

When we turn to later interviews and memoirs, we see a strong emphasis on hopes of social reform as crucial in the decision to join the movement. For Louise Irvine, a woman teacher who joined in 1936 and became Birmingham women's organizer, the British Union stood for 'a highly patriotic kind of socialism' capable of solving the horrific housing conditions she had encountered in the city. Yolande McShane, in her autobiography, *Daughter of Evil*, gives similar reasons for the decision which eventually led to her becoming women's organizer for Merseyside: 'I found Mosley's ideas attractive — they seemed to promise a better life for the poor . . . Joining the Blackshirts seemed to bring nearer the day when all children would have enough to eat, and also be able to enjoy the country and sea I loved so much.' At a more rank and file level, Mrs Pugh, an ex-member interviewed in 1988, joined the Smethwick branch at the age of about 15 as a result of a woman's speech to her Church Youth Group about how Mosley's movement was working for 'a better world with peace as the main objective and the end of the Depression'.[50]

If some members were attracted by the desire for social reform or peace, others recall that they joined for more personal reasons. The *Guardian* in 1978 published the reminiscences of a former member who had joined as a teenager, partly because of the telling off she received from her mother when she first bought the movement's paper. This had determined her to join: 'It was the most exciting period of my life, the feeling of doing something that was secret to everyone in my family'.[51] In addition, as with all political organizations, particularly youth ones, physical attraction played its part. This is an element in the account in the *Guardian* and also appeared in Stuart Rawnsley's researches into northern Fascism when the former Women's Section Leader in Moss Side, Manchester, told him that she had originally joined because of her attraction to one of the Blackshirts whom she later married.[52] (The possibilities of romantic entanglement, of course, were not only an influence on women Fascists. In a recent article, a man involved with William Joyce's National Socialist splinter group of the thirties attributed it to his adolescent attraction to one of its young women supporters.[53])

Amid this constellation of reasons for membership — some overtly political, others entwined with the rhythms and demands of adolescence — one factor is notably absent. When we look, for instance, at the British Union press in 1937 we find Anne Brock Griggs's electoral contest described as a fight against 'Jewry' just as in the previous year a woman member's account of women speakers at Bethnal Green began by describing a bus conductor's question. '"Are you having a meeting tonight? Well, we certainly need you, this part is absolutely infested with them!" We were not left in doubt as to his meaning. As the bus stopped a family of Jews struggled to climb aboard without first allowing us to alight.'[54] Both these examples concern the East End and the later years of the British Union's development, and it may be that women members recruited in the early thirties or in particular areas of the country paid little or no attention to the movement's anti-Semitism. According to McShane's Liverpool reminiscences, that Mosley was 'anti-Jew' appeared far less important to her than his support for 'Equal opportunities for all', partly because she 'knew no Jews'.[55] But in other accounts, anti-Semitism as a crucial factor in the BUF is often strangely absent.

More research is needed before we can discuss the role of women in the BUF with confidence, but certainly the movement itself needs to be re-evaluated in the light of its policy towards women. Both feminist and non-feminist writers have argued that a crucial element in Fascism is hostility to women's equality and a defence of male privilege,[56] and an examination of Fascism in countries where it came to power gives strong support to such a view. Yet in the British Fascist movement of the thirties, this aspect of Fascism was often muted in favour of an appeal to women which emphasized the equality of the sexes in a Corporate State and which tried to hold in uneasy combination notions of woman as mother and woman as citizen. When it addressed motherhood, the movement was capable of sounding like a socialist campaigner for maternity provision or a feminist campaigner for peace. When it spoke to women as citizens, its propagandists might emphasize the suffragette past of a woman such as Mary Richardson or express surprise that it could be seen as anti-feminist. In the serried ranks of men who made up its leadership and in many of the views of the men (and women) it recruited, British Fascism in the thirties was as patriarchal as its Continental equivalents. But, in important ways, above all with regard to equal pay and to peace, BUF attitudes to women were far more complex than we would expect.

MARTIN DURHAM
The Polytechnic, Wolverhampton

NOTES

I would like to thank David Mayall and Jill Liddington for their valuable comments on an earlier draft of this article.

1. G.C. Webber, 'Patterns of Membership and Support for the British Union of Fascists', *Journal of Contemporary History*, vol.19 (Oct. 1984); Richard Thurlow, *Fascism in Britain. A History 1918–1985* (Oxford, 1987) chs.5, 6.
2. See, for instance, Claudia Koonz, *Mothers in the Fatherland: Women, the Family and Nazi Politics* (London, 1987); Jill Stephenson, *The Nazi Organisation of Women*

(London, 1981); Alexander De Grand, 'Women under Italian Fascism', *Historical Journal*, vol.19 (1976); Veronica Ware, *Women and the National Front* (Birmingham, 1978).

3. The main discussion of both aspects to date is to be found in D.S. Lewis, *Illusions of Grandeur: Mosley, Fascism and British Society, 1931–81* (Manchester, 1987), pp.78–80, 83–84.

4. See, for instance, Richard J. Evans, 'German Women and the Triumph of Hitler', demand publication article, *Journal of Modern History*, (Mar. 1976); Helen L. Boak, 'Women in Weimar Germany: The "Frauenfrage" and the Female Vote' in Richard Bessel and E.J. Feuchtwanger (eds.), *Social Change and Political Development in Weimar Germany* (London, 1981); Tim Mason, 'Women in Nazi Germany', *History Workshop*, 1 (Spring 1976), pp.90, 109–10; Stein Ugelvik Larsen, Bernt Hagtvet and Jan Peter Myklebust (eds.), *Who Were the Fascists?* (Bergen, 1980) pp.218–20, 431, 709–11.

5. See, for instance, Kate Millet, *Sexual Politics* (London, 1971) pp.157–68.

6. Oswald Mosley, *The Greater Britain* (London, 1932) pp.40–42.

7. Anne Brocks Griggs, *Women and Fascism* (London, 1935). On the left and maternity in the thirties, see Jane Lewis, *The Politics of Motherhood* (London, 1980).

8. *British Union Quarterly* (April–July 1937); Oswald Mosley, *Tomorrow We Live* (London, 1938) p.16.

9. Griggs, op cit., pp.2–3.

10. *Blackshirt*, 19 Aug. 1933.

11. Ibid., 23 Jan. 1937.

12. *Action*, 18 Sept. 1937.

13. *Blackshirt*, 22 Feb. 1935, 2 Nov. 1934.

14. See, for instance, *Action*, 26 Dec. 1936, 2 July 1938; *British Union Quarterly*, (Spring 1940).

15. Oswald Mosley, *Fascism: 100 Questions Asked and Answered* (London, 1936) question 76.

16. Stuart Rawnsley, 'The Membership of the British Union of Fascists' in Kenneth Lunn and Richard Thurlow (eds.), *British Fascism* (London, 1980) pp.161–3; Robert Skidelsky, *Oswald Mosley* (London, 1975) pp.347–8; Colin Cross, *The Fascists in Britain* (London, 1961) pp.187–8.

17. *National Life*, Mar. 1934, 2 Dec. 1935.

18. *Action*, 7 Mar. 1940; *British Union Quarterly* (July–Sept. 1937).

19. *Fascist Quarterly* (July 1935).

20. *Action*, 26 Mar. 1938.

21. Ibid., 22 Apr. 1939.

22. Ibid., 4 Apr. 1940.

23. Ibid., 6 May 1939.

24. Jill Liddington, *The Life and Times of a Respectable Rebel: Selina Cooper 1864–1946* (London, 1984) pp.409–10.

25. Thurlow, op cit., caption to photo facing p.142.

26. Mosley (1932), op cit., pp.40–41.

27. Cross, op cit., p.76; Nicholas Mosley, *Rules of the Game* (London, 1982) p.257; Nicholas Mosley, *Beyond the Pale* (London, 1983) p.91; *Blackshirt*, 7 Sept. 1934. Published sources are rather contradictory on the early leadership of the Women's Section. According to David Pryce-Jones, Lady Cynthia, Mosley's first wife, was titular head of the Section until her death in May 1933. Another titled figure, Lady Makgill, is described by one of his interviewees as running the Women's Section at the BUF's National Headquarters, and Lady Makgill herself told him that 'I created the women's section of the BUF in Lady Cynthia's day' but left shortly after her death. She was described in the BUF press, however, nearly a year later, as leader of the Women's Section. According to a MI5 report on British Fascism, she resigned from her position in May 1934 following a dispute over 'serious deficiencies in the funds of the Women's Section'. David Pryce-Jones, *Unity Mitford. A Quest* (London, 1976) pp.43, 72; *Fascist Week*, 13 Apr. 1934; PRO HO 144/20140 p.112.

28. She was not the only former suffragette to join the BUF, and three others — Norah Elam, Mercedes Barrington and Mary Allen — were also active in the movement. Like Richardson, Elam was keen to argue in the BUF press that there was no tension between fighting for women's emancipation and fighting for Fascism. Many other veterans of the suffragette movement, however, strongly opposed Fascism, ranging from the socialist Sylvia Pankhurst to Flora Drummond, leader of the right-wing Women's Guild of Empire. See Cross, op cit., pp.179–80; Thurlow, op cit., p.70; Sue Bruley, *Leninism, Stalinism and the Women's Movement in Britain, 1920–1939* (London, 1986) pp.249–50; Brian Harrison, *Separate Spheres: The Opposition to Women's Suffrage in Britain* (London, 1978) p.233; *Blackshirt*, 29 June 1934, 25 Sept. 1937; *Fascist Quarterly* (July 1935).
29. *Fascist Week*, 22–28 Dec. 1933.
30. *Blackshirt*, 1 June 1934.
31. Ibid., 6 July 1934.
32. See ibid 23–29 Mar., 6 July, 20 July 1934.
33. Ibid., 7 Sept. 1934.
34. Ibid., 21 Sept., 28 Sept., 5 Oct., 19 Oct., 16 Nov. 1934.
35. *Action*, 21 Nov. 1936.
36. See, however, the extract from a letter of Lady Maud Mosley's in early 1935 in which personal tensions — above all in regard to 'Miss R- with her dishonest inefficiency' — are very much to the fore. Nicholas Mosley (1983), op cit., p.92.
37. See Cross, op cit., pp.179–80, 165–67.
38. *Blackshirt*, 27 Mar. 1937.
39. Ibid., , 6 Sept. 1935.
40. *Action*, 1 Oct., 8 Oct. 1938.
41. Ibid, 13 May, 20 May, 16 Sept. 1939.
42. Ibid, 18 Jan., 4 Apr., 11 Apr., 18 Apr., 16 May 1940.
43. For women's propaganda marches, see, for instance, *Action*, 9 Apr. 1938; for the Women's Drums Corps, see *Action*, 2 July 1938.
44. Lewis, op cit., pp.79–80.
45. *Action*, 25 June 1938.
46. W.F. Mandle, 'The Leadership of the British Union of Fascists', *Australian Journal of Politics and History*, vol.12 (Dec. 1966); Rawnsley, op cit., p.156.
47. *Action*, 29 July, 12 Aug., 19 Aug., 26 Aug. 1939.
48. *Blackshirt*, 16 Nov. 1934.
49. *Action*, 5 Dec. 1936; 23 Jan., 2 Jan. 1937.
50. *Mosley's Blackshirts. The Inside Story of the British Union of Fascists, 1932–1940* (London, 1986) pp.46–7; Yolande McShane, *Daughter of Evil* (London, 1980) p.30; Interview by author, Mrs J. Pugh, 7 Apr. 1988.
51. *Guardian*, 4 Mar. 1978.
52. Rawnsley, op cit., p.155.
53. *Spectator*, 6 Aug. 1983.
54. *Blackshirt*, 23 May 1936, 20 Mar. 1937.
55. McShane, op cit.
56. See, for instance, Stanley G. Payne in Larsen et al, op cit., pp.20–21; Millet, op cit.

Rescued from the Shadows of Exile: Nellie Driver, Autobiography and the British Union of Fascists

The article critically uses the unpublished memoirs of Nellie Driver, Woman District Leader of the Nelson branch of the British Union of Fascists, in order to focus upon the nature of provincial Fascism in one of the main centres of Lancashires's textile industry and also to locate the experience of Fascist activity in the life of an individual. Autobiographies are shown to have both empirical and theoretical value to the historian by informing debates from new perspectives and permitting an insight into the meaning of events and beliefs to an active member of the blackshirt movement.

I

In 1980 Nelson District Library acquired a substantial typewritten autobiography which was subsequently brought to wider notice through the pioneering work of Stuart Rawnsley into northern Fascism, and the name of Nellie Driver now appears with some frequency in a number of secondary texts on the British Union of Fascists. However, the treatment of this memoir tends to be brief and cursory, failing to discover the full flavour and insights which it offers on regional Fascist activity and the personal implications, motivation and outcome of joining Mosley's movement. Before considering the content of the work and its value, though, it is necessary to place this personal record of a life within a broader discussion of source material on Fascism and the relevance and importance of autobiographical items.

Historians of the Fascist movement in Britain between the wars continue to face the problem of sources and access to sensitive material. Robert Skidelsky noted in the bibliographical appendix to his biography of Oswald Mosley the difficulty in finding, preserving and obtaining the right to view the Mosley papers, and successive governments are still reluctant to make available all the Home Office records on the BUF.[1] The period of closure is regularly extended and, although historians' appetites are occasionally whetted by the release of certain files, most recently in 1986, there remains a greater interest in, and speculation about, the items still held back for some future release. Also, one can only regret the loss of files that have been weeded, shredded or otherwise lost to the researcher in the intervening decades, including around 700 Home Office files on BUF members destroyed under

section 3(6) of the Public Records Act.[2] As a consequence, much
of the written work on Mosley and the BUF tends to be based
around a similar combination of essential source material, including the
official records considered acceptable for release, printed information
originating from the movement itself and documentation provided by
anti-Fascist organisations, notably the Communist Party of Great Britain
and the Board of Deputies of British Jews.

Perhaps one of the most striking absences is the dearth of eye-witness
and autobiographical accounts written by men and women who were at
some time members of Mosley's party. This is an absence made all the
more remarkable by the fact that it highlights a reluctance and silence
that does not appear to afflict other major parties and movements.
Almost every significant political organisation of the last two hundred
years has inspired works written by persons keen to provide an account
of their active involvement. This is true for national political parties
and their leaders as well as for the obscure and unknown rank and file
activists from the time of early trade unionism and Chartism through
to the present. It is surprising, then, that the BUF does not appear to
have had among their members a similar proportion of activists and
sympathisers eager to provide a record of their efforts on behalf of the
party or of their commitment to the ideology of the extreme right. This
relative silence is made more striking when placed alongside the number
of autobiographies and memoirs written by both the leaders and ordinary
members of the Communist Party. Extensive research into working
class autobiographies has revealed 57 memoirs by members or former
members of the CP covering the inter-war period. The total number
of Fascist autobiographies, written by persons of varied backgrounds,
amounts to only perhaps one-tenth of that figure.[3] This a discrepancy
which cannot be explained by differences in size of membership of the
respective parties or in terms of the working class proportion of that
membership, but which perhaps instead reflects a desire not to make
public an association with the Radical Right or possibly an unwillingness
on the part of the literary establishment to publish such items for fear of
guilt by association.[4]

Nevertheless, despite this shortage of Fascist memoirs, it is increasingly
the case that historians are now turning to autobiographies in an
endeavour to throw new light on old questions.[5] This development
is partly the product of an improved awareness of the existence and
availability of such material, and with this has come a movement
away from a previous tendency either to disregard such material
or relegate it to a position of minor importance in the hierarchy
of historical sources. References to the memoirs of Philip Snowden,
Phil Piratin and Margaret McCarthy are now appearing with greater
frequency, together with the more familiar works of Oswald and Diana
Mosley, and the lesser-known, and relatively inaccessible, unpublished
memoirs of Richard Reynall Bellamy and Nellie Driver. Even such a
short list taken from the bibliographies of recent publications on British

Fascism includes sympathisers, anti-Fascists and members of the political establishment, and in each case the political memoir is being looked at in the hope of finding new insights and details. Familiar works are being re-examined with new questions in mind and new discoveries always offer the possibility of a fresh perspective. But each time the question is asked whether autobiographies are reliable. To what extent are the personal observations, anecdotes and stories recorded in an autobiography valuable insights and acceptable historical facts or merely private musings, speculation and individual interpretation?

The essential problem of the autobiography is that it is the record of a life seen and understood backwards, so that descriptions and analysis of events, both public and private, are inevitably coloured by opinions formed later. Primarily for this reason many commentators on historical method view the autobiography as existing somewhere in the twilight zone between primary and secondary source, exhibiting the strengths of neither and the weaknesses of both.[6] Little discussion is offered of the merits or otherwise of this type of document beyond general criticisms that the subjectivity of autobiographies means that they can be no more than a highly personal record of experiences and thoughts, often written to justify actions, and composed long after the events described. To add to this, they are usually considered inaccurate in factual details and prone to gross distortion, perhaps because of a conscious desire to inflate one's own importance, to embroider and embellish the mundane and unimportant, or to suppress and edit the dubious and reprehensible. Inaccuracy and distortion could result also from a combination of unfortunate occurrences to which all writers are prone, notably accidental and unconscious editing, poor memory and misunderstanding. Apart from these problems concerning factual accuracy there is also the question whether the story of one person's life has any broader consequence and validity, and it is often asked if autobiographers can be regarded as typical and representative of the generation, class or organisation from which they are writing. The mere fact of writing a life history makes the autobiographer in some ways exceptional and atypical, but the real issue is whether this invalidates or qualifies any general implications or conclusions that can be inferred from the text. The list of criticisms therefore appears comprehensive and serious doubts are raised as to the historical value of the memoir. Central to the problem is the extent to which the inevitable subjectivity and selectivity invalidate its value as a tool in the attempt to recreate the past.

Clearly, autobiographies are not the only type of source material susceptible to these problems and no account or report can claim to be entirely objective, representative or comprehensive. A verbatim transcription of, for example, a speech can give an accurate record of what was said but it cannot provide a full picture because it does not reveal tone, inflexion, irony or reception. While the government records that survive in the Public Record Office are generally regarded as essential reading for any serious researcher, they represent only the weeded and un-shredded tip of a vast and ever-expanding iceberg of potential official information. Moreover, the writers of any type of document are to some extent constrained by the accepted limitations and conventions of the genre in which they are working, whether government enquiry, newspaper article or personal memoir.[7] This ever-present tendency towards a degree of subjectivity and selectivity demands that any source has to be read with a critical and perceptive eye for the sub-text, or unwitting testimony. The complaint usually levelled against the autobiography is not just that these elements are present in their starkest form, but that they become more of a problem the greater the distance that exists between the time of writing and the events described. Such a view is based on the presupposition that an immediate record is more objective, more accurate, and so of greater value. Yet there would appear to be no sound rationale or proof for the argument that an account written during or immediately after an event is less prone to distortion or subjective interpretation than anything written after a lapse of many years.

There can be no disputing that hindsight and opinions formed later in life can affect understanding and analysis of early experiences, and the editing and changed emphasis that the autobiographers bring to their memories may indeed obscure and discolour. Equally, though, this could also lead to an improved, not diminished, objectivity and clarity resulting from the ability to look back from a position which allows a wide perspective and broader understanding. It is the task of the historian to identify the tone and extent of discoloration and to illuminate the obscure by treating the subjectivity and selectivity of memoirs as worthy of consideration in their own right. If handled with care and sympathy the treatment of episodes, and the sentiments and reactions exposed, can be as revealing as any factual or verbatim account. Likewise, omissions from the text are as important as the topics eventually chosen for inclusion. It is the autobiographers, usually without the assistance or guidance of an interviewer, co-writer or editor, who are deciding what is important and relevant, giving their own weight and interpretation to particular themes, and who are concerned with providing not merely descriptions but an insight into the impact of events on an individual life. It is through precisely the subjectivity and selectivity of the memoir that we are able to penetrate the previously hidden area of private attitudes and fears, hopes and expectations.

A final weakness of the criticisms levelled against autobiographies is the tendency to dismiss them all as equally guilty of the various faults. Against this it is important to recognise the subtleties of variety with this genre of writing. A personal memoir is as individual and distinctive as the fingerprints of the author, not only in the obvious area of life details but also in terms of the methods of, and reasons for, composition. A life history may be composed entirely from memory; with the help of notes and diaries kept at the time; by interviewing and tape-recording; with the aid of a researcher or family; and with or without reference to other primary and secondary material. Similarly, it may have been written deliberately for publication; to fill empty retirement or unemployed years; to reveal the 'truth'; to make money; for personal or public reasons; for the eyes only of grandchildren and family; to improve literacy skills; for propagandist purposes (political or evangelical); or as justification and explanation of a life and career. Each of these variables will necessarily affect the content in different ways and have to be considered when assessing the strengths and weaknesses of any memoir, and especially the specific genre of political autobiography. In the main these are accounts of public life, written by persons who had achieved some notoriety, repute or distinction, and intended for a wide public readership. In relation to the present study the memoirs of Oswald Mosley are the most obvious example. In 1968 he published his long-awaited autobiography, *My Life*, a volume which was to be greeted with a mixed response by admirers, critics, historians and political commentators. Although Robert Skidelsky is perhaps the most charitable in his use of this work, acknowledging that his biographical appraisal was helpfully informed by the material provided by Mosley, he does not uncritically accept all of Mosley's claims and indeed recognises that Mosley was inevitably and naturally emphasising only what was of importance to him.[8] Other commentators, less favourably disposed to this particular example of subjectivity and selectivity in autobiography, have accused Mosley of writing a book that was bland, unrevealing, a deliberate distortion and prone to crude omissions.[9] Particular attention is given to Mosley's explanation of the BUF's adoption of anti-Semitism and use of political violence as a tactic. These areas form the basis of much heated debate, with disagreement over timing, nature, origins and reasons for such a policy. It was hoped that Mosley would throw important new light on these shadowy topics but, in the view of Vernon Bogdanor, his comments and analysis were not even remotely convincing. In short, the tendency is to dismiss *My Life* as a whitewash, an attempt to obscure the controversial, to smooth the rough and unpleasant edges of the BUF, to present it as just another political party and to secure the political rehabilitation of Mosley himself. Even though Mosley has evidently not succeeded in this, his memoirs are accused of falling into, by choice or otherwise, all the traps that await the autobiographer and in so doing has confirmed the fears of all those with doubts about the validity of political reminiscences. This need to 'set the facts straight', to excuse or justify behaviour, to exaggerate or underplay a personal role when appropriate and to obscure and ignore embarrassments is thought to be a feature present in the memoirs of all major political figures influential in public life. However, it would be wrong to taint all autobiographies with the same sullied brush. Such needs and desires are less in evidence in the writings of the minor actors on the large political stage, who achieved little or nothing in the way of national recognition. In many cases the works of these people were never published or perhaps reached only a limited and local market. The content of the political memoir would necessarily have been affected by these differences in motivation for writing and the different expectations concerning the diffusion and longevity of the memoirs. Some clearly expected their life histories to be used as the definite and comprehensive record of a period and events, whereas others accepted a more modest and almost obscure place for their memories.

In the early 1960s, more or less the same time as Mosley was recording his own reminiscences, a former Fascist from the small weaving town of Nelson in Lancashire was also sitting down to put her life history on paper. While Nellie Driver's work is not the subject of such bitter condemnation and dismissal as that of Mosley, partly due to her position in the movement and the relative inaccessibility of her memoirs, there nevertheless exists a degree of uncertainty and unease over how to regard her writings, a consequence of the traditional approach to the political autobiography in general and that of Mosley in particular. The tendency has been to extract the objective facts and impressions of the BUF which can then, ideally, be checked for accuracy and generality against existing knowledge. This has proved possible with some of the information she provides, but there also remains much that has to remain tantalisingly unsubstantiated. This problem of verification has led one historian of the BUF to preface his use of some material from the autobiography with the phrases 'claims were made' and 'reputedly', but elsewhere he is prepared to accept without any such qualification Driver's apparently unconfirmed story of Mosley physically attacking a fellow member of the BUF.[10] Similarly, Rawnsley acknowledges that Driver's memoirs, written and tape-recorded, were indispensable in the writing of his thesis and yet he limits himself to extracting only the occasional quotation for illustrative purposes and an uncritical acceptance of her comments regarding membership. While showing the necessary caution, both Thurlow and Rawnsley are by this approach highlighting the dilemma which historians face over the weight and emphasis to be given to comments and anecdotes contained in such a highly personal document as a life history. In contrast with Mosley's memoirs, though, Driver is not accused of the crimes of blatant whitewash and distortion. Although both were writing within the constraints imposed by the conventions of this particular literary genre, their finished memoirs are very different in a number of important respects.

Both writers describe a significant moment of political activity, but with the essential difference that Mosley was writing as founder and leader of the movement, on whom the onus of responsibility for explanation would necessarily fall most heavily.[11] He was expected to write his memoirs and his personal account was awaited eagerly by contemporaries, associates, opponents and historians. It was assured of publicity, publication and a wide readership. The contrast with Driver's memoirs could hardly be more direct. She was writing not from the London heart of Fascism but from the regional backwaters of Nelson, thereby providing a different focus to the more customary emphasis on the metropolis. Also, she was writing as a woman, from a background of working class poverty, both being elements which give to her memoirs a distinctive tone and flavour. Moreover, her motives for recording her life contrast with Mosley, evidencing a considerably more personal and introspective reflection. There is no indication that the work was intended for a readership other than, perhaps, immediate family, and the impression is that she wrote from a strong desire to make clear to herself the meaning of her life and to try to pull the various strands of her existence into a coherent whole. She did not expect her work to be read by a mass audience, or even an audience at all, and so criticisms of distortion, falsification and whitewashing would seem misplaced as they could serve no real purpose other than self-delusion. The only bias of which she can fairly be accused is that common to all autobiographers of selecting and ordering only those events and episodes which had some significance in her life.

It is apparent, then, that autobiographies certainly need to be treated with as much critical evaluation as historians take to all their material, but there is an equal need not to take a limited view of their usefulness and search only for new or supplementary pieces of factual information and to dismiss them if they seem to contain errors or bias. The autobiography should be read as a work of literature and eye-witness documentary evidence; as a personal assessment of a life and a source for detail on specific events. Above all, the reader needs to be sympathetic, not necessarily to the author or the content of the work, but rather to the form of writing, its conventions, limitations and strengths. The memoirs of Nellie Driver provide not only direct and first-hand information concerning the nature of the provincial BUF but can also locate Fascism in the context of an individual life, in this instance the life of an ordinary, working class, female activist.

II

Nellie Driver was born shortly after the declaration of the First World War of poor but religious parents, with her father having some claim to French aristocratic descent. Following demobilisation he took the family to Middlesbrough in order to obtain employment in the booming post-war shipping industry. Soon after starting construction work in the shipyards he began to suffer from attacks of vertigo and, with no possibility of alternative employment in this part of the North-East, the family returned to Nelson. They remained there only briefly, however, before moving out to the nearby countryside in an endeavour to find a cure for their daughter's ill-health. Again their stay was only temporary, as a small inheritance from Nellie Driver's paternal grandparents enticed the family back to Nelson to set up a grocery business. Bad debts and competition quickly caused this new venture to fail and the family to move once more, this time to neighbouring Borrowford and work in the local mill. Shortly afterwards Nellie's father became seriously ill and died, forcing her mother to return to work as a chainbeamer and Nellie, at the age of 14, to take her first job in a sweet factory, Nelson's only other major industry apart from weaving and related trades. She was forced to leave at 16 in line with the unofficial unemployment policies then in operation and, unable to find further work, Nellie and her widowed mother fell into extreme hardship, relying on driftwood for fires and food left on the doorstep by kindly neighbours.[12] Following some years of material deprivation, unemployment and bleak prospects, both Nellie and her mother joined the BUF in 1935, at the time of Mosley's Lancashire campaign.[13]

The inability of the BUF to break into mainstream political life in the first two years of its existence had caused the leadership to rethink their strategy, with the favoured new direction being based around the attempt to win significant mass support by offering solutions to local and regional problems. The Lancashire cotton campaign, usually said to span the years 1934 to 1936, but especially concentrated in the months from November 1934 to April 1935, is one aspect of this move towards revitalisation.[14] It was thought that a modern political party with new and direct proposals for the regeneration of the textile industry could win important backing from the unemployed and the desperate cotton operatives of the North-West. The BUF sought to exploit what was believed to be a growing sense of disillusionment, rooted in the failure of established parties and the trade union movement to offer even the hope of recovery and improvement, by presenting both an analysis of the problems and a solution which promised a future for the textile industry and the North-West region.[15] Emphasis was placed firmly on local issues in a style and language that could easily be understood, with responsibility for decline attributed to the self-interested actions of employers, financiers and politicians.[16] In contrast, the BUF presented itself as the champion of the ordinary man, appealing to an instinctive common sense of injustice and a tradition of contempt for the long-established structures of capitalist power and authority. At the heart of the critique was the belief that high profits were made at the expense of the worker, who was suffering working conditions unchanged for a century, using antiquated machinery and caught in the trap of low wages. As was commented in the Fascist *Action*: '. . . the workers in one of the most important industries in Britain [are] looked upon as of less account than the cloth they weave . . .'.[17]

Such a condemnation of exploitative capitalism showed many features in common with the arguments of their socialist opponents, appearing as the creed of the ordinary man and woman suffering at the hands of an impersonal system. Similarly, in some of the components of its proposed programme it differed little from the demands of the socialists, calling for 100 per cent trade unionism, good wages, holidays with pay, shorter working hours and a higher standard of living.[18] Presented in this way it is possible to see how Driver could assert that '. . . the working class have nothing to fear from fascism and everything to gain'.[19] The sting in the tail came with the less-publicised methods to be adopted to achieve this and the nature of the proposed Corporate State, both representing a radical departure from the policies of the left.

The analysis, then, seemed reasonable, the promises attractive, while the solution or method of fulfilling the programme was at the very least dynamic and modern, offering a positive and radical alternative. The content and tone of the BUF message appeared logical and rational, calculated to appeal to parochial sentiments and to offer some release from the suffering created by the crisis in the cotton industry. The potential therefore existed for support, with people attracted by any or all of these components, and the BUF, nationally and locally, strenuously sought to realise this by organising meetings, distributing pamphlets and with the national leaders, including Mosley, conducting a series of speaking tours around the textile districts of Lancashire. As mentioned previously, much of this activity took place in 1934/5, but this represents only the early peak of a more continuous effort throughout the period up to the outbreak of war. In Nelson the correspondence columns of the local newspaper were regularly used to publicise the BUF arguments and meetings were frequently held. Indeed, local activity did not perhaps peak until as late as 1938, when in February of that year over 200 meetings were organised throughout Lancashire, and a series of smaller gatherings were held in September in Nelson as a preliminary to the address given by Mosley at the Palace Theatre on 16 October on the Fascist cure for cotton.[20] On this occasion the local press accorded Mosley the privilege of a full verbatim account of his speech, providing a detailed and accessible exposition of BUF policy to a large, local audience.

The campaign, then, was long-lasting and, given the circumstances and conditions existing in the North-West and the methods and emotive appeal of the BUF propagandists, at the very least there existed the potential for significant recruitment to the Fascist movement. However, the extent of their success would appear to be open to some discussion. Both Richard Thurlow and Stuart Rawnsley believe some inroads were made by the BUF, with the former referring to some 'considerable headway' in 1934 but followed by decline thereafter, and the latter talking of a 'quite high level' of recruitment among the unemployed and threatened operatives in both Lancashire and Yorkshire.[21] However, it has been estimated that by 1937 the total active BUF membership of the North-West, including Manchester and Liverpool, was no more than 100.[22] The impression for the region as a whole, then, is of some positive response initially followed by decline from around 1935. While this assessment of the Lancashire situation remains general and impressionistic, the particular case of Nelson may assist in providing some indication of actual and potential trends.

Robert Skidelsky suggests that it was only in Blackburn, Burnley and Nelson/Colne that the BUF made any significant impact in the North-West.[23] Yet he was writing when the memoirs of Nellie Driver were still undiscovered and so was unable to incorporate into his analysis any of the insights provided concerning the last-named branch. Even so, while this omission can now be corrected, it is still possible to identify contrasting pictures of Fascist activity in this small weaving town. On the one hand, the Nelson branch can be seen as flourishing by the mid-1930s, with a growing membership, support from local businessmen and a newly-appointed Woman District Leader and Assistant District Organiser (Propaganda). The branch had its own meeting room and bookshop and was active in organising public debates, undertaking diverse propaganda activity and selling the Fascist newspaper. The claim, originating from Rawnsley's interviews with Driver in December 1976, that membership peaked at 100 is repeated without further comment in many secondary texts.[24] This picture of a thriving and efficient Fascist movement in Nelson requires some qualification.

The membership figure may or may not be accurate. The interview took place more than 40 years after the period being described and there is the possibility that Driver romanticised or exaggerated the numbers for the benefit of the interviewer. No corroborative evidence is provided by Rawnsley and, interestingly, there is no relevant numerical material in Driver's written memoirs, composed some 13 or so years before the interview took place.[25] However, if this figure can be accepted as accurate there is still no reason to infer that either this level of membership was long-lasting or that it represented a high level of commitment to Fascism from within the town. Indeed, it is likely, though this has to remain speculation, that any such peak was of very short duration. Support for this interpretation can be found in the tone of the memoir, which is one of disillusion in failing to attract support rather than enthusiasm inspired by vigorous and lasting growth. Driver declined a suggestion from Richard Reynall Bellamy, who led the BUF in the North, that she should stand as a candidate in the local elections as she did not believe she could win more than ten votes in her own ward. To add further to this picture of failure, the branch seemed unable to sell more than one paper to the Nelson public on Saturday evenings.[26] Driver was forced to concede in her written memoirs that the local people rejected the BUF: 'In Nelson progress was slow and far from satisfactory . . . Often we wondered whether it was all worth it. People did not want our "steel creed of the iron age".'[27]

Even more difficult to determine than the actual membership of the local BUF is the extent of active and passive support given to the movement. That interest certainly existed is given substantial weight by the size of the audience which attended Mosley's meetings in 1938, filling the local theatre to its 2,000 capacity, though clearly drawn from the neighbouring towns in the North-West as well as Nelson itself. Although only minor and isolated instances of dissent and opposition were recorded as having taken place at these gatherings, this is not to suggest that all those present necessarily gave their backing to the BUF. However, these meetings do indicate the level of curiosity generated by the presence of the BUF leader, an interest which the local branch evidently was unable to sustain once Mosley had left the district. Indeed, throughout the 1930s the party machine in Nelson failed to win mass support, achieve financial solvency, or even maintain cohesion and harmony among the few members it had managed to attract. Driver herself makes the contrast between the well-run and powerful BUF organisation in London and its weaker northern character, a feature which she attributes to the strong independent nature of the northern people, which is illustrated by their refusal to follow the simple party procedures of saluting fellow-members and officers, selling newspapers on a regular basis or participating in other activities insisted upon by the national headquarters.[28] Local meetings were marked by factional fighting between the diverse groups and individuals who made up the membership, and it is becoming one of the most popular quotations from Driver's memoirs that the Nelson BUF consisted of ex-Communists, Catholics, Christadelphians and others who disagreed over interests, priorities, tactics and organisation. This uncomfortable diversity led Driver to liken the persistent clashes within the branch to the performance of comic opera. Moreover, this was presented not as evidence of the broad appeal of Fascism but rather of its ability to attract society's cranks, faddists, and outsiders with 'waste paper basket ideas', seen by Driver as a 'dreadful nuisance' and serious obstacle to the progress of the movement. The meetings in Nelson and throughout other areas of the North-West were often ill-attended 'flops', and on more than one occasion ended in chaos. Yet, 'carefully-cooked' reports were sent to party headquarters describing them as highly successful, evidencing a clear intention to please Mosley and further the impression of a dynamic movement.[29] Furthermore, while the BUF saw the advantages of giving titles and status to their members, these could be more glamorous in name than in practice. The chief duty of Nelson's Assistant District Organiser (Propaganda) appears to have been as a graffiti-writer, daubing the gate-posts of a local clergymen suspected of left-wing tendencies! This impression of the relative ineffectiveness of the BUF in Nelson also gains some support from the contemporary response from one part of the labour movement. Despite the local Weavers' Union having a reputation for militancy, they nevertheless gave permission for Nellie Driver's mother to teach her daughter, already a known and active Fascist, the trade of chainbeaming. It would seem, then, that against the picture of BUF organisation, efficiency and growth there can also be placed a picture of division, inefficiency and limited appeal. This apparent failure in one of Lancashire's main textile areas needs to be explained.

When considering what the BUF was offering in terms of the practical objectives and promises outlined earlier, it is possible to understand how this could have an appeal. Yet these promises to the Lancashire people could not be divorced from the other well-documented aspects of the party which were likely to have an opposite effect. The operatives of the North-West, as elsewhere, were suspicious of a party which practised anti-Semitism, was associated with Mussolini and Hitler, adopted tactics of violence and confrontation and planned to radically restructure society. These negative qualities, the weakness of their arguments and the hollowness of their promises were well exploited by their opponents.

The theorists from the Communist Party highlighted the flaws in the BUF's analysis of cotton's decline, pointed to the practical impossibility both of excluding Japanese goods from India and of subduing India's own textile industry, and stressed the association of Fascist proposals not with improved working conditions but with wage cuts.[30] These critiques formed the basis of an organised offensive campaign by the Communist Party in Lancashire, leading to conferences, meetings and the distribution of, allegedly, 10,000 copies of the pamphlet 'Mosley and Lancashire'. The fight was even taken to the correspondence columns of the local newspapers with Fascists, Communists and representatives of the National Unemployed Workers' Movement engaging in many and often lengthy written confrontations on several points of policy and programme, and which on occasion also spilled over into face-to-face street conflict.[31] However, while anti-Fascist activity was undeniably present, there is no direct evidence that either their demonstrations or theoretical and polemical discourses served as the main factor in restricting Fascist activity and recruitment. The general failure of both the British Union of Fascists and the Communist Party to attract widespread support in this part of the North-West would indicate that the reasons for the weakness of extremist politics were more deeply embedded in the economic and political complexion of the town.

While it is necessary to avoid making any simple or single causal connection between economic distress and political extremism, it is also the case that a drastic downturn in economic fortunes, combined with ineffective government action, can make previously rejected policies and parties a more attractive proposition and alternative. The uncertain and changing face of national politics in these years was reflected in many constituencies throughout the country. In 1931, for example, the comfortable parliamentary majority enjoyed by the Labour Party in the Nelson and Colne constituency was overturned, and the monocled, cigar-smoking, bowler-hatted Linton Thorp unseated Arthur Greenwood by a margin of 7,686. While political allegiances may not have been permanently shifting there is contained in this large swing an indication of the growing desperation of the local electorate borne out of the crisis facing local industry. A Board of Trade report commented that the scale and rapidity of the decline in the cotton industry was without parallel, creating not only mass unemployment but also serious underemployment.[32] But the political shift of 1931, while significant, was not permanent and in 1935 Sidney Silverman was returned as the Labour candidate and continued to represent the area until his death in 1968.[33] While the crisis in textiles was severe it does not appear to have been sufficiently wide or deep to bring about a permanent fissure in the local body politic or fundamentally to threaten traditional allegiances. However, this is to remain at a rather general level. It is important not to homogenise the experience of the textile industry between the wars, for there were major regional variations in the scale and tempo of the decline, dependent largely upon such variables as the quality of the yarn and the market for the products. In Nelson many small firms were forced out of existence and there was a reduction in the number of looms, but the impact of the crisis was not as serious as in neighbouring areas. The spinners of medium yarn from Oldham suffered to a far greater extent than the weavers from Nelson producing high quality cloth for the home and Dominion markets.[34] Throughout the 1920s the rate of unemployment in Nelson remained below the national average at around the six per cent mark and, although hit badly by the 1929 crash, the figure still managed to keep below the average level for the industry as a whole. In 1931 over 33 per cent of Burnley weavers were unemployed compared to 25 per cent in Nelson, dropping to 18 per cent in 1932 and 12 per cent in 1936/7.[35] These statistics suggest that the cotton crisis in the Nelson district peaked before the emergence of the BUF and that the problem, rather than worsening, was in fact showing signs of moderate improvement by the early- to mid-1930s. Even so, this argument linking economic decline, relative and absolute, with radical politics is to rest on unproven and questionable assumptions. The base of the explanation needs to be widened to take account not only of the performance of industry but also of its structure, and the nature of the political institutions, relationships and traditions to which it gave rise.

Although primarily a one-industry town, Nelson managed to avoid the same level of paternalism normally associated with that variety of industrial organisation by its dependence on the room and power system in which a large number of small employers leased rooms in a big mill shed.[36] The direct contact and negotiation that resulted between employer and worker meant that the minor demands could be satisfied quickly and without resort to the cumbersome and slow trade union bureaucracy.[37] When the issues became more serious, as with the opposition to wage reductions and the introduction of the 'more looms' system into weaving, the Weavers' Association, considered to be the most radical of the Lancashire cotton trade unions, was eager to continue their tradition of militancy in taking the fight to the employers.[38] When needed, the Association was prepared to respond. The solid rock of the trade union movement in the district of Nelson seemed unmoved by the economic crisis, continuing the long history of a vital and active labour movement. The Social Democratic Federation, Independent Labour Party, Labour Party and trade unionism all had a long and deep background in the area and, despite the exceptional occurrence of the election of Linton Thorp in 1931, there was continued and regular support for Labour representatives in both national and local elections.[39] Commentators frequently refer to the strong socialist culture and high level of labour consciousness which existed in the town.[40] The decline of the cotton industry was unable to undermine this culture or threaten the core of this consciousness, and so left an infertile and inhospitable soil in which Fascism failed to take root.

III

Thus far I have extracted from the memoir what Driver tells us about the BUF, and have placed this in its general and specific context. That is, looking at Fascism as a national political movement but in its local setting. In this way some important insights, points of detail and impressions can usefully be taken from the section of the autobiography covering BUF activity between 1935 and 1940. But this account is also in many ways a disappointment. The section on Fascism is relatively brief, with Driver devoting only 45 pages of a 168 page memoir to this five year period, contrasting with the 90 or so pages describing her 21 month term of internment. Also, her treatment is selective in that it fails to mention a number of features and issues of central interest to historians of the movement. Notable by their absence are any discussions of tactics, ideology, policies, organisation, finances, policing, public order, or profiles of individual members or supporters. Fleeting glimpses are occasionally provided, but little of substance on any of these topics. One explanation for these significant omissions is that she was being careful to edit, in the manner of Mosley, the controversial and sensitive. However, this then raises the troublesome question why she felt a need to be selective in this way given that her memoirs were not intended for mass consumption. It has to be remembered that Driver is not telling us what we necessarily want to hear, and she is certainly not answering all the questions we would wish to ask. Instead, she was writing about what was important to her, and in order to make some personal assessment of the key episodes in her life. This, then, is to locate her activity for the BUF in the context of the rest of her life, and her memories provide a rare and valuable insight into the meaning of Fascism for the individual.

Driver has been described as 'one of the driving forces of fascism in Lancashire',[41] and to understand how and why this was achieved we need to return to the problem of her membership and motivation. When Driver came to join the BUF in 1935 her political consciousness was at best ill-formed and immature, with no previous experience of, or interest in, the politics of the day. However, she had carried through her early life a broad sympathy with the underprivileged, and her recent personal experience of unemployment and hardship gave to this general sense of injustice a more vibrant and urgent note: 'Family hardships and the sufferings of the people all around me . . . caused me to rebel against the prevailing poor social conditions.'[42] This rebelliousness eventually found its outlet in Fascism, but not before other options had been tried. While Fascism came to her as a method of ending the sufferings of herself and others it also answered a more personal and introspective search which had begun much earlier. Up to 1935 Driver had sought relief from such material deprivation through the sanctuary of religion. She had been raised a Nonconformist, but even at a young age she rebelled against the drabness of the Baptists and felt drawn to what she believed to be the colour and romance of the established Church. In religion she found some compensation for a lonely childhood and adolescence, during which she also suffered from a serious illness which left her emaciated and with a permanent heart condition. Failing to find any joy in her impoverished home and school life, this pattern continued at work where she became the target of persecution by her workmates, for reasons which are left unexplained. Isolated and outcast, her young life lacked any focus other than religion. A newly-formed branch of the Christian Endeavour provided the opportunity for active work in Christ's cause, but this collapsed after only a few weeks, forcing her to transfer her devotions to an independent Methodist chapel. Again, though, this left her still unsettled, for '. . . organised religion seemed so cold and empty'.[43] Both she and her mother then tried other chapels, revivalist and evangelical meetings, and spiritualist seances, but each failed to provide the light and the spiritual comforts they were seeking. It was at this point of growing disillusionment with religion, coupled with her appalling material circumstances, that Nellie Driver received a letter from a friend in Manchester who was Woman District Leader of the Hulme branch, enclosing BUF literature and urging her to join. As mentioned previously, there is no indication that before this Driver had given any thought to matters of politics and yet she snatched at this offering, gripping with both hands the emblems of this organisation, and '. . . from henceforward politics and social reform were to be my religion'.[44]

Fascism had become for Driver her new philosophy of life and Mosley her new object of worship, giving him a faith and devotion which she never entirely abandoned even during the trials of internment and the post-war victimisation of former Fascists. The BUF provided the romance and colour Driver had sought earlier in established religion, with the drum corps, salutes, standards, emblems, uniforms, devotions and demonstrations replacing the symbols and icons of the chapel and church. It appeared as the answer not only to physical deprivation and suffering but also to her own emotional and spiritual poverty. Once she had become a member of the movement, however, a significant transformation took place. Although political considerations and ideological commitment perhaps appeared as relatively minor factors in Driver's decision to join the BUF it cannot be argued that these elements remained unimportant or undeveloped.

Driver was promoted to Woman District Leader of the Nelson branch shortly after joining, achieving this position when only just into her twenties. The generally accepted understanding of gender roles within the BUF would be that Driver was given, by this appointment,

responsibility only over other women members, with overall control of
the local branch resting with the male District Leader, a local weaver.
In practice, though, the roles were swept aside by Driver's enthusiasm
and energy and it was she who assumed effective leadership and control
over the whole branch, causing Richard Reynall Bellamy to comment
that the 'ineffectual' District Leader was simply clay in her hands.[45]
Before Driver joined in 1935 the BUF in Nelson consisted of only
a few isolated members and, despite the qualifications to the size
of membership discussed earlier, it was largely through her personal
efforts that a Fascist organisation and branch existed at all in the town.
She attended and organised local meetings throughout the North-West,
became involved in several violent confrontations with anti-Fascists,
helped to run the Fascist bookshop and was even fined for defacing
railway posters with BUF propaganda. She travelled the North-West
in order to listen to Mosley at rallies and to confirm her position as
a member of the inner band of the northern Fascist elite. She gained
important recognition within the movement when she was awarded a
medal for her services to the party and was entitled to put HS (Honoured
for Service) after her name on official documents. Plans were also made
for her transfer to the London headquarters but these were shelved as a
result of the change to austerity within the party. Driver was a regular
and frequent contributor to the local press, effectively using the available
mass media to outline BUF policies and showing sufficient confidence
to reply to her opponents on such issues as the reasons for cotton's
decline, protectionism, unemployment, internationalism and foreign
policy. The young girl with just an instinctive sense of injustice had
come a long way in a very short time. Although much of her writing
is little more than plagiarism or loose paraphrase of BUF literature,
there is also much that originates from her own imagination, thoughts
and experiences. It becomes increasingly apparent that Driver had not
only listened to Mosley's rhetoric but had also swallowed it, especially
where it addressed Lancashire's problems. In short, Driver's life had
been effectively transformed. The isolation and spiritual sparseness
of her early years had been replaced by a movement which gave
meaning and direction to her life, and also ensured a position of
local prominence and status within the organisation, unthinkable and
unattainable elsewhere. While, as indicated previously, much of this
was hollow in that the local branch of the BUF rested on a relatively
small base, to Driver the benefits of belonging to the movement were
paramount. Failing to find emotional or spiritual comfort in her early
experiences of nonconformist religion, Driver turned to seek them in
nonconformist politics. From 1935 to 1940 the BUF offered the home,
the comradeship, the sense of purpose and the light for which she had
been searching since childhood. The status and authority she acquired
within the branch was the positive return for her commitment to the
Fascist cause. Far from relegating this woman member to a subordinate
and minor position within the party, the BUF instead gave to Driver a

self-respect and importance that was inconceivable in almost any other context, political or otherwise.[46] The war was to bring this to a rude and sudden end.

In October 1940 Driver was arrested under Defence Regulation 18b (1a) following the decision of the Government in the previous spring to intern the leading national and local officials of the BUF. The state was now to take control of Driver's life, moulding its direction and shape for the next 21 months, in a way similar to the previous external, determining influences of the BUF and religion. She was taken first to Holloway Jail in London before being transferred, in June 1941, to Port Erin on the Isle of Man. It was during this period of internment that her political commitment to Fascism, although not her personal devotion to Mosley, came under increasing challenge. At first she seemed intent on holding on to her new-found political faith, expressing a reluctance to abandon and deny everything she had come to believe in so fervently. Gradually, though, this reluctance began to crumble. While in Holloway she was drawn less to her fellow BUF internees and instead found kindness and friendship from the prostitutes, Catholics and, perhaps surprisingly, Jews. Her fear of isolation and tendency to engage in soul-searching returned as the symbols and activity of the BUF were taken away. Driver was progressively pulled towards the lure of religious faith once more: 'I knew instinctively I could not pit my will against the Eternal God'.[47] She began to attend Catholic services and the Roman faith edged her Fascist beliefs into the background.[48] Even the harsh conditions of her internment, described in some detail in the memoirs, became bearable because of her new-found spiritual strength. Her transfer to the Isle of Man brought some improvement in the material circumstances of imprisonment and Driver found in this unlikely environment a level of intimacy and loyalty in her friendships that had previously been missing from her life. She greeted the news of her impending release, set for June 1942, with some sadness and regret for it meant a return to the isolation and loneliness of her former existence: 'When Euston Station was reached the Government had finished with me. From now on I had to look after myself. No longer would I be pilotted and directed at every step under escort. Almost panic-stricken I stood alone whilst people rushed about in every direction . . .'.[49] On returning to Nelson she eventually found employment in an electrical engineering factory, having experienced numerous rejections because of the former Fascist associations, and succour in the Catholic faith. The absence of any discussion of her life from 1947 on is itself a revealing exclusion. She was to die, single and childless, in 1981, fittingly within a few months of Mosley himself.[50]

IV

Despite the quantitative and qualitative limitations of Driver's auto-biography discussed earlier, its value, other than by virtue of its scarcity as a Fascist memoir, is that it can operate and inform on a number of levels. As well as providing facts and anecdotes for cross-checking, the autobiography can also be used as the basis for constructing a biographical portrait which uses the subjectivity and selectivity contained in the reminiscences as a positive and worthy feature. By considering her own thoughts, impressions, use of language and metaphor, and assessment of a life, balanced against the more customary historical records, it is possible to obtain a glimpse into the character and motivation of an active member of the BUF in a northern, working-class setting. Her comments on such matters as membership and party activity cause us to give further consideration to the nature of provincial Fascism and the impact of the cotton campaign, to move away from casual generalisations and to scratch beneath the veneer of superficial assumptions and impressions. Moreover, it serves to take attention away from the national leadership and London location of the BUF, and towards rank and file activity in a small Lancashire town. Useful perspectives are provided on the relative failure of Fascism in this particular district, with interesting if undeveloped remarks on the relationship between the centre and periphery of the party and the staunch independence of the northern character which the Fascist vision was unable to penetrate.

As well as providing this fairly detailed, if selective, view of provincial Fascism, Driver's autobiography, by means of its subjectivity and highly personal reflection and retrospection, permits some glimpse into how the experience of Fascist activity fitted into the overall pattern of an individual life. Driver's Fascism has to be seen and understood as coming sandwiched between two thick slices of religion. She was drawn to it not merely, or even mainly, because of her personal experiences of material deprivation and vague sense of injustice, nor was she attracted primarily by the political arguments and solutions of the BUF. At least initially, Fascism, Mosley, the party and its organisation gave the leadership, guidance and structure which religion had failed to provide in her early years. The themes and language of the narrative, with stories of early escapes from death, disabling illnesses, and the search for the flame to lighten a dark and empty soul, have more in common with the spiritual autobiographies of the eighteenth and nineteenth centuries than the political memoirs of the twentieth. When religion was found wanting Driver turned to the secular alternative of politics rather than indulging in drink and gambling, as was typical of the nineteenth century backsliders; but this proved, for her as for them, only a temporary aberration from the pathway to enlightenment.

However, this apparent relegation of her Fascist beliefs and activity to a position of relatively minor importance in her life should not blind us to the possibility that without the outbreak of war her devotion to Mosley and right-wing politics may have been maintained. Also, although spanning a comparatively short period, Driver gained immeasurably from her experience. If she was hoping to find a faith, commitment, comradeship, home, sense of worth, status, direction and purpose, then she was not to be disappointed.

While Driver's motivation for joining the BUF, and her subsequent activity on behalf of the movement, may have been without parallel, her memoirs do suggest certain preconditions in which Fascism can take root and it would be a mistake to ignore the possibility of generalising from the particular and personal. The memoir highlights the materialist conditions which can act as a stimulus, set against the attitudes, values and hopes of an individual. While this is to move somewhat uncomfortably and tentatively towards the minefield of psycho-history, it should at least indicate the collision of circumstances, general and specific, common and private, in which political extremism can breed. Ideally it would be desirable to test Driver's experiences against those of others similarly attracted to the Fascist cause. While we await the discovery of other such items, we are left for the moment with this rare and absorbing account which permits a most important penetration into the private thoughts of an individual who saw in Mosley the means of local, national and personal salvation.

DAVID MAYALL
Sheffield City Polytechnic

NOTES

I am most grateful to Martin Durham, Colin Holmes and Frank Lennon for their valuable comments on early drafts of this paper, and to Richard Thurlow and the staff of Nelson District Library for their helpful assistance with references and information.

1. R. Skidelsky, *Oswald Mosley* (London, 1975).
2. Nellie Driver's internment file was not among those released by the PRO in February 1986 and it is probable that it was among those destroyed. I am grateful to Richard Thurlow for this information. For further discussion of this see C. Holmes, 'Internment, Fascism and Public Records', *Bulletin of the Society for the Study of Labour History*, no.52, part 1 (Apr. 1987), pp.17–23.
3. For published autobiographies see Y. McShane, *Daughter of Evil. The True Story* (London, 1980); O. Mosley, *My Life* (London, 1968); D. Mosley, *A Life of Contrasts* (London, 1977). For unpublished memoirs see R. R. Bellamy, 'Marching with Mosley'; R. Saunders, 'A Tiller of Several Soils'; N. Driver, 'From the Shadows of Exile. An unpublished autobiography by Nellie Driver, Woman District Leader of the Nelson branch of the BUF, 1935–1940'. For autobiographical fragments see L. Wise (ed.), *Mosley's Blackshirts* (London, 1986); A. K. Chesterton, *Why I Left Mosley* (London, 1938); *Blackshirt*, 16 Nov. 1934 (though note Martin Durham's reservations about the authenticity of these accounts in his article in this volume); *Action*, 29 July, 12 Aug., 19 Aug., 26 Aug. 1939; R. W. Jones, 'I was a Blackshirt menace', *Spectator*, 6 Aug. 1983. Note also the use of tape-recorded reminiscences. An interview with a former Fascist appeared in *The Guardian*, 4 Mar. 1978, and both Stuart Rawnsley and John Brewer interviewed a small number of Mosleyites for their studies of the BUF in the north–west and West Midlands respectively. See S. Rawnsley, 'Fascism and Fascists in Britain in the 1930s: A case study of Fascism in the North of England in a period of economic and political change', unpublished PhD thesis, University of Bradford, 1981; J. Brewer, *Mosley's Men. The British Union of*

Fascists in the West Midlands (London, 1984). Finally, an organisation called 'The Friends of OM', who publish a journal with the same title, repeatedly stress the need for personal documentation of the 'great days' and it is apparent that there exist a number of scattered personal reminiscences which still await discovery.

4. For details of autobiographies by Communists and former Communists, and other items which include some comment on Mosley and British Fascism, see J. Burnett, D. Vincent and D. Mayall (eds.), *The Autobiography of the Working Class: An Annotated Critical Bibliography, Volume 1, 1790–1900* (Brighton, 1984) and *Volume 2, 1900–1945* (Brighton, 1987).

5. For example, note the use of the autobiography in challenging former assumptions and adding new dimensions to the debate concerning the BUF, anti-Semitism and political violence. See J. Jacobs, *Out of the Ghetto: My Youth in the East End, Communism and Fascism 1913–1939* (London, 1978); R. Skidelsky, 'Reflections on Mosley and British Fascism', in K. Lunn and R. Thurlow (eds.), *British Fascism, essays on the Radical Right in Inter-War Britain* (London, 1980) pp.78–99; V. Bogdanor, 'A deeply flawed hero: on Skidelsky's biography of Mosley', *Encounter*, vol.44 (June 1975) pp.69–77. Also, R. Thurlow, *Fascism in Britain: A History, 1918–1985* (Oxford, 1987) and D. S. Lewis, *Illusions of Grandeur: Mosley, Fascism and British Society 1931–1981* (Manchester, 1987) make frequent reference to autobiographical material.

6. See, for example, the comments in A. Marwick, *The Nature of History* (London, 1970) p.134, and J. Tosh, *The Pursuit of History: aims, methods and new directions in the study of history* (London, 1984) pp.32, 54–5. Many other surveys of source material fail even to mention autobiography.

7. For a fuller discussion see D. Vincent, *Bread, Knowledge and Freedom: a Study of 19th Century Working Class Autobiography* (London, 1982). My own comments on this are based to a large degree on the pioneering work of David Vincent and John Burnett into this genre of writing.

8. Skidelsky, *Oswald Mosley*, p.14.

9. See Bogdanor, loc. cit.; Thurlow op. cit., p.121.

10. Thurlow, op. cit., pp.94, 99.

11. It should also be noted that the political content of Driver's memoirs forms only a relatively small proportion of the total. This selectivity and weighting is discussed later. A more extreme example of this is provided by Yolande McShane, Women's Organiser for Merseyside 1936–7, who confines her account of Fascist activity to a brief explanation of why she was attracted to Fascism and short observations on the clashes with Communists at a rally in Liverpool stadium. See *Daughter of Evil*, pp.29–30, 44.

12. Driver, 'Shadows of Exile', pp.13–16.

13. The memoir is regrettably deficient in certain points of detail and vague in chronology, making it impossible to determine the length of time she spent working in the textile industry or the duration of her experience of unemployment between 1935 and 1940.

14. Most of the secondary texts deal only briefly with this topic and the most useful account of the campaign is to be found in Rawnsley, 'Fascism and Fascists', especially chs. 2 and 3. See also Skidelsky, *Oswald Mosley*, p.325; Thurlow, op. cit., p.93; R. Palme Dutt, 'The cotton industry and the Fascist offensive in Lancashire', *Labour Monthly*, vol.17, no.4 (Apr. 1935) p.232.

15. See N. Driver, 'Cotton's rise and fall: a woman looks at Lancashire', *Action*, no.118, 21 May 1938, p.14.

16. See letter from Nellie Driver in the *Nelson Leader*, 22 July 1938, p.7.

17. N. Driver, 'Unhappy Lancashire Weavers', *Action*, no.92, 18 Nov. 1937, p.14.

18. Letter from Nellie Driver in the *Nelson Leader*, 2 June 1939, p.7.

19. Letter from Nellie Driver in ibid., 1 July 1938, p.7.

20. See Lewis, op. cit., p.73; N. Driver, 'Aftermath of Cotton Campaign', *Action*, no.109, 19 Mar. 1938, p.20; N. Driver, 'On the British Union Front: Packed Cinema hears Mosley at Nelson', *Action*, no.140, 22 Oct. 1938, p.17; *Nelson Leader*, 21 Oct. 1938, p.10.

21. Thurlow, op. cit., pp.93, 126; S. Rawnsley, 'The membership of the British Union of Fascists', in Lunn and Thurlow (eds.), op. cit., pp.150–165.
22. Thurlow, op. cit., p.123.
23. Skidelsky, *Oswald Mosley,* p.325.
24. See Rawnsley, 'The membership of the British Union of Fascists,' in Lunn and Thurlow (eds.), op. cit., and 'Fascism and Fascists', pp.236–7, 239, chs.8, 9.
25. In relation to this problem note Thurlow's criticism of the Trevelyan Scholarship Project Report on Yorkshire Fascism for their acceptance of estimates of BUF membership in Leeds provided by a former Fascist. See Thurlow, op. cit., p.123.
26. Driver, 'Shadows of Exile', p.45.
27. Ibid., p.64.
28. Ibid., p.33.
29. Ibid., pp.29, 32–3, 44.
30. R. Palme Dutt, loc. cit.; W. Rust, 'Mosley and Lancashire', *Labour Monthly*, vol.17, no.5 (May 1935), pp.291–9; W. Rust, 'Cotton and the Left: a Reply to the "Fascist Quarterly"', *Labour Monthly*, vol.17, no.11 (Nov. 1935) pp.696–6.
31. Note for example the written exchanges between Nellie Driver and Vincent Myles of the NUWM in the correspondence columns of the *Nelson Leader*, the street confrontations in Nelson, and opposition to Mosley's Nelson meetings in 1938 and 1939. See N. Driver, 'Shadows of Exile', pp.36–7, 51–61; *Nelson Leader*, 24 Mar. 1939, p.10; N. Driver, 'On the British Union Front: Nelson and Colne', *Action*, no.127, 23 July 1938, p.17; N. Driver, 'On the British Union Front: Packed Cinema hears Mosley in Nelson', *Action*, no.140, 22 Oct. 1938, p.17; N. Driver, 'Amazing scenes in Lancashire: thousands fail to gain admittance to packed Nelson meeting', ibid., no.161, 25 Mar. 1939, p.7; N. Driver, 'Aftermath of Cotton Campaign', ibid., no.109, 19 Mar. 1938, p.10.
32. Board of Trade, *Working Party Reports: Cotton* (London, 1946) p.6.
33. For a biographical portrait see E. Hughes, *Sydney Silverman, Rebel in Parliament* (London, 1969).
34. L.H.C. Tippett, *A Portrait of the Lancashire Textile Industry* (London, 1969) p.6.
35. A. and L. Fowler, *The History of the Nelson Weavers' Association* (Nelson, 1984), pp.69–70; *Nelson Leader*, 31 July 1939, p.9; J. Liddington, *The Life and Times of a Respectable Rebel: Selina Cooper, 1864–1946* (London, 1984).
36. Liddington, op. cit., p.32ff.; Fowler, op. cit., pp.2–3.
37. J.Weinroth, 'Little Moscow', unpublished typescript, pp.2–9.
38. See Fowler, op. cit.; Weinroth, 'Little Moscow'.
39. See Liddington, op. cit., pp.132–4; 345; P. Snowden, *An Autobiography,* 2 vols. (London, 1934).
40. Liddington, op. cit., p.134; Weinroth, 'Little Moscow', pp.2, 24; Fowler, op. cit.; W. Bennett *The History of Marsden and Nelson* (Nelson, 1957), pp.211–2.
41. Thurlow, op. cit., p.121.
42. Driver, 'Shadows of Exile', p.28.
43. Ibid., p.27.
44. Ibid., p.29.
45. Quoted in Rawnsley, 'Fascism and Fascists', p.61.
46. For further discussion of women and Fascism, and comments on factors motivating female membership which draw on written and oral reminiscences, see the article by Martin Durham elsewhere in this volume.
47. Driver, 'Shadows of Exile', p.108.
48. For an interesting discussion of the appeal of the BUF to Catholics and of the parallels between the Catholic Church and the Fascist movement in terms of structure, organisations, authoritarianism and dogmatism, see Skidelsky, *Oswald Mosley*, p.347; Rawnsley, 'Fascism and Fascists', pp.254–5.
49. Driver, 'Shadows of Exile, p.162.
50. See short obituary notice in *Action!*, no.288, Feb. 1981, p.2.

'Colonel' Barker: A Case Study in
the Contradictions of Fascism

*In 1929 'Colonel' Barker, known as a leading light in a
British Fascist organization, the National Fascisti, appeared
in a London court on two counts of perjury. The 'Colonel'
was soon revealed as Valerie Arkell-Smith, a woman who
had married her lover, Elfreda Haward, in a Brighton
Parish church and literally convinced hundreds of men with
her disguise. The press coverage devoted to Valerie Arkell-
Smith's sensational trial for her activities as 'Colonel' Barker,
reveals the intricate and complex workings of gender ideology
in the late 1920s. This paper also explore the reasons why, in
the post-war era, notions of female emancipation became so
closely linked with militarism that Fascism appealed directly
to women.*

In March 1929 'Colonel' Ivor Gauntlett Bligh Barker was arrested for
failure to appear on a bankruptcy summons and was soon revealed to
the world as Valerie Arkell-Smith. As 'Colonel' Barker she had married
Elfreda Haward in a Brighton church in 1923 and later became assistant
to National Fascisti president, Colonel H. Rippon-Seymour. There she
acted as boxing instructor at the south London headquarters and urged
her second 'wife' Dorothea to join the organization. 'I quite enjoyed the
life and was always ready to join the fracas the young men had with the
Communists', the 'Colonel' said of her experience with the Fascists. 'I
am told I became rather well known.'

The press coverage devoted to Valerie Arkell-Smith's sensational trial
for her activities as 'Colonel' Barker reveals the intricate and complex
workings of gender ideology in the late 1920s. But it also suggests that,
in this post-war era, women's emancipation had become so linked with
assumption of previously masculine roles that even a Fascist uniform
could signal liberation. By 1934, English traveller, explorer and writer,
Rosita Forbes, was claiming in her magazine, *Women of Many Lands*,
that military uniforms were 'the modern idea' that promised them
equality with their male counterparts.

At the same time there was growing concern that, as women increasingly moved into the public sphere with their new-found political
power, the gender hierarchy was about to crumble. With so many
men dead or permanently disabled because of the War, many social
commentators asked, was Britain about to experience an Amazonian
coup? 'The war has bred a new spirit amongst the rising generation',
wrote a Liverpool journalist in 1919. '[Woman] has imbibed the spirit of

our own gallant masculine youth and she is clamouring for an outlet for the newly-inherited spirit of adventure.'[1] If their demands were ignored, the future for Britain remained unclear.

Valerie Arkell-Smith was the living embodiment of this anxiety. She claimed to have adopted her male disguise to escape from her common-law husband, Earnest Pearce-Crouch, an Australian officer given to drink and brutal beatings. 'The woman known as Valerie Arkell-Smith would vanish', she wrote of her decision to become the 'Colonel'. 'I [would] be free of Pearce-Crouch who would surely never think of looking for me as a man; and I would be free to take on any work that comes my way as a man. Had I not already mixed with men and done a man's work in the Army?' It was even less likely that Pearce-Crouch would look for his wife and mother of his two children among the leadership of the National Fascisti or in an ex-officers' club. It was a disturbing thought.

But the security a masculine persona guaranteed was only a partial motive for Valerie's masquerade. Her rejection of femininity was unequivocal as she told the press: 'behind the change from woman to man I [was] able to screen myself against all the tortures, miseries and difficulties of the past and work out my own salvation'.[2] It was an era when gender roles were in upheaval. Ironically, organizations like the National Fascisti were the most vociferous advocates of ensuring women's place in the domestic realm and least sympathetic to Valerie's plight. However, her act of rebellion followed its own logic; since she had come to identify so completely as a man, she had a vested interest in maintaining the social structures that would ensure her new-found masculine power. Although her case represented a myriad of conflicting interests, Valerie Arkell-Smith, in part, came to symbolize women's rejection of the domestic ideology that had fettered them before the War.

The following discussion will give a brief overview of the NF's beliefs and aims as a background to Colonel Barker's story. It will then focus on the press coverage of Colonel Barker's 1929 trial to explore the complex contradictions she presented and the public's ambiguous attitude towards her rebellion. Colonel Barker's masquerade, however, must be viewed within the light of a wide-spread fascination about women as soldiers that was fostered during the First World War in a country where their role was militarily confined to support services. Music-hall singers like Vesta Tilley regularly appeared on stage dressed in officer's uniforms, acting out a popular female fantasy. Newspaper reports often revealed that women — like Dorothy Lawrence in 1915 and 'Albert F.' in 1917 — were attempting to enlist to join 'the great adventure' overseas. Flora Sandes, an English Red Cross nurse turned soldier in the Serbian Army, became a celebrity when she returned home on leave in 1916.

In her uniform the 'Colonel' had not only duped her fellow Fascists but, as one British Army officer stated, 'it was the most complex hoax the

West End had ever seen'. By assuming a military persona in a post-war period the 'Colonel' found an avenue to the male power and privilege still denied women. As she told the *Sunday Dispatch*, 'Trousers make a wonderful difference in the outlook on life. I know that dressed as a man I did not, as I do now I am wearing skirts again, feel hopeless and helpless.'[3] The 'Colonel', when revealed as a woman, shattered every ideal that the officer and gentleman she mimicked was supposed to believe. Valerie Arkell-Smith had simply found a way to use it to her own ends. But, before examining how these issues were represented in the British press, it is important to examine briefly the history of the National Fascisti itself.

Formed in 1924 to pursue a more radical Fascist policy than its parent organization, the British Fascists, the National Fascisti was a small but highly-visible group. Male members wore black shirts, modelled after the Italians, utilized prevalent Fascist myths and symbols and professed to draw their inspiration from Mussolini. They adopted the Roman fasces — symbol of authority — as an emblem and there was evidence of members practicing military drilling in London. Although its membership was never large, according to Robert Benewick 'it had a broader base then the anti-Communist groups and the British Fascists in that it included a thuggish element'.[4] Claiming they were more interested in actions than words the NF continued to disrupt Socialist meetings in Hyde Park throughout 1925. Reports conflicted wildly on the numbers involved — the *Evening News* reported 2,000 had watched the fight, while the *Daily Herald* stated the 30 Fascisti had attacked 25 Socialists — but the National Fascisti seemed adept at attracting publicity.

The *Daily Herald* ran an article on the 'dust-up' and sent a reporter to 'penetrate' the NF headquarters in Edgware Road. Accompanying the subsequent article was a front page photo of three Fascisti outside their West London hut armed with swords. A NF member was quoted as saying, 'We shall meet the Communists, blow for blow'. Chief political officer Fisher responded in an interview: 'No, two blows for blow. We shall meet them with their own weapons. But we shall fight clean — with our fists — and no kicking below the belt, like the Communists kick. [But] we are out to smash the reds and pinks.'[5]

An official of the British Fascists refused to comment on these statements but stressed that his organization, unlike the NF, believed in free speech. On other occasions the British Fascists took even greater pains to divorce themselves from the NF's more violent actions, reinforcing the political divide between the two groups.[6]

The Herald's penetration of the NF office also revealed the organisation's overtures towards egalitarianism. In reply to a *Herald* story about the NF, a representative claimed that 'within this organization the class of each is the class of all. All are equal except for our own administration'.[7] Despite these protestations of equality, the *Herald* reporter noted a young woman seated at a typewriter in the Fascisti's headquarters who was dressed in civilian clothes rather than the blackshirt uniform.

The NF, like the British Fascists, supported a separate women's organization which encouraged women to join. They were expected to perform administrative and domestic duties and, like the British Fascists — the parent organization upon which it was modelled — they supported a traditional dichotomy between public and private divisions of gender. Female leaders in the BF were entrusted with organizing the domestic sphere; Rotha Lintorn Orman, for example, devoted her energies to encouraging self-reliance in women, combating Socialist Sunday Schools and establishing children's clubs. Nesta Webster, who served on the BF Grand Council for three months, established a library where the ultra-right could read about the Communist menace.[8] In Scotland, Edinburgh Area Commander Miss Blake organized kitchen meetings as a counter to socialist activities aimed at women with children. The appeal to the middle-class could be seen most visibly in letters to the *Fascist Bulletin* that called for putting Fascist children into boy scouting and girl guide movements since their aims were considered to be almost identical.[9]

The NF's numbers are difficult to estimate although it is clear from several accounts that they never attracted a large following. But they were highly visible provocateurs and, in 1925, came to symbolize what many social commentators feared was the Government's failure to curb a growing threat to the British system of political democracy. As the *Daily Herald* had uncovered, the NF were not only armed but ready to fight. They openly declared, 'comrades, under the shadow of our banners, it is beautiful to live, but if it is necessary, it is still more beautiful to die'.

Two months after the newspaper exposé of the NF that had resulted in eviction from their Edgware road office, four men armed with revolvers hijacked a *Daily Herald* delivery van *en route* to Euston station with 8,000 copies of the newspaper. Driver J. R. Bayfield was forced into the street at gun-point before the men climbed into the van and drove off. Police found it a few hours later and on 28 October four NF members appeared in the dock of a London court and read the following statement: 'We the undersigned, being loyal subjects to his Majesty the King, having noted of late that a certain paper known as the *Daily Herald* has been publishing certain matters which did not lead us to suppose that it is loyal to this country considered that some action should be taken.'[10]

The NF claimed that they hoped to draw police attention to the 'subversive nature of the publication' by delaying the paper's distribution by a few hours. Finding insufficient evidence to support a charge of larceny, the Director of Public Prosecution, Sir Archibald Bodkin, reduced it to one of 'creating a public nuisance'. Labour MPs, Labour Party locals, the Trades Union Congress and socialist authors such as George Bernard Shaw and Arnold Bennett were outraged at Bodkin's decision. Bennett attacked it as 'monstrous' and Walter Citrine, TUC secretary, spoke of the 'disquieting feeling [that] has arisen amongst

Trade Unionists at the failure of the responsible authorities to deal firmly with the fascists'.[11] The Newspaper Proprietors Association protested to the Prime Minister and the *Herald* received hundreds of letters of support. Bodkin's decision made the Government appear 'soft' on the Fascists. No such sympathy was reserved for 12 Communist leaders charged with seditious libel and incitement to mutiny for urging soldiers and sailors to join the Communist cause in the event of revolution.

The NF survived the publicity surrounding the *Daily Herald* case and by 1927 had moved its headquarters to Hogarth Road, Earl's Court. Members continued to disrupt Socialist meetings but now had the added responsibility of 'protecting' Conservative speakers from angry crowds at public forums. Although this duty afforded them police protection, the Fascisti ran a boxing and fencing club to train its members for their skirmishes. That year 'Colonel' Victor Barker DSO became secretary to NF president, Colonel Rippon-Seymour, and took on the training of young male recruits. Along with these martial skills the 'Colonel' gave 'his' charges advice on other matters. '[I] gave them lessons on life with a capital L, telling the young fellows of the snares and pitfalls to avoid', the 'Colonel' told *The Sunday Dispatch* in 1929. 'I used to get two or three of them together and talked to them . . . about the folly of getting mixed up with women.' Paradoxically, the 'Colonel' was teaching boys how to become men, thus legitimating her assumed identity.

However, the organization was torn by a power struggle during the winter of 1926/27 which brought the NF to the attention of local police. 'Colonel' Barker's employer, Colonel Seymour, was charged with committing common assault on Charles Eyres, leader of the NF's Croydon branch. Eyres accused Seymour of misappropriating the organization's funds and changing the constitution to give himself increased powers. In a flash of rage, Seymour drew a sword and pointed an unlicensed gun at his accuser.[12] On a police raid at NF Headquarters a few weeks later a handgun with a forged firearms certificate that belonged to Barker was seized and the 'Colonel' subsequently charged with unlawful possession of an automatic pistol. After Barker's acquittal in May 1927, the 'Colonel' was quoted as saying the NF was folding for lack of support but that it 'hopes to reorganize very shortly on very careful lines'.[13] Despite this optimistic statement, the organization was moribund.

The British press rediscovered the Fascisti two years later when the 'Colonel' was arrested in March 1929 after failing to appear in court on a bankruptcy summons. At Brixton the prison doctor had discovered her well-kept secret and she was promptly transferred to Holloway. Valerie Arkell-Smith was then further charged with giving false testimony on a public document in connection with her 1923 marriage in a Brighton church to Elfreda Haward. Her six-year career masquerading as an officer, an actor, a dog-breeder, farmer, scout-master and cricket captain revealed a remarkable talent for disguise. Her press testimonials, moreover, exposed the limits experienced by the 'new woman' of the 1920s; it was not that the court or public believed that Valerie Arkell-Smith was forced by the spectre of unemployment to assume her disguise, but as an officer and a gentleman it was all so much easier. Her involvement with an organization like the NF that emphasized her 'manly' values and caricatured masculinity was perceived as a rejection of feminine weakness and powerlessness.

'Colonel' Barker, however, was not an anomaly. Throughout the war years press reports often assumed that women who took up arms were breaking down the barriers of sexual repression. Albert F., a woman who successfully lived and worked as a male printer in North London, was conscripted in 1916. Her story echoed the 'Colonel' since Albert F. claimed the call to national service was 'a godsend'. She sought anonymity in male disguise and hoped that in the army 'there was chance of getting where my husband would never find me'.[14] When her identity was revealed at the Mill Hill barracks, Albert F. immediately went into hiding.

Women's flight from femininity through the adoption of a male identity cropped up in popular magazines into the 1930s. It was promulgated by writers like Rosita Forbes who was hailed as 'a torch of inspiration for the women of those post-war years, now emancipated in large measure, (who) still gingerly feel their way along the paths trodden heretofore only by men'.[15] To assume the quintessential masculine profession seemed the most vivid realization of equality to Forbes, who followed the burgeoning of women's military involvement in her weekly magazine. An article on Chinese women entitled, 'From Lily Foot to Army Boot' identified the army as a great liberating force. Young women and girls happily displayed their ranks in Spain's Republican militia, while a Somaliland woman shouldered a gun across her naked chest and modern Turkish women at the University of Ankara were reported to 'have taken quickly and with eagerness to the modern idea of uniforms'.[16]

Revolutionaries and Fascists were thrown together under Forbes' category of those who trod new paths to freedom, even though she realized the fragile promise of equality that women's military involvement held out. Underlying the image of a woman with the gun was the illusion that her service would entitle her to power and a political voice.[17] The parallels with 'Colonel' Barker's case, although her actual military involvement was confined to her work at a remount depot, did not escape the press. As she wrote of her war experience, 'in a way it was a man's job and certainly I savoured the friendship of men and became accustomed to living like a man'.[18] In the post-war era, there were thousands of women who expressed similar sentiments and even a few who took action to ensure their hard-won independence.

In 1919 Liverpool was rocked by scandal when several women were tried for attempting to stowaway on foreign-bound ships in sailors' clothes. It seemed, according to many press reports, another example of women's unbound desire for sexual revolution. '[Woman] would have fought on the battlefield and was not allowed to, although she managed to get to the fringe', mused one writer. 'The love of adventure is so strong in them that they are willing to make the greatest sacrifices in order to carry through such an adventure.'[19] One of the stowaways was a war widow who had served four years as a transport driver in France. The judge recognized that she 'could not settle again to domesticity, she pined for adventure [and] she too rigged herself in trousers' and risked boarding an American ship.

A sympathetic magistrate interviewed about this phenomenon acknowledged the constraints against which the female stowaways were clearly fighting. 'The trouble is, these girls want an outlet for their enthusiasm', he was quoted as saying. 'They want freedom from restraint, an opportunity to enjoy life and not to be compelled to spend their days in a bandbox tied up with pink ribbons. They want to come out and be in touch with realities.'[20] Since alternatives to 'pink ribbons' were still in short supply, women continued to register their individual protest by claiming male privileges for themselves.

During the war many 'real-life' female soldiers had used patriotic rhetoric or claimed romantic motives for their disguise to make their transgression of gender boundaries acceptable. They were often portrayed in biographies or news stories as devoutly loyal wives or lovers who braved the rigours of battle to follow their men. When 'Colonel' Barker's true identity was first revealed, *The Daily Herald* subscribed to this convention. 'Why did she do it?' a reporter asked in an article on 6 March 1929:

> That question . . . was answered for me in a whisper by one of her friends and the answer is given as it was spoken. "The man she loved had died, I don't know in what circumstances, and she made a solemn vow by the side of his body that she would take his name and live the same kind of life he lived, (which was easy for he was a clean living fellow) and be unchanged when they met again. She had some belief in spiritualism".[21]

This gesture of love, however, was fraught with contradictions. Those women who assumed a dead lover's identity, or adopted a male persona to follow him into battle, also assumed masculine privileges. During 'Colonel' Barker's trial it soon became clear that, for her, this extended into the realm of lesbian sexuality.

Revelations that Valerie Arkell-Smith had married Elfreda Haward and that they had lived 'as husband and wife' greatly undercut the 'Colonel's' appeal as a misguided patriot. Although the female soldiers often reported visiting brothels with their comrades, they were never expected to do more than pretend to flirt with the women.[22] The ultimate male privilege — women's sexual love — was denied them if they wished to survive in the ranks which secured their imitative role. The 'Colonel' had ignored this. Following only four months after Hall's *Well of Loneliness*, was banned from the UK, the 'Colonel' was easily identified as part of the new breed of 'mannish lesbian'.

These women were not content to play at their female sexual relationships; Hall and other feminists of the period wore male clothes as a statement of their scepticism towards gender categories.[23] It was a rebellion against the male order. Although the 'Colonel' shared Hall's need to shed the trappings of femininity, politically they were diametrically opposed. The 'Colonel' denied her lesbianism by embracing an extreme right-wing ideology that actually reinforced women's role as mother and helpmate. Her defending lawyer, Mr Freke Palmer, attempted to portray his client as a hapless victim of a brutal husband who assumed her male disguise to support her children. As Palmer told the court, 'There has been a great deal of publicity in this matter because a woman has been bold enough and has succeeded in earning a living as a man when she could not do it as a woman. It seems to shock some people but there is no law against it'.

The public may have believed that Valerie Arkell-Smith had, as prosecutor Sir Ernest Wild stated, 'profaned the House of God . . . outraged the decencies of nature and broken the laws of man'. But her decision to join the NF was actually an attempt psychologically to cover up her traces. In her uniform, as the 'Colonel', she trained men to fight against the 'pinks and reds' whose politics were far more sympathetic to her plights. Instead, she identified with the oppressors and assumed she was safe within their camp. The National Fascisti allowed her to 'prove' her masculinity with its tough posturing. As she told the *Sunday Dispatch*, 'Today when the whole world knows my secret I feel more a man than a woman . . . I actually felt that I was a man and there is no one who can say that I ever failed to act as a man, whether it was working on a farm or fighting in the Fascisti or even when I was on the stage.' To Valerie the only alternative to living her miserable feminine existence was the wholesale adoption of a masculine persona, complete with masculine swaggering and 'Blimpish' gestures.

The importance of this machismo to the fascist ideology was reflected in the British Fascists' response to 'Colonel' Barker's trial. An article in their newspaper, *The British Lion* criticized the NF for behaving as 'a little bunch of "men"'. They were denounced as 'hot heads' who refused to take their responsibilities as Fascists seriously.[24] Moreover, they implied that the NF existed merely to give its members an opportunity to play at soldiering and 'Colonel' Barker was a prime example of its artifice. The British Fascists dissociated themselves from Barker by stating that she had never been a member. Even so, that a woman had infiltrated the Fascisti's ranks, usurping its privileges and authority, was highly embarrassing to the BF. The 'Colonel' made a mockery of the Fascists' attempts to reinforce the hierarchy of gender that seemed threatened by women's new-found political power.

'Colonel' Barker's experience offers greater insights into Fascism's appeal to men than women. However, Barker's desire to escape from the confines of domesticity by penetrating a highly masculine organization was understood, emulated and articulated by women elsewhere. While writers such as Rosita Forbes and Radclyffe Hall realized the importance of the claim to male clothes and occupations, women elsewhere continued to disguise themselves to achieve this end. But without a political structure to support their struggle for equality, these individual Amazons brought real change for women no closer. Rather, they became caught, like 'Colonel' Barker, in the need to support the oppressive structures against which they had fought so vigorously. The women who chose the individual route to freedom soon realized that it was short-lived and always paid at a very high cost.

JULIE WHEELWRIGHT
London

NOTES

1. See also Sandra M. Gilbert, 'Soldier's Heart: Literary Men, Literary Women, and the Great War', *Signs: Journal of Women in Culture and Society*, vol.8, no.31 (1983) for more on post-war gender anxiety; and Diana Condell and Jean Liddiard, *Working for Victory? Images of Women in the First World War, 1914–1918* (London, 1987) for women's work during the war.
2. 'My Amazing Masquerade — A wife confesses', *Empire News and Sunday Chronicle*, 19 Feb. 1956.
3. *Sunday Dispatch*, 31 Mar. 1929.
4. Robert Benewick, *The Fascist Movement in Britain* (London, 1972) p.36.
5. 'Blackshirts — Blacklegs?' *The Daily Herald*, 31 July 1925.
6. 'British Fascists Repudiate National Fascisti', *The Daily Herald*, 19 Nov. 1925.
7. 'Black outlook for Reds', *The Daily Herald, 31 July 1925*.
8. Richard Thurlow, *Fascism in Britain: A History, 1918–1985* (Oxford, 1987) p.52–54.
9. *The Fascist Bulletin*, 19 Sept. 1925.
10. 'Four black shirts in the dock', *Daily Herald*, 29 Oct. 1925.
11. 'TUC and Fascists', *Daily Herald*, 11 Nov. 1925.
12. Thurlow, op. cit., p.54.
13. 'Fascists Finish', *The Daily Sketch,* 19 May 1927.
14. 'Woman Tries to Join the Army', *Illustrated Sunday Herald*, 13 Aug. 1916.
15. Introduction by E. Royston Pike, Rosita Forbes (ed.), 'Some women of my travels', *Women of Many Lands: Their Charm, Culture and Characteristics* (London, 1938).
16. Ibid, 'Rifle Practice', p.132; 'Woman-at-Arms', p.9; and 'Miss Turkey Steps Out', p.189.
17. Julie Wheelwright, *Amazons and Military Maids: Women Who Dressed as Men in Pursuit of Life, Liberty and Happiness* (London, 1989) p.190–194.
18. 'My Amazing Masquerade', *Empire News and Sunday Chronicle*, 19 Feb. 1956.
19. 'Girls Love of Adventure', *Liverpool Weekly Courier*, 13 Dec. 1919.
20. Ibid.
21. 'Woman's Strange Life as Man', *Daily Herald*, 6 Mar. 1929.
22. See, for example, discussion of this in Flora Sandes, *The Autobiography of a Woman Soldier* (London, 1927) p.80.
23. Esther Newton, 'The Mythic Mannish Lesbian: Radclyffe Hall and the New Woman', *Signs*, vol. 9, no. 4 (Summer 1984) pp.558–575.
24. *The British Lion*, Apr. 1929.

Politics and Race, Gender and Class: Refugees, Fascists and Domestic Service in Britain, 1933–1940 [1]

Between 1933 and the outbreak of the Second World War 20,000 Jewish women escaped from Nazi Europe to become refugee domestics in Britain. At the same time some 'native' domestic servants were attracted to the British Fascist movement. Both groups of women have been ignored by historians. This article suggests that this is a serious omission which has led to an incomplete view of the refugee and Fascist movements in Britain. Indeed consideration of class and gender issues sheds valuable light both on the relative failure of Fascism in Britain and British responses to the Jewish refugee crisis in the 1930s.

Well over half the Jewish refugees from Nazi Europe who escaped to Britain during the 1930s were women. In the same decade it has been estimated that at least 20 per cent of the British Union of Fascists' (BUF) membership was female.[2] Nevertheless the gender aspects of both movements have received scant attention. On the one hand, the experiences of the (largely male) élite émigrés have been emphasized, at the expense of the ordinary (largely female) refugee.[3] On the other, titles such as 'Mosley's Men' and 'The Boys in Black' indicate the chauvinist tendencies in recent historiography on British Fascism.[4] This brief essay will address both shortcomings through the subject of domestic service, where, by a series of bizarre paradoxes and contradictions of class, ethnicity, politics and gender, refugee and Fascist experience coincided.

In 1980 Stuart Rawnsley rightly complained about the 'complete lack of interest by historians in the ordinary membership of the BUF'. Since then, some progress has been made in rediscovering the grass-roots support of the movement, but distinct limitations are still apparent. One of these lies in the issue of gender. Brewer's small sample of 15 former Fascists from the West Midlands includes only one woman — a reflection on his skewed sample rather than the sexual make-up of the BUF.[5] Other secondary work by Thurlow, Cullen and Lewis has also ignored working-class women's support of Fascism and has concentrated solely on ex-suffragette '"spirited" middle-class women' who were members of the BUF.[6] Nellie Driver, the real force behind Fascism in Nelson is indeed the only working-class female member to achieve any attention in the existing literature on British Fascism.[7]

The recent release of government material, the so-called 'Mosley papers' has added to this class distortion. Of 15 Fascist internment files released, only three are women — Lady Mosley, Commander Mary Allen and Nora Briscoe (a member of the anti-Semitic Right Club). All were members of the middle classes or aristocracy. Although a few files have been retained by the Home Office, the vast majority have been destroyed.[8] If government files are thus unable to reveal the nature of working-class women's support for the BUF, other sources are still available to the historian. Oral history is one solution, although it is a difficult one, given the reluctance of ex-members to come forward and admit to their past associations. Far more accessible are the BUF's own publications, which, although including their own problems and limitations, have not, surprisingly, been exploited for the material they contain on Fascist support. This latter source is by no means inclusive or without in-built biases, but it gives not only an indication of female working-class membership of the BUF, but also the previously neglected issue of class conflict within the movement.

In his initial Fascist manifesto, *The Greater Britain* (1932), Oswald Mosley first addressed the issue of Fascism and women. Here the question of women who wished to pursue careers in the professions, industry and politics was regarded as a minor point. The 'greater question' was that of 'normal women', who, for 'the future of the race' would 'seek the important career of motherhood'. Mosley's classically Fascist doctrine on gender, that the female's place was in the home, was summarized by the phrase '*We want men who are men and women who are women*'. By 1938, however, Mosley had, to an extent, revised this crude domestic determinism. Women would still be represented in the future Fascist Parliament through their 'interests' as mothers and housewifes but 'This does not mean that we seek to relegate women purely to the home, which is a charge denied in practice by the fact that we present to-day a larger proportion of women candidates to the electorate than any other party'.[9]

This change in the Fascist leader's stance on the women's role itself reflected the increasing role of women in the BUF as the 1930s progressed. It was evident in 1935 with the publication of a pamphlet, *Women and Fascism* by Anne Brock Griggs (the BUF's Woman Propaganda Officer). As Martin Durham points out elsewhere in this volume, this marked a clear departure from Mosley's statement three years earlier. Equal pay, encouragement to enter the professions and the end of sex discrimination were all features of Griggs' programme.[10]

In her pamphlet, under a section 'Trades and Professions for Women', Griggs devoted a paragraph to domestic servants outlining a training programme in domestic science. Employers would be forced to allow sufficient time for such training and from this 'Certificated workers would raise the standard throughout the whole of this profession'. In addition workers would be represented in Parliament through a domestic corporation which 'would ensure reasonable hours and abolish the unregulated drudgery which prevails at present'.[11] Griggs, although herself middle class, was making an appeal designed to attract both mistress and maid. The mistress would gain in terms of better service, and the servant through improved hours and conditions of work. Thus, through the pursuit of a 'modernist' tendency in Fascism, class differences would be overcome. Nevertheless, such theoretical niceties were lost on the actual membership of the BUF. Indeed debate on domestic service was to reveal the class conflict and contradiction inherent within the Fascist movement — what D.S. Lewis has recently described as the simultaneous existence of 'reactionary and radical elements' in the BUF.[12]

In the BUF's populist organ, *Blackshirt*, in December 1934, Margaret Burgess revealed the radical aspect of BUF ideology. Her article, entitled 'A Revelation of Domestic Slavery' attacked the present conditions of domestic service, its lowering of wages and standards which led to girls who were 'overworked and heavy-eyed, under-fed and under-paid'. It was clear from Burgess's article where the blame was to be placed — on the mistress who with her 'snobbish tendencies' took advantage of the glut in the labour market, holding captive the servant who, fearing a bad reference and not allowed to qualify for unemployment pay, was unable to move on. Burgess concluded by asking 'how many servants could honestly describe hers as the perfect mistress[?]'.[13]

This radical attack on exploitation and 'domestic slavery' did not go unchallenged. A 'Potential Fascist' from south-east London protested that it was in fact impossible to get servants. Despite offering 'a good home, our own food . . . 17/6 a week, three half-days a week and four weeks' holiday', she had 'been let down by thieves, liars, and back-biters'.[14] There was thus conflict between those middle- and upper-class women supporters of the BUF who saw the movement as a bulwark against socialism and labour militancy and wanted a cheaper, more malleable servant workforce, and the domestics themselves, who were attracted to Fascism because it campaigned for their rights. Not until the latter part of 1938, with the influx of refugee domestics, was the BUF able to address this dilemma. However, before examining the Fascist's response to these Jewish refugees, it will be necessary to ask how successful the BUF was in recruiting domestic servants.

Claudia Koonz has recently commented that 'many [domestic] servants had supported Hitler and anticipated the Third Reich would usher in a new era for them. The appeal to a classless society and "Aryan" solidarity had formed the core of Hitler's promises . . . The family servant believed the "Socialist" component of National Socialism would dignify her humble status.'[15] In Germany and Britain domestic service had followed a similar pattern after 1918. The occupation was increasingly unpopular, wages and conditions changed little, but due to lack of economic alternatives many women remained in the occupation — in Germany there were 1.3 million domestics in 1925, the same number as Britain in 1931.[16] How far then was the BUF successful in emulating the Nazis in recruiting domestic servants?

Theoretically it is possible to see the appeal of Fascism to British domestic servants. On one level there was little alternative for those who wanted to protest about conditions of work. Attempts to unionize domestic servants had always been short-lived and it was not until 1937/8 that the TUC's Women's Department sponsored the formation of a National Union of Domestic Workers (NUDW).[17] In the world of British politics the major parties showed little interest in the occupation. Moreover, government enquiries in 1919 and 1923 generally took the side of the employers, who were more concerned to increase the number of servants rather than improve the employees' working conditions.[18] On another level the failure to unionize domestics (the NUDW, even with the support of the TUC, only attracted a tiny fraction of the total servant population) was indicative of the peculiar nature of domestic service. Pam Taylor has argued that many domestic servants were unwilling to challenge the class-based hierarchical nature of their occupation. Many were forced into domestic service through family pressure in the depressed inter-war period and accepted their employer's ideology of domestic service — that is, the inevitable existence of class divisions in society and, from this, the natural status of 'service'.[19] A former domestic servant, when asked if she felt that her employers were better than her, replied 'Oh yes. Without them we wouldn't have had a job', which illustrates the problems for those on the left trying to organize resistance to the occupation on class grounds.[20] Nevertheless, many domestic servants did harbour grievances about the nature of their work, the hard labour, long hours and poor wages. This, in conjunction with the BUF's appeal above class grounds, could have made Fascism attractive to the vast army of the normally apolitical domestics in Britain during the 1930s.

The BUF was aware of this potential and attention was increasingly drawn to the plight of domestic servants in its publications throughout the decade.[21] Such efforts were not without success and there is indication of support from domestic servants for the BUF in its journals and local studies of BUF membership.[22] In turn, this support helped radicalize BUF policy on this 'profession' so that, by 1938, the Fascists might have claimed to have more progressive policies on domestic service than the Labour Party![23] The support of domestic servants for Fascism in Britain is thus significant and had implications in the consideration of the class and gender make-up of the BUF. There is, however, a danger in putting too much emphasis on the question 'Who were the Fascists?' in the British context. As Gerry Webber has recently argued, 'instead of constructing elaborate theories to explain why a few thousand people *did* support the fascist movement in Britain, it might be more profitable to ask why so many millions *didn't*'.[24] Even with a generous estimate it is doubtful whether more than several thousand domestic servants were members or even passive supporters of the BUF — thus the vast majority did not support the movement. It has been possible to outline several reasons why Fascism might have appealed to domestics. Moreover, it is evident that the Nazis in Germany were successful in this area and that in Austria 'domestic personnel . . . [were] strongly over represented' in the Nazi party.[25] So why did the BUF fail to recruit, on a *substantial* scale, members of the occupation?

The first factor to consider is that the disparate nature of the workforce, spread across the whole of the British Isles, made domestic servants notoriously difficult to organize. The BUF simply did not have a sufficient network of local branches to enable recruitment on a massive scale. Its propaganda network was also insufficient to overcome the barriers of isolation as regards domestics. An effective media black-out of the BUF in the second half of the 1930s intensified the movement's problems. Thus it must be suggested that the lack of large scale Fascist movements and organizations during the 1920s in Britain hindered potential recruitment in the following decade.[26] Domestic servants largely remained beyond the reach of the BUF. Second, internal problems within the BUF limited potential interest. It might be argued that class considerations of some prominent women in the BUF led to insufficient time being spent on the problems of domestic service. More energy was devoted to another non-unionized women's occupation — nursing — where class self-interest was perhaps less important.[27] In the early days of Nazi Germany, Claudia Koonz has suggested that 'Servants anticipated a very different sort of society from their mistresses'. Evidence of middle-class self-interest over domestic service within the British Fascist movement or, in short, its *reactionary* tendencies, lessened the attraction of the *radical* aspects of the BUF policy.[28]

Only in 1938 and 1939 did the BUF address this dilemma between the radical and the reactionary — one that had lessened its appeal to both mistress and maid. As with so many areas of BUF policy, contradictions and shortcomings in theory were papered over with the use of anti-Semitic arguments. On the one hand, the plight of young girls 'forced by economic necessity to leave their homes' and then made to endure miserable conditions as domestic servants was blamed on the exploitation of 'certain alien households'.[29] On the other hand, the poor standard of servants was blamed on the influx of Jewish refugee women into the occupation, who, according to one Fascist mistress, 'simply get into this Country as domestics as an excuse, and once they are in are prepared to do nothing'.[30] A kennel-maid supporter of the BUF shared this distrust, doubting whether the refugees had really been persecuted. Nevertheless, rather than seeing the refugees as pushing up wage rates, she complained that these foreign Jewish women are 'exploiters rather than refugees, and that the wages and conditions of English domestic workers are in process of being lowered to accommodate aliens'.[31] The BUF was certainly keen in the last year before the war to attract domestic servants by claiming that 'the wholesale importation of foreigners was throwing our own countrywomen out of work'.[32] To summarize, the BUF, which attempted to attract both working- and middle-class women, dealt with the problem of satisfying the contradictory demands for 'The Perfect Servant' and 'The Perfect Mistress' by the use of anti-Semitism.

The cohesive role of anti-Semitism was thus important in holding a diverse group of women together in the BUF. Nevertheless, the appeal of its anti-Semitism was limited — not because it was somehow unrespectable in 'tolerant' Britain, but in fact the converse. Whilst John Vincent's claim that the BUF's anti-Semitism was 'carrying coals to Newcastle' and thus ineffective is not applicable to all the BUF's policies and activities, it is clear that both mistress and maid were able to maintain hostility to Jews *within* mainstream society — attacks on refugee domestics were as likely to appear in the Beaverbrook press as in a Mosleyite organ.[33] Apart from the misery that their new occupation carried with it, Jewish refugee domestics had to face the anti-Semitism of both their employers and fellow employees.[34] Moreover, at a union level, refugees were banned from the newly-created National Union of Domestic Workers due to pressure from its members and potential members who feared that foreigners would push down wage rates and conditions of work.[35]

The position of women in Fascist countries had received scant attention from historians. It is remarkable, however, that those who have recently tried to rescue this experience have ignored the plight of Jewish women.[36] In the British context it is thus vital that those who address neglected issues of gender do not forget the persecuting aspect of Fascism, or, indeed, its impact on those whom it persecutes. For example, the achievements of a working-class activist, such as Nellie Driver, in the BUF must not obscure the fact that she joined an organization that would have willingly have expelled hundreds of thousands of women in Britain simply because of their religious, ethnic or racial background.[37]

During the 1930s, a combination of Nazi anti-Semitic discrimination and the reluctance of the outside world to accept Jewish refugees forced many middle-class German Jewish women to seek positions as domestic servants outside Germany.[38] Britain was one country which, partly due to pressure from middle-class professional groups as well as from the openly anti-Semitic BUF, refused (at least up to the end of 1938) to accept anything other than a trickle of refugees. The only major exceptions to this policy of exclusion were the two occupations where a major shortage of labour occurred — domestic service and nursing. Thus, rather than a generous policy of asylum, Britain's admittance of some 20,000 refugee domestic servants from 1933–39 was more designed to meet the demands of middle-class women in this period. Ministry of Labour and then Home Office regulations ensured that these refugees could only enter on condition that they remained as domestic servants.[39] With some exceptions, the former middle-class Jewish women were treated merely as a source of scarce labour, rather than as victims of Fascist oppression. Whilst the BUF and its members cast doubt on the reality of the persecution these dispossessed women had fled from, the majority of the mistress class, by exploiting the refugees in a manner consistent with the nature of domestic service, in effect also withheld any sympathy.[40] As a refugee recalls: 'anyone who came as a domestic, was treated as a domestic. There was no quarter given'.[41] The refugee women, on top of the pressures resulting from their loss of prestige — many had previously employed servants themselves — had other stresses to face. They were often, despite their pitifully low wages, the chief bread-winner and source of emotional support for family now settled in Britain. Many male refugees (former lawyers, doctors and accountants), unable to practise in Britain due to professional hostility, could not cope either physically or mentally with their loss of status. In a remarkable reversal of their previous role as subservient middle-class housewives or daughters, these Jewish women took responsibility as the stronger partner.[42] Moreover, they faced the worry of relatives and friends left behind in Europe. Although usually powerless to help, the refugee domestics were often regarded by those trapped in Germany and Austria as the last chance of escape.[43] Yet rarely were these added psychological burdens taken account of by the mistress class. Margareta Burkill, an organizer of refugee domestics in Cambridge, made a point of telling employers 'the whole story . . . who the people were, what their background was, and so on'. She was thus stunned to find that 'dons' wives could treat somebody who was in every way as good as them in an absolutely terrible manner'.[44] Refugee domestics soon therefore learned to stop referring to their past experiences of persecution under the Nazis.

Furthermore, the xenophobia and anti-Semitism displayed by the National Union of Domestic Workers and the BUF, as well as within individual households, made impossible a united campaign against the abuses of domestic service. The importance of this factor should not be minimized as the refugees, for reasons of politics and status, did not accept the ideology of domestic service. Therefore, their potential as leaders of domestic servants was great. As it was, refugees were forced to rely on their own networks of clubs to resist their exploitation.[45] With the outbreak of war, they were left exposed and vulnerable. Up to half were sacked at the outbreak of war, and a significant number interned in the invasion panic of the spring of 1940 (when class, ethnic and gender prejudices of sections of the state, press and public united to demand the removal of freedom for Jewish refugees in British society).[46]

Ironically, the demands for internment of aliens, partly caused by the anti-Semitism of the BUF, were matched by that for the internment of Fascists. In Holloway prison, and later the camps of the Isle of Man, the women Fascists, who had done their utmost to exclude and remove the female refugees, were made to share the latter's company.[47] This was, perhaps, the final paradox in the bizarre and tragic events of the 1930s. Nazi barbarism and the indifference of the outside world forced tens of thousands of middle-class German and Austrian Jewish women into the hardship of domestic service. At the same time, in Britain, some middle-class women in the BUF were opposing the entry of these women of their same class, yet supporting the aspirations of working-class domestic servants in this country. Others in the same organization were, however, opposed to this radical aspect of Fascism and supported the interests of the mistress rather than the maid. Certainly individuals such as Lady Mosley (whose autobiography reveals a hatred of mixing with working-class women in her period of internment, and who tellingly never refers to domestic servants by name) indicates one reason why Fascism failed to recruit dramatically among the working-class women of Britain.[48] Gender solidarity thus did not always overcome class divisions in the name of Fascism. Nevertheless, working-class women, as this study has indicated in the case of domestic servants, *were* recruited and did play a significant role in the BUF. It is extremely doubtful, however, whether the male chauvinistic and class biases inherent in the movement would have been removed had the BUF achieved power. Indeed, these divisions of gender and class were only ever overcome by Fascism in action in its persecuting role, as the horrors of the holocaust graphically illustrate.[49]

TONY KUSHNER
University of Southampton

NOTES

1. I would like to thank Graham Heaney and Charles Esdaile for comments on this paper.
2. Some 41,400 of the 75,000 Austrians and Germans in Britain at the outbreak of war were female. See R. Stent, *A Bespattered Page? The Internment of 'His Majesty's Most Loyal Enemy Aliens'* (London, 1980) pp.11, 191–2. For the Fascist percentage see R. Thurlow, *Fascism in Britain: A History, 1918–1985* (Oxford, 1987) facing p.142.
3. G. Hirschfeld (ed.), *Exile in Great Britain* (London, 1984) rarely mentions issues of gender.
4. J. Brewer, *Mosley's Men* (Aldershot, 1984); Thurlow, op.cit., ch.6.
5. S. Rawnsley in K. Lunn and R. Thurlow (eds.), *British Fascism* (London, 1980) p.150; Brewer, op.cit., p.5.
6. Thurlow, op.cit., pp.70 and 130; S. Cullen, 'The Development of the Ideas and Policy of the British Union of Fascists, 1932–40', *Journal of Contemporary History* XXII (Jan. 1987) p.133; D.S. Lewis, *Illusions of Grandeur: Mosley, Fascism and British Society 1931–81* (Manchester, 1987) pp.78–9.
7. For Driver, see David Mayall's contribution in this volume.
8. The Public Record Office has a catalogue of the 'Mosley Papers', including a list of 18-B detainee files.
9. O. Mosley, *The Greater Britain* (London, 1932) pp.41–2; *Tomorrow We Live* (London, 1938) p.16.
10. A. Brock Griggs, *Women and Fascism* (London, 1935) pp.2–3.
11. Ibid., p.3.
12. For modernist tendencies see Cullen, op.cit.; Lewis, op.cit., p.55.
13. *Blackshirt*, 7 Dec. 1934.
14. Ibid., 14 Dec. 1934.
15. C. Koonz, *Mothers in the Fatherland: Women, the Family and Nazi Politics* (London, 1987) pp.162–3.
16. For German figures see T. Mason, 'Women in Germany, 1925–1940: Family, Welfare and Work pt 1' *History Workshop* I (Spring 1976) p.79; for Britain see A. Chapman

and R. Knight, *Wages and Salaries in the United Kingdom 1920–1938* (Cambridge, 1953) pp.215–7.

17. See N. Soldon, *Women in British Trade Unions 1874–1976* (Dublin, 1978) p.144 or S. Lewenhak, *Women and Trades Unions* (London, 1977) pp.181–4, 230–1.

18. See Ministry of Reconstruction, 'Report of the Women's Advisory Committee on the Domestic Service Problem' (London, 1919 Cmd 67); Ministry of Labour, 'Report to the Ministry of Labour of the Committee Appointed to Enquire into the Present Conditions as to the Supply of Female Domestic Servants (London, 1923).

19. P. Taylor,'Women Domestic Servants 1919–1939: The Final Phase' (MA, Birmingham University, 1978) passim. See L. Davidoff, 'Mastered for Life: Servant and Wife in Victorian and Edwardian England', *Journal of Social History* (Summer 1974) pp.406–28 for an earlier period.

20. A Welsh ex-domestic servant interviewed on 'Women Working', Channel 4, 3 Aug. 1988.

21. See, for example, Olive Hawks, 'Position of Domestic Servants', *Blackshirt*, 9 Oct. 1937; 'Woman's World' in *Action*, 23 July 1938; Phyllis Aldridge, 'Women Demand Results', *Action*, 11 June 1938; *Action*, 8 July 1939.

22. *Blackshirt*, 7 Dec. 1934, 8 Feb. 1935; *Action*, 3 June 1939, 8 July 1939. See the comments of the BUF's Birmingham female section organizer that the movement attracted 'teachers, secretaries and office workers, nurses, shop assistants, waitresses, domestic workers, housewives etc.' Quoted by Brewer, op.cit., p.13.

23. For Ernest Bevin and Labour's late discovery of the conditions in domestic service see A. Calder, *The People's War* (London, 1969) p.401.

24. See S. Larsen et al., *Who Were the Fascists* (Bergen, 1980); G. Webber in *The Social Basis of European Fascist Movements* (London, 1987) p.152. J. Brewer, 'Looking Back at Fascism: A Phenomenological Analysis of BUF membership', *Sociological Review* XXXII (1984) pp.747–8 indirectly approaches this question.

25. For Germany see Koonz, op.cit.; for Austria, G. Botz in Larsen, op.cit., p.218.

26. Ken Lunn has recently argued that the British Fascists were more mass-based than has been previously allowed for. See his article in T. Kushner and K. Lunn (eds.) *Traditions of Intolerance: Fascism and Race Discourse in Britain* (Manchester, 1989) pp.140–154. This is a significant point but should not obscure the essential weakness of Fascism in Britain by the turn of the decade.

27. The involvement of nurses in the BUF is also worthy of more research. Nurses were another working-class group, intimidated from forming unions, who the BUF attempted to attract through the use of anti-Semitism directed towards refugee nurses. See Lewenhak, op.cit., pp.230–1 for trade unions and nurses: *Action*, 6 Aug. 1938 for hostility to refugee nurses and Z. Josephs, *Survivors* (Birmingham, 1988) pp.123–32 for the experience of these refugees.

28. Koonz, op.cit., p.162.

29. *Action*, 11 June 1938.

30. Letter from 'Pilgrim' in *Action*, 8 July 1939.

31. Letter from 'E.S.' in *Action*, 25 Feb. 1939.

32. *Action*, 3 June 1939.

33. J. Vincent in *The Times Literary Supplement*, 4 Apr. 1975. *Action*, 3 June 1939 carried a letter which had first appeared in the *Evening Standard* from a domestic servant attacking the refugees. The BUF's attacks on Jewish employers were also echoed more popularly — see the correspondence in the *Jewish Chronicle*, 2 Dec. 1938–6 Jan. 1939.

34. For anti-Semitism from the mistress class see A. Stevens, *The Dispossessed* (London, 1975) pp.167–8; from fellow employees see Imperial War Museum (IWM) refugee tape no.3816 or 'Our English Colleagues and Us', 1939, in TUC Archive Box 54.76 (4).

35. See Union minutes, 7 Dec. 1938 in TUC Archive 54.76 (4) and further comments in T. Kushner, 'Asylum or Servitude? Refugee Domestics in Britain, 1933–1945', *Bulletin of the Society for the Study of Labour History* LIII (winter 1988) pp.19–26.

36. J. Stephenson's *Women in Nazi Society* (London, 1975) and *The Nazi Organisation*

of Women (London, 1981) rarely deal with questions of anti-Semitism or Jewish women. Koonz, op.cit., xiv–xv comments that her chapter on Jewish women was added on later and, as Tim Mason has suggested, this section is one of the weakest in this remarkable overview. See *History Workshop* no.26 (Autumn 1988) p.202.

37. Mosley made it clear in his '18B' interview that all 'foreigners', including Jews, would be expelled from Britain under a Fascist regime. See P.R.O. HO 283/13/40.
38. See. H. Strauss, 'Jewish Emigration from Germany — Nazi Policies and Jewish Response pt II', *Leo Baeck Institute Year Book* XXVI (1981) p.400.
39. Kushner, 'Asylum or Servitude?' deals with government policy on refugee domestics.
40. For BUF doubts see *Action*, 8 July 1939 and more generally in my other contribution in this volume.
41. Isabelle Beck, letter to the author, 16 Feb. 1988.
42. See L. Segal, *Other People's Houses* (London, 1965) for an account of this process with her own parents. Jillian Davidson, 'German–Jewish Women in England', a paper delivered at a conference at Cambridge University, Sept. 1988: 'The History of German-Speaking Jews in the United Kingdom' deals with the changing status role of men and women.
43. H. Gerrard 'We Were Lucky', Museum of London Jewish Life, 34/84, gives a moving account of these pressures.
44. IWM refugee tape no.4588.
45. For refugee resistance, see TUC Archives, 54.76 (4).
46. Kushner, 'Asylum or Servitude' for the internment panic.
47. For internment see Thurlow, op.cit., ch.9 and T. Kushner, *The Persistence of Prejudice: Anti-Semitism in British Society During the Second World War* (Manchester, 1989) chs.1 and 5.
48. D. Mosley, *A Life of Contrasts* (London, 1977) passim, particularly p.181 where she relates how she disliked eating with the ordinary BUF women in Holloway: 'As soon as I decently could I abandoned the communal style of living' — upstairs and downstairs had to be kept apart!'
49. For Jewish women in the holocaust see V. Laska (ed.), *Women in the Resistance and in the Holocaust. The Voices of Eyewitnesses* (Westport, 1983) and Sybil Milton, 'Women and the Holocaust' in Renate Bridenthal, Anita Grossman and Marion Kaplan (eds.), *When Biology Became Destiny: Women in Weimar and Nazi Germany* (New York, 1984) pp.297–333.

II WAR AND MINORITIES

An Embattled Minority: the Jews in Britain During the First World War

Previous research on the impact of the First World War on Jews in Britain has concentrated on its effects on German or Russian immigrants. This article examines how English Jews were affected, analysing the dilemmas and complexities deriving from Jewish identity at a time of extreme nationalism. On policy regarding the oppression of Jews in Russia, the creation of all-Jewish units, special facilities for orthodox Jews and the conscription of foreign Jews, the Anglo-Jewish minority found itself at odds with the ethnic majority. The resulting tension contributed to outbreaks of anti-Jewish violence in 1917 and eroded the position of Jews in British society.

It is now widely accepted that the First World War engendered a serious deterioration in the position of the Jews in British society and a number of recent studies have contributed to the delineation of this decline.[1] However, existing research has concentrated almost exclusively on the impact of the war on immigrant Jews, whether enemy aliens or friendly aliens. Hostility to German Jews, the confusion of Germans with other Jewish immigrants and the resentment towards Russian-born Jews — who, although subjects of an allied power, were nevertheless able to avoid military service — has been well charted.[2] On several occasions this antipathy was expressed in major incidents of street violence; these, too, have been extensively chronicled and ascribed chiefly to the presence of Russian-born Jews of military age who were not yet in uniform.[3] While all of these studies have broadened our awareness of anti-Jewish currents specific to the war years, they have concentrated upon the immigrant Jews and neglected the impact of the war on the Jewish population of Britain in general.

The Great War reached so deeply into the social entrails of the participant countries that no minority or marginal group escaped its influence; yet, as Jay Winter has shown, it affected different sections of the British people in substantially different ways: the likelihood of death or degree of discomfort could be regionally, generationally or socially specific.[4] Jews in Britain experienced the War in ways that were significantly divergent from the majority of the population, ways that were determined by the very fact that they were a minority, and one which had highly individual characteristics.

The Jewish population was part of a supra-national group and this unavoidably provoked questions of identity and allegiance. Jews born in other countries faced the most obvious and immediate conflict of loyalties, but British-born Jews were not immune from such quandaries. Before 1914, the persecution of Jews in Russia had been a central preoccupation of Jewish international aid and lobbying organisations. As a result of the pattern of wartime alliances it ceased to be feasible to criticise the Tsarist regime, yet the ill-treatment of Russian Jews did not cease. For over two years, British Jews were compelled to walk a tightrope between transgressing their loyalty to the allied cause and abnegating responsibility for their fellow Jews.

British Jews were also ineluctably embroiled in the perplexities of foreign-born Jews in Britain. The representative, social and welfare organisations of Anglo-Jewry were obliged to formulate policy with respect to alien Jews, forcing British Jews to make painful choices between a straight British identity and a more complex one, embracing Jews who were not British and might even be enemies. The question of military service was crucial for Russian-born Jews, but it also played tortuously upon the identity of Jews born in Britain. When the creation of an all-Jewish unit was suggested as a device to encourage the recruitment of foreign-born Jews, British Jews split bitterly over the merits of the idea. Argument raged over whether Jews should fight as Jews or as citizens — a conundrum which exposed awkward questions about the nature of Jewish identity and the relations of Jews to the wider society.

Social and economic strains, which increased as the war dragged on, highlighted still further the differences between Jews and the majority population. Rationing had a particularly harsh effect on the Jews, whose patterns of food consumption were constrained by religious dietary laws. Yet attempts to modify government regulations exposed them to accusations of special pleading. Air-raids, too, had a differential impact since the bombing was concentrated on areas of dense Jewish settlement and gave salience to the response of Jews in particular.

The war thus threw up acute dilemmas for Britain's Jewish minority. British Jews were under enormous presure to show that they were loyal citizens. At the same time, they were expected to police their minority group and were held responsible for the misdemeanours of any of its members, no matter how tenuous their identification with Britain or with other Jews happened to be. If sections of the Jewish population behaved badly in the eyes of the majority, British Jews could either disassociate themselves from the erring element or intervene to discipline them. If they disclaimed responsibility, the majority population — the British — still held them accountable (and viewed them with added contempt for deserting their own people). If British Jews chose to align with other Jews, they could do so either through expressions and gestures of solidarity or the enforcement of unpopular measures, depending on their view of what technique would succeed best in ameliorating the pressure of the majority. In either case, it was a 'no-win' situation.[5]

This paper will show how the war turned the spotlight relentlessly onto all the points of difference between Jews and non-Jews. It will argue that, although the years 1914–18 created new solidarities and common experiences,[6] their cumulative effect was to drive a wedge into relations between Jews and the majority population. Less obvious were the effects on Jewish society. Jewish existence as a minority in Britain rested on a carefully worked out set of agreed criteria covering citizenship, culture and religion. The war called this compact into question, ruptured the shared values and agreed meanings which constituted the ascribed character of the Anglo-Jew and shattered the precarious bonding which held together Jewish society in Britain. It tested the relations between the Jews and British society and, in the process, exposed the delicate fabric of the Anglo-Jewish identity which had been constructed over the preceeding 75 years.[7] It is only by examining the War's impact in its entirety that it becomes possible to discern the true scale of the crisis which it provoked.

I

The peculiar and uncomfortable position of the Jews in British society became evident in the opening days of the War in terms of British Jewry's attitude towards Russia. After the assassination of the Archduke Franz Ferdinand, and Austria–Hungary's ultimatum to Serbia, the *Jewish Chronicle*, the semi-official voice of Anglo-Jewry edited by Leopold Greenberg, declared 'a feeling of sympathy with both sides'. Greenberg noted that the Jews had fared well in both countries and was dismayed at the prospect of a conflagration that would pitch Jew against Jew. Above all, he asserted that it was desirable to avoid any British entanglement on the same side as Russia, Serbia's ally: 'For England to fight alongside of Russia would be as wicked as for her to fight against Germany, with whom she has no quarrel.'[8] In the following week, Greenberg was thrown into full reverse, arguing that the German violation of Belgian neutrality was an adequate justification for an alliance with Russia and war on Germany.

Despite reports of the continuing persecution of Jews in Russia, publication of the newsheet *In Darkest Russia*, edited by Lucien Wolf, was suspended.[9] In its report on the year 1914, the Anglo-Jewish Association (AJA), which had formerly campaigned hard for Russian Jewish rights, refused to pass any comment on the matter.[10] Although it began to print statements from impeccable sources testifying to the continued suffering of Russian Jews, the AJA remained extremely guarded on the subject.[11] Behind the scenes Wolf, who acted as the full-time lobbyist on international affairs for the AJA and the Board of Deputies of British Jews, persisted in reminding the Foreign Office of the misery of Russian Jewry. Wolf, in memoranda to the Foreign Office, and Greenberg, in his paper, argued that, by virtue of their loyal war service, the Jews of Russia showed that they deserved emancipation. They also pointed to the effect of Jewish suffering in Russia on the opinion of American Jews, whom the Foreign Office were eager to win over to the cause of the allies as part of its effort to bring America into the war.[12]

This was a delicate balancing act and often entailed ungainly compromises. In his leader and comment columns, Greenberg devised an explanation for Russian ill-treatment of the Jews that verged on the apologetic. He argued that 'From the Russian people Jews have never experienced anything but the deepest sympathy, and with the Russian people they have ever felt on mutually agreeable terms'. It was the threat of German expansionism that had produced internal repression. Russian Jews understood this: 'They see that it has been the militarism of Russia's next-door neighbour that has in the main been responsible for the reactionary spirit.'[13] Greenberg did not entirely suspend criticism of the Tsarist authorities. He seized upon reports from neutral and, especially, Russian sources that were critical of the brutal handling of Jews in the war zone: 'What men in the front rank of the Russian nation say cannot be treasonable in the mouths of Englishmen.'[14] Yet he simultaneously maintained the fiction that the Germans were responsible for anti-Jewish policy in Russia.

Greenberg's ratiocinations did not escape criticism. He was chided by less timerous English Jews and lashed by the American Jewish press for his 'perverse theory' which they ascribed to fear of offending British opinion by attacking an allied power. In reply, Greenberg went so far as to say that the persecution and suffering of Russian Jews 'form after all a smaller question, a localised question, when compared to the great issues that are at stake in the war'.[15] This was an astounding defence in view of the unequivocal denunciation of Russia before 1914 and illustrates the pressure of majority opinion on Jewish loyalties. The succour of Russian Jewry, an expression of Jewish international solidarity, was one of the less obvious casualties of wartime intolerance.

II

The intense nationalism of the War not surprisingly incited a high level of chauvinism and hostility towards enemy aliens. Unnaturalised enemy aliens of military age were interned in 1914 and 1915; after the sinking of the *Lusitania,* anti-alienism became more fevered and internment and deportation were extended to women, children and old people.[16] Jews from enemy alien countries were caught by these regulations. Despite the fact that they had been resident in Britain for many years and had left their countries of origin in search of a better, freer life in liberal Britain, they were torn from their families and their livelihoods. However, the Anglo-Jewish leadership showed little direct concern for these men and their families. It refused to offer assistance to interned enemy aliens, even though the government set up tribunals to consider hard cases at which the Jewish community might have been officially represented.[17] Nor did the Board of Deputies accept the offer of aid to innocent

Russian and Rumanian Jewish victims of the anti-German riots after the *Lusitania* sinking.[18]

The President of the Board, David Alexander, and its solicitor, Henry Henriques, argued that the treatment of 'enemy aliens' was not a specifically Jewish matter. A majority of deputies supported them. The Jewish friendly societies and the B'nai Brith (a national organisation of the Jewish middle class), protested against the Board's official indifference, but failed to obtain a change of policy. When the matter was raised at the Board, Leopold Greenberg commented that the debate was 'marked by a nervous terror of the impugnment of Jewish patriotism which played havoc with the logical facilities of the members'.[19] As a result, the friendly societies and the B'nai Brith themselves represented Jews on aliens' advisory tribunals. In non-London Jewish centres local representative bodies were hastily established to mediate between Jewish aliens and the authorities.[20] The Board remained aloof even when anti-alien orders were extended and tightened up, such as the barring of enemy alien Jews from certain parts of the country.[21] Yet its position was understandable when seen against the background of jingoism and xenophobia that increased as the fighting wore on. Jews and Germans were regularly conflated in the press and in openly anti-Semitic journals. Physical violence against Jews occurred in several towns and cities in 1914 and 1915; Jewish shopkeepers around the country were so afraid that they took to displaying in their shop windows their naturalisation papers or old photographs of themselves in the Russian army.[22]

III

A general level of anti-Jewish feeling, the 'background' anti-Semitism of the pre-war years, was evident in the treatment of Jewish volunteers from the earliest days of the war. There were reports of discrimination and abuse against Jews from several recruiting depots and word spread that Jews were unwelcome in certain units.[23] Claims that the Jews were not doing their bit were made frequently. In the closing days of voluntary enlistment Lord Derby, the minister responsible for recruitment, described the Jewish response as 'patchy', an allegation echoed by *The Times*.[24] It was partly to allay these charges that the *Jewish Chronicle* published weekly the names of all Jewish volunteers in its Honour Record and, later, prominently listed casualties as well as Jews earning medals or promotions.[25]

If British-born Jews were the victims of peace-time prejudice carried into the ranks, foreign-born Jews encountered a more specific form of discrimination. There was a great deal of confusion among recruiting officers as to the status of foreign-born volunteers: non-naturalised Jews were turned away if they tried to enlist, but there was also evidence that naturalised British Jews were refused. The central recruitment office had to issue circulars clarifying the situation, but not before some Jews had become disheartened, while others took the news of denials as a convenient pretext for not attempting to enlist.[26] During 1915–1916, as it appeared that large numbers of eligible foreign-born Jews were not enlisting, there was increasing press comment about Jewish 'shirkers'. This created discomfort among British Jews who started recruitment campaigns in order to remedy the deficiency.[27] Other palliatives were considered, such as an all-Jewish unit dedicated to foreign-born Jews, which will be dealt with in greater detail below.

The inauguration of conscription was greeted with relief by Anglo-Jews since it was anticipated that, by eliminating the possibility of British Jews choosing not to enroll, it would end the carping about Jewish war service. Instead, it opened up a new set of difficulties. Jews who were subject to the Military Service Act began to appear before conscription tribunals pleading exemption on the grounds that they were Jewish conscientious objectors or were unable to serve because they were *cohanim*. The whole country was racked by the conscription/concientious objection debate, but it had a differential impact on the Jews. The Jewish population was bitterly divided over these appeals, which raised previously dormant issues of the relative weight of Jewish as against British loyalties, the competing claims of religious observance and the duties of citizenship.[28]

The official leadership, with the authority of the Chief Rabbi, J. H. Hertz, declared that there were no specifically Jewish grounds for conscientious objection. Rabbis and *cohanim,* they argued, could serve, if not in combat roles.[29] There were many other Jews, however, who disagreed. A group of eminent rabbis in Leeds disputed Hertz's decision and mounted a serious challenge to his authority.[30] A *cause celebre* developed around the minister of the Liverpool Old Hebrew Congregation, Rev. John Harris, who was summarily dismissed from his post because he had testified at a conscription tribunal on behalf of a Jewish conscientious objector. In fact, Harris disavowed Jewish motives for his action, claiming that he was arguing on general principles and on this basis he won measured support from the *Jewish Chronicle*.[31] Throughout the course of these controversies, the Jewish leadership and press were at pains to distance Judaism from conscientious objection: a Jew could seek exemption as a citizen, but not as a Jewish believer.[32] The identity of the Jewish citizen was split into separate parts under the pressure of events and the fear of intolerance.

IV

While conscription created circumstances which set apart Jews eligible for military service, it also heightened the anomaly of Russian-born, friendly alien Jews of military age who were ineligible for military service. Around 25–30,000 Jews fell into this catagory and they became the target for increasingly scathing press comment and popular hostility once they were the only group of young, able-bodied men left in British cities. The government's clumsy and halting efforts to deal with this have been well-researched but less attention has been paid to the Anglo-Jewish dimension of this ostensibly immigrant question.[33]

In May 1916, the War Office announced that it would accept friendly-alien volunteers into the British Army. Anglo-Jews greeted this with mixed feelings. While they welcomed the clear-cut decision in favour of Russian-born Jews, they were worried by the voluntaristic aspect of the arrangement. Lucien Wolf, for example, recommended to the War Office that it make service compulsory. He and Greenberg shared an apprehension that voluntary service would be a failure. Moreover, they disliked the element of special treatment: they preferred conscription hand in hand with naturalisation, bringing foreign-born Jews into line with other citizens.[34]

After two months of recruitment drives, it was apparent that Russian Jews were not responding overmuch to the opportunity offered to them. As a result, the Government declared that 'voluntary' enlistment would be backed up by the threat of deportation for those not 'choosing' to serve in the British Army. Although Wolf and Greenberg were dismayed by the lacklustre performance of Russian-born Jews, they were indignant at the new step. The prospect of Jews being deported back to the country which they had fled years ago, of which young Jews had very little knowledge and for which they had no affection was disturbing. It was a clearly discriminatory measure and Greenberg demanded that, instead, Russian-born Jews should be conscripted and made into full citizens.[35]

The official leadership had fewer scruples regarding foreign Jews in Britain. Henry Henriques defended the War Office position, although he hoped that Jews who did serve would get citizenship eventually. To underline the urgency for action, Henriques pointed to the growing antagonism towards Jews in British cities. Other members of the Board of Deputies deplored the leadership's acquiescence to forced repatriation. A storm of opposition broke and the Board's officers were to forced to concede that it would give no official endorsement to the policy. Russian-born Jews themselves formed a Foreign Jews Protection Committee (FJPC) which organised an effective protest campaign that won the support of Liberal MPs and newspapers. After widespread protests and deputations to the Home Office the Damoclean sword of deportation was dropped.[36]

The issue was complicated by the fact that the Home Secretary who was responsible for the measure was a Jew. Defending the Government's policy at the Board, Lionel de Rothschild argued that, as a Jew, Herbert Samuel must have the best interests of the Jews at heart. Many deputies thought that, on the contrary, it was because Samuel was a Jew that he was compelled to act harshly so as to avoid any taint of bias. Samuel was in an exquisitely agonising position: in his public capacity he acted as an Englishman and treated Russian Jews purely as foreigners; but his critics upbraided him for abjuring Jewish ties and, worse, adopting illiberal practices in order to forestall hostile judgements that he showed favouritism towards his own people.[37]

The problem of what to do with friendly-alien Jews festered on through the autumn and winter of 1916. Russian Jews had been given until 30 September to attest or apply for exemption, but there was such a poor response that the deadline was set back to 25 October in the vain hope that more would sign up. Instead, recruitment drives were disrupted and Russian Jews, led by the FJPC, resisted the blandishments of the Jewish press and the Chief Rabbi.[38] Less than one per cent of eligible Jews in the London area attested and accusations of shirking peppered the local and national press. Jews were also being increasingly labelled with 'job snatching'.[39] However, in January 1917 it emerged that the Government was in negotiation with the Russian authorities to arrange legal means by which Russian subjects could be compelled to serve in the British Army or returned to Russia to serve there and, after much delay, a scheme was announced in March 1917.[40]

The Anglo-Russian Convention was fraught with difficulties and met a mixed response from British Jews. There was relief that, at last, the vacillation and confusion was over, combined with alarm at the conditions under which Russian Jews would be conscripted into the British forces. In particular, objections were raised to the absence of any promise that Russian Jews would receive naturalisation if they served under the British flag.[41] The Russian Revolution seemed miraculously to deliver British Jews from this continuing torment by ending the disabilities of Jews in Russian society and, hence, any aversion to their voluntary or obligatory return. The *Jewish Chronicle* opined that 'The whole question is no longer specifically a Jewish question at all . . .' Jews in Britain need have no more qualms about the forcible return of Russian Jews to their country of origin than they did about the repatriation of Belgians or Italians. Furthermore, it was anticipated that Russian Jews would now drop their objections to fighting in the British ranks and that many others would willingly return to their country of origin — as hundreds, in fact, did.[42]

Yet it was not so simple. The agreement with the Russian government took two months to conclude, during which time the FJPC kept up its agitation and antipathy towards Jewish 'shirkers' escalated. Greenberg was forced to revise his previous optimism and noted that 'the trouble that may ensue to Anglo-Jewry by the attitude of a number of recalcitrants who, unhappily, are being misled, is eminently one for Jewish consideration and, if necessary, Jewish action'.[43] When the Convention was embodied in law by the Military Service (Convention With Allied States) Bill it failed to meet earlier Jewish objections concerning the absence of provision for naturalisation. While Herbert Samuel told the House of Commons that the anti-Russian Jewish agitation was 'a strong and most legitimate feeling' he was concerned that, without the extension of immediate naturalisation to Russian Jews opting to serve in the British Army, the conditions of service would be unjustly exceptional.[44] His apprehension was shared by Greenberg who, ever sensitive to discrimination, observed that Russian Jews would not be eligible for commissions.[45]

This point was more than a quibble: it reveals the root of Jewish anxieties. The Convention threatened to discriminate against Jews in Britain, even if they were not British Jews; the principle of equality before the law, which affected all Jews, was at stake. Greenberg was, consequently, pleased that naturalisation was included in the final version of the Bill, even if it was made subject to the normal requirements of residence and other considerations. In spite of the embarrassment which the stubborn resistance of Russian Jews had caused, the *Jewish Chronicle* trenchantly defended their right to treatment on a par with other soldiers. Ever vigilant, the paper commented with concern about the failure to provide maintenance for the kin of Russian Jews who returned to Russia. It expressed resentment when evidence arose that the Convention tribunals were not providing proper medical examinations and denounced rumours that Russian Jews would be confined to labour battalions.[46]

At the same time, Greenberg and the majority of Anglo-Jewish opinion had absolutely no sympathy for continued war-resistance by the FJPC and greeted with equanimity the arrest of its leaders.[47] In like manner Greenberg was outraged by the persistent attempts of Russian Jews to gain exemption before the specially established tribunals. The *Jewish Chronicle* took particular exception to the appearance of men claiming membership of the ministry. These cases multiplied and led to renewed conflict between the Jewish ecclesiastical authorities in London and venerable rabbis in Leeds whose perspective they did not share.[48] The central Jewish organisations regarded Russian Jews who resisted enlistment or eschewed service in the British Army with unconcealed contempt. In March 1917, the Jewish Board of Guardians announced that its soup kitchen would operate a policy of 'No khaki, No soup'. This move was intended to pressurise Russian Jews to enlist, but it ruptured a self-professed tradition of philanthropy between Jews. The Board of Guardians also refused to give any financial aid to the dependants of men who had returned to Russia.[49] It was symptomatic of the procrustean bed on which Anglo-Jews found themselves pinned that they could display such a keen awareness of discrimination against fellow Jews, on the grounds that they were citizens or potential citizens, only to implement prejudicial policies of their own according to definitions of what they believed constituted acceptable forms of Jewish belief and practice in the light of majority opinion.

V

Issues of identity and equality also underlay the violent controversies surrounding the creation of separate Jewish units to serve in the British Army. The idea of an all-Jewish unit was first raised in the opening weeks of the War by an energetic and eclectic British Jew, Captain Webber. He organised a meeting in the East End with the aim of recruiting 2,000 Russian-born, Yiddish-speaking Jews into a Foreign Legion to fight with the British. This initiative enraged the Jewish establishment, which saw it as separatist and a dangerous precedent. The senior Jewish Chaplain, Rev. Michael Adler, appealed to the Jewish public not to assist in the venture and intervened personally at the War Office to scotch the enterprise. Edmund Sebag-Montefiore, the Jewish liaison with the War Office, protested in the *Jewish Chronicle* that the formation of a special Jewish unit would imply that Jews were reluctant to serve in regular formations for fear of prejudice or out of a greater sense of attachment to other Jews. If prejudice did exist, Jews would get the better of it by entering the widest possible range of units and showing their fellows what they could do.[50]

Leopold Greenberg was one of the leading advocates of the Jewish battalion idea and gave it the support of the *Jewish Chronicle*. He was annoyed by Adler's interference, arguing that a Jewish unit was no different to public school regiments, pals brigades and other 'fancy units' that lacked a territorial base. Although prejudice was not the main rationale for such a unit, rumours about discrimination did act as a deterrent and a Jewish unit seemed the best way of maximising Jewish willingness to fight. Greenberg, as his models showed, believed in the *a priori* existence of bonding amongst British Jews that justified the creation of a Jewish fighting formation.[51]

Webber's activities and the campaign for a Jewish battalion stirred up deep acrimony in Jewish circles. Finally, in December 1914, a meeting was held in a London hotel between the rival camps. Webber was joined by Joseph Cowan and David Eder, and could point to the support of the novelist Israel Zangwill — all of whom were Jewish nationalists of one hue or another. The Rev. Adler was in the company of Sir Philip Magnus MP, Sir Stuart Samuel MP, the Rev. J. F. Stern, Dr Redcliffe Salaman, Meyer Spielman, Lucien Wolf and other representative members of the upper crust of Anglo-Jewish society. The latter argued the typical 'assimilationist' line that a Jewish unit would be a 'ghetto unit', setting Jews apart on the basis of religion and a tacit acceptance of discrimination. They were hostile to the notion that the Jews constituted anything more than a denominational group and, while the issue of Jewish nationality was not raised, it was most likely on the covert agenda of both parties.[52] The War Office prevaricated in the face of these divergent views and, once 'fancy units' had gone out of fashion, allowed the proposal to die.

The idea of a Jewish battalion was resurrected in June 1916 by Vladimir Jabotinsky — the Polish Jewish Zionist leader who had organised Jewish refugees from Palestine in Egypt into the Zion Mule Corps — in a letter published in the *Jewish Chronicle* in June 1916. He saw it as a way to induce recalcitrant Russian Jews to enter the ranks as well as a propaganda coup for Zionism. However, Jabotinsky envisaged that the unit would serve only in non-combat, home-defence roles. This suggestion was quickly rejected by Greenberg who spoke for many Jews when he expressed distaste for the idea of a Jewish unit which would function on a different basis from the rest of the British Army.[53] Jabotinsky won qualified support from the *Jewish Chronicle* and a few of the English Zionists, but his campaign for a Jewish unit eventually foundered on the same obstacles as in 1914: the hostility of Anglo-Jewry and the indifference of the Government.[54]

Then, in July 1917, to the surprise of Jews in Britain, the War Office suddenly announced that it desired the creation of a Jewish regiment. The original proponents of the idea were both delighted and disturbed by the manner and the content of the proposition. There had been no prior consultation between the War Office and Jewish representatives; it was also unclear whether the unit was merely a device to assist the induction of unwilling Russian Jews or whether it was to be dedicated to some expressly Jewish purpose, such as the campaign in Palestine. Above all, there were violent objections to the unit's designation as 'The Jewish Regiment' and the use of the Star of David for its insignia.[55]

The use of the title 'The Jewish Regiment' stirred British Jews into a frenzy. It was rounded on at a meeting of the Board of Deputies during which the President, Sir Stuart Samuel, said 'it was quite impossible to conceive greater opposition to the idea than it had received'.[56] Greenberg wrote an open letter to Lord Derby saying that 'It threatened to divide Anglo-Jewry into segments, because it is cutting athwart the community . . .' Greenberg noted that all sections of the Jewish population were split on this issue, with nationalists, anti-Zionists, orthodox and Liberal, immigrant and British Jews ranged on either side.[57] Rival deputations attended upon Lord Derby, who only confused matters by implying that the regiment was intended to ease the absorption of 'non-assimilated' Jews and might or might not go to Palestine. Afterwards, the *Jewish Chronicle* complained that the Jewish regiment as planned was 'a trifling with the Jewish idea and one that does at least savour of discrimination and differentiation'.[58]

The title and insignia of the Jewish Regiment triggered such controversy because they touched on the raw nerve of Anglo-Jewish identity. Greenberg, who had championed the idea of a volunteer unit, now argued that 'when a Jewish soldier dons the British or the French or the Russian uniform, he does so as a British, French, or a Russian soldier, and not as a Jewish soldier. There is, therefore, neither point nor relevancy — there will, we fear, be grounds for actual offence — in imposing the symbol of Jews or Judaism upon his accoutrements'. This would be especially so if the symbol of Judaism came to be associated with a unit composed of reluctant, foreign-born Jewish conscripts. Jews had fought and died voluntarily under the flags of their respective countries thus far and it was because 'the proposal of the government seems to ignore this fact and to set up a new standard of loyalty for a cause which Jews have gladly suffered, that we venture to question both the propriety and the wisdom of the proposed distinctive sign'. Unless the unit was to be dedicated to a specific Jewish purpose, the emblem and appellation should be removed.[59]

As a result of Anglo-Jewish opposition, the unit was finally designated numerically as one of the line battalions of the Royal Fusiliers and distinguished by a seven-branched candelabrum, symbol of the ancient Hebrew State and the Maccabeans. In fact, the 38th and 40th Royal Fusiliers soon became known as 'The Judaeans' and were a cause for great pride among Jews in Britain. They were held up by the *Jewish Chronicle* as a 'living refutation' of anti-Jewish calumnies about cowardice and shirking. Regardless of the gravity with which the rival camps in the Jewish world regarded the question of a Jewish military unit, the unit did little to alter popular perceptions of the Jews. After the Judaeans had conducted a ceremonial march through the City of London in February 1918, rumours circulated that Jewish soldiers had used the parade as an opportunity to desert.[60]

VI

The controversy surrounding the military service of Russian-born Jews has been commonly linked with the major anti-Jewish riots in Leeds in June, and Bethnal Green in September, 1917. There is without doubt a strong connection, but the explosive question of war service has tended to draw attention away from more mundane matters that highlighted differences between Jews and non-Jews, which generated an awareness of the 'other' and, frequently, outright antagonism. Equally, the focus on the riots has blurred the continuity of anti-Jewish feeling and led to the irruptions of hostility being treated as the expression of particular interactions, with discrete causes, rather than as the nodal points for long-running waves of antipathy.[61]

The British economy was severely disrupted by the outbreak of war and many workers were temporarily unemployed and exposed to hardship. The 'Jewish trades' — clothing, footwear and furniture — were hard hit but, while non-Jewish workers were given access to the Prince of Wales National Relief Fund (NRF), immigrant Jews were barred. The NRF thus perpetuated the discriminatory treatment of alien workers, who were denied the benefits of state welfare aid even though they paid taxes and national insurance contributions. After some agitation, Jewish representatives were appointed to local NRF committees and ensured that unemployed Jewish workers did get assistance.[62] Yet, at the same time as they protested, the Jewish authorities responded in the traditional manner by taking up the burden themselves. Added to this, British Jews pledged to support Belgian Jewish refugees who poured into London in 1914 and were housed and maintained by British Jews at substantial cost.[63]

By early 1915, the allotment of army contracts for uniforms, boots, saddles and straps, ammunition boxes and prefabricated huts brought an extended period of prosperity to the Jewish trades. Over the following two years the shortage of labour, combined with the 'khaki boom', led to an unprecedented rise in the wages and living standards of Jewish workers.[64] Young employed Jewish men and women embarked on a consumer spending spree and took advantage of newly affordable amenities to take trips and holidays in large numbers for the first time. Before long there were complaints in local papers from the residents of areas like Clapton Common and the Surrey Hills who objected to the 'invasion' of exuberant and smartly dressed Jewish youths from London's East End.[65]

During 1916, a country-wide campaign against Sunday trading emerged that may have been related to the sudden prosperity of Jewish people and also to the issue of Russian Jews. It appears to have begun in autumn 1916, when traders in East London started calling for the enforcement of Sunday trading regulations, referring explicitly to Jewish businesses. By the end of the year it had spread to Manchester and Leeds.[66] In early 1917, police and local councils announced a crack-down on Sunday trading in Grimsby and Lincoln, followed by renewed efforts in Leeds and Manchester. The East London press revived the question in the spring of 1917.[67] Concurrent with these movements was a sustained flow of adverse comment about Jewish 'profiteering' and 'job snatching'. This could range from attacks in *New Witness* on Sir Marcus Samuel, head of Shell, to anonymous leaflets circulated in the East End advocating a boycott of Jewish traders.[68] The claim that Jews were taking the jobs of men at the front — clearly associated with the presence of Russian Jews — was publicised in London and the north, particularly in Leeds.[69]

The effects of the German submarine blockade from early 1917 contributed to such tensions in unexpected ways. Shortages, food substitution and rationing all had a differential impact on the Jews in Britain.[70] For example, the inauguration of 'meatless Thursdays' — when butchers were obliged to close — posed special difficulties for Jewish women who traditionally did their pre-Sabbath shopping on a Thursday. In the winter months, when Jewish butchers closed at around 3.00pm on Friday, this left only a brief opportunity to buy meat and prepare it before the Sabbath commenced.[71] When beef and mutton began to run short, the Food Controller advised people to replace them with bacon, hare and tinned meat, options that were not available to devout Jews. They were forced to petition local food committees for extra supplies of beef, which gave the appearance of seeking favoured treatment.[72]

With the introduction of coupons for certain foodstuffs, the situation worsened. Jews had to ask permission to transfer bacon coupons to beef and for *kosher* butchers to have special deliveries of *kosher* meat. Again, this had to be explained and defended against the imputation of favouritism.[73] When word circulated that Jewish butchers had extra supplies, they began to attract non-Jews from outside the areas of Jewish residence. The *kosher* butchers, however, knew their clientele and turned away the newcomers. This provoked angry scenes outside Jewish butchers' shops and accusations that there was a 'Jewish ring'.[74]

Shortages and food controls also brought singular problems for the celebration of Jewish festivals, particularly Passover. Unusually large quantities of sugar were required for seasonal dishes and, it was claimed, to replace the loss of nutrition consequent upon the abstention from the normal consumption of bread. Oil was likewise needed in large amounts for cooking the many fried foods for which purpose lard was not a suitable substitute. The all-important unleavened bread (*matzoh*) was understood mistakenly by the Food Controller to be a cake or a biscuit and deemed a 'precluded product', the manufacture of which required a special, expensive licence.[75] There were persistent difficulties during late 1917 and throughout 1918 with the pricing of *kosher* bread. The food control authorities fixed a price for bread, but Jewish bakers asserted that their products cost more to make. No one at all was sure how to fix the price of *matzoh*. As a result, there were frequent and publicised prosecutions of Jewish bakers and retailers who were held to have violated the price codes enforced by the food controllers.[76]

The onset of heavy air-raids against London in the summer of 1917 further aggravated relations between Jews and non-Jews in the capital. The Jewish population was concentrated in one of the Germans' target areas, east London. After the first raids, large numbers of Jews sought safety in towns along the south coast, in the Home Counties and as far afield as Cardiff, Birmingham and Manchester. The raids, therefore, had a ripple effect that spread far beyond where the bombs actually fell. The national and local press described an 'exodus' of Jews and featured grumbles by residents in Surbiton, Maidenhead and Brighton to the effect that the influx of Jews from east London was causing a shortage of housing, pushing up rents and bringing disease and dirt.[77] Back in the East End, those Jews who stayed were criticised for crowding the air-raid shelters and the tube stations in anticipation of bombing attacks and accused of spreading panic.[78]

The *Jewish Chronicle* swung between condemning expressions of antipathy towards Jews and admonishing the victims to mend their ways according to the strictures of their critics. In October 1917, it devoted the sermon of the week to 'Against Giving Way to Panic', while Greenberg lashed out at those who claimed that Jews were behaving in a cowardly fashion: 'parading the supposed cowardice of East End Jews does not prove ones own courage'.[79] But, later, he wrote 'Is it not possible to impress upon these people a greater measure of self-restraint than is visible, say, in the violent attacks of their assailants?'[80]

In the spring of 1918, a related charge was added to this litany. Jews were held responsible for the overcrowding on trains carrying commuters to and from London daily and at weekends. Furthermore, letters in the press and editorial comment lighted upon the presence of Jews who played cards and ate fried fish in the compartments or talked in an animated fashion.[81] Popular feeling reached such a pitch that, in May 1918, several MPs demanded the imposition of passes on south-east commuter lines. These would only be issued to people who had been resident in the area before January 1917 — a transparent device to exclude London Jews who had moved out of London to take refuge from the bombing.[82] In fact, the overcrowding on the trains was probably due to the cut-backs in services and rolling stock due to labour shortages and military requirements.[83]

Thus, even without the issue of military service, the War supplied a plethora of instances in which Jews were rendered distinctive and 'problematic'. In the locations where rioting occurred there had been a long history of friction specific to the war, not to mention a longer pre-history of conflict. This was outstandingly so in the case of Leeds. There the Jewish war record was held up to scrutiny from August 1914 onwards and, after the introduction of conscription, the press reported in detail Jewish appeals to tribunals for exemption. In 1916 there was a minor scandal over a Jewish teacher who allegedly kept his pupils in class while other school children were marking Empire Day and saluting the Union Jack. Leeds' butchers waged a campaign against Sunday trading at the end of 1916 while, at the same time, a city councillor stated that Jews were not pulling their weight in the war effort. A Jewish munitions worker was prosecuted in January 1917 for refusing to work on the Sabbath and, in the same month, members of the Council of Trades took up cudgels against Sunday trading.[84] The riots of June 1917 were not simply a reaction to alleged 'shirking' by Russian Jews and they were certainly not due to 'purely accidental circumstances'. The disturbances need to be understood in a more subtle and highly textured context of social and economic relations and, above all, the inability to accommodate Jewish difference.[85]

VII

The war years savagely eroded the status of Jews in Britain, a loss of standing that has been understood largely in terms of anti-Germanism, anti-alienism and anti-Bolshevism. The position of immigrant, alien Jews has been made central to all of these currents of hostility. What has been less well comprehended is the impact of the war on British Jews as well, through their involvement in issues concerning the immigrants and as a consequence of the questions which the War posed for their own identification as Jews. British Jews were obliged inexorably to take a position towards the immigrants, forcing them to make painful and virtually impossible choices between Jewish ties and what the majority laid down as the correct forms of patriotic behaviour.

The official Jewish communal organisations were sundered on a succession of issues deriving from the pressures of war. With regard

to enemy-alien, Russian-born Jews, and Jews associated with the
pacifist or socialist movements, a section of British Jewry was willing
to renounce the previously intimate and highly-charged bonds which
joined Jews together. A similar line of fracture divided Jews on
questions of international Jewish solidarity, embracing the issues
of Zionism and attitudes towards Russian Jewry under Tsarism or
Bolshevism. Since the rival factions within Anglo-Jewry prosecuted
their views within communal organisations the years between 1914 and
1918 were punctuated by intense in-fighting ending with a substantial
restructuring of the power relations between different sections of the
Jewish population.[86]

The differential pressures which the war exerted on Jews in Britain as
against the rest of society were, almost entirely, the result of popular
prejudice and the unintended consequences of policy decisions at local
and national level. However, the measures which, in effect, selected the
Jews cannot be dismissed as 'accidental' just because their ramifications
were unforeseen. There was no intention to discriminate, but there
was little accommodation made for minorities and still less thought
for the implications which public policy might have for them. This
flowed inevitably from an unwillingness, an inability, to comprehend
and accept the differences of minorities within society. In this sense,
the problematic exists not at the level of specific instances of conflict,
at the level of 'interaction' between social groups, but in the realm of
ideology. It was acceptable and desirable for British Jews to fight and die
for their country; they were often praised for their patriotism. But they
fought and died for an England and an idea of Englishness that remained
stubbornly impermeable to the particular needs and aspirations of the
varied peoples which comprised the country's true population.[87]

DAVID CESARANI
Wiener Library, London

NOTES

This chapter forms part of a larger work in progress. I would like to thank Tony Kushner
for his comments on an earlier draft.

1. C. Holmes, *Anti-Semitism in British Society, 1879–1939* (London, 1979) ch.8;
    L. Poliakov, *A History of Anti-Semitism*, vol.4, *Suicidal Europe, 1870–1933* (Oxford,
    1985) ch.6; S. Almog, 'Antisemitism as a Dynamic Phenomenon; "The Jewish
    Question" in England at the End of the First World War', *Patterns of Prejudice*, 21:4
    (1987) pp.3–18. World War One is also treated in S. Bayme, 'Jewish Leadership and
    Anti-Semitism in Britain, 1898–1918', unpublished PhD thesis, Columbia University,
    New York, 1977 and telegraphically in G. Alderman, *The Jewish Community in British
    Politics* (Oxford, 1983) pp.88–89.
2. On anti-Germanism, see C.C. Aronsfeld, 'Jewish Enemy Aliens in England During
    the First World War,' *Jewish Social Studies*, 18 (1956) pp.275–83; also, S. Yarrow,
    'Germans in England and the First World War', unpublished MA thesis, Middlesex
    Polytechnic, 1987 and her contribution in this volume. Poliakov and Holmes deal

with this in detail. On the Jews and anti-alienism, see D. Cesarani, 'Anti-Alienism in Britain After the First World War', *Immigrants and Minorities*, 6:1 (1987), pp.5–29. On the treatment of Russian-born Jews in Britain, see C. Bermant, *London's East End. Point of Arrival* (London, 1975) pp.222–230; Holmes, *Anti-Semitism in British Society*, pp.126–136; S. Cohen, *English Zionists and British Jews. The Communal Politics of Anglo-Jewry. 1895–1920* (Princeton, 1982), pp.252–254 and J. Bush, *Behind the Lines. East London Labour. 1914–1919* (London, 1984) ch.6, esp. pp.173–184. This matter also receives consideration in S. Kadish, 'Bolsheviks and British Jews: The Anglo-Jewish Community, Britain and the Russian Revolution', unpublished DPhil thesis, Oxford University, 1987.

3. See Holmes, *Anti-Semitism in British Society*, pp.130–132, 134–136 and Bush, *Behind the Lines*, pp.181–182. Also, A. Gilam, 'The Leeds Anti-Jewish Riots in 1917', *Jewish Quarterly*, 29:1 (1978) pp.34–7 and N. Grizzard, *Leeds Jewry and the Great War 1914–1918* (Leeds, 1981) pp.8–11. Other incidents of violence are touched upon in A. Marwick, *The Deluge. British Society and the First World War* (New York, 1970) p.131 and J. Williams, *The Home Fronts. Britain, France and Germany, 1914–1918* (London, 1972) pp.65–66.

4. J. Winter, *The Great War and the British People*, (London, 1985).

5. This analysis draws heavily on G. Dench, *Minorities In The Open Society. Prisoners of Ambivalence* (Oxford, 1986).

6. Bush, *Behind the Lines*, pp.189–190.

7. On the construction of an Anglo-Jewish identity, see I. Finestein, *Post-Emancipation Jewry: The Anglo-Jewish Experience* (Oxford, 1980); T. Endelman, 'Communal Solidarity Among the Jewish Elite of Victorian London' *Victorian Studies*, 28:3 (1985) pp.491–526; B. Cheyette, 'From Apology to Revolt: Benjamin Farjoen, Amy Levy and the Post-Emancipation Anglo-Jewish Novel, 1880–1900', *Transactions of the Jewish Historical Society of England*, vol. 29 (London, 1988) pp.253–65.

8. *Jewish Chronicle* (hereafter, *JC*), 31 July 1914, p.7. Leopold Greenberg, 1862–1930, b. Birmingham; journalist and publisher; aid to Theodore Herzl and co-founder of English Zionist Federation, 1899; editor *Jewish Chronicle*, 1907–30.

9. *JC*, 7 Aug. 1914, p.5. The newsheet monitored the oppression of Russian Jews. Lucien Wolf, 1857–1930, b. London; journalist, assistant editor *Daily Graphic*, editor *Jewish World*, 1900–09; [co-founder of Jewish Historical Society, 1893;] secretary, Board of Deputies Conjoint Foreign Committee 1903–17 and Joint Foreign Committee, 1918–28; member of Jewish Territorial Organization and anti-Zionist.

10. *43rd Annual Report of the Anglo-Jewish Association, 1913–1914* (London, 1914) pp.5–6. (Hereafter abbreviated to *AJA 43rd Annual Report, 1913–1914*, etc.)

11. *AJA 44th Annual Report, 1914–1915*, pp.5–6 and 9–12.

12. The situation of Russian Jewry and Wolf's diplomacy has been described by D. Vital, *Zionism: The Crucial Phase* (Oxford, 1986) pp.108–119. See also, M. Levine, 'Lucien Wolf: A Study in Anglo-Jewish Diplomacy, 1914–1919', unpublished DPhil thesis, Oxford, 1986.

13. *JC*, 4 Sept. 1914, p.7.

14. *JC*, 23 Apr. 1915, p.7.

15. Comment in *American Hebrew* as reported in the *JC* and reply, *JC*, 25 June 1915, p.9. See also the corruscating *American Israelite* which accused the *JC* of 'inconsistency' and 'cringing', *JC*, 8 Oct. 1915, pp.7–8. Greenberg had domestic critics too, see letter from Albert Hyamson, *JC*, 7 May 1915, p.21.

16. See Holmes, *Anti-Semitism in British Society*, pp.121–26; Yarrow, 'Germans in England and the First World War', pp.40–57.

17. Board of Deputies minute book, vol.16, 15 Nov. 1914, Board of Deputies Archive, (hereafter, BOD, vol.16, 15 Nov. 1914 etc.). The Board did intervene selectively, to help extract interned rabbis, for example.

18. *JC*, 21 May 1915, p.5 leader comment and 28 May 1915, p.16 on the response of the Board of Deputies; BOD, vol.16, 13 June 1915.

19. BOD, vol.16, 13 June 1915. For Greenberg's comments, *JC* 18 June 1915, p.7 and a similar plea for official Jewish action, 2 July 1915, p.7. David Lindo Alexander,

1842–1922, b. London; barrister; President, Board of Deputies, 1903–17. Henry S. Q. Henriques, 1866–1925, b. London, barrister and author; Honorary Secretary and Solicitor, Board of Deputies.

20. For reports of friendly society action and local initiatives, *JC*, 2 July 1915, p.15; 23 July 1915, p.6 and pp.17–18; 6 Aug. 1915, p.18. Further protests were raised at the Board when it met in July, BOD, vol.16, 22 July 1915. By October 1915, two friendly societies had dealt with over 3,200 cases alone, *JC*, 1 Oct. 1915, p.21.

21. BOD, vol.17, 20 Feb. 1916; BOD, vol.17, 26 Mar. 1916, and 30 Apr. 1916.

22. See Holmes, *Anti-Semitism in British Society*, pp.121–122; Marwick, *The Deluge*, p.131. For contemporary reports of anti-Jewish violence, *JC*, 11 Sept. 1914, p.13; Liverpool, 14 May 1915, p.18; Tonypandy and Poplar, 28 May 1915, pp.19–20; Hull, 2 July 1915, p.22. For loyalty displays, see *JC*, 2 Oct. 1914, p.19 on north, north-east and east London; 16 Oct. 1914, p.21 on east London; 28 May 1915, p.20 in Poplar; 30 July 1915, p.19 for north and north-east London.

23. Hackney depot appears to have been notorious, although it was claimed that Jewish volunteers 'bellyached' about conditions there and so induced an off-hand or overtly hostile attitude towards other Jews, *JC*, 9 Oct. 1914, pp.5 and 17, 23 Oct. 1914, p.8. The 4th (Reserve) City of London Battalion, London Regiment, turned away a Jew and later told inquirers that Jews were not wanted. In fact, there were Jews in the unit and others were allowed to join — but not until after it had acquired a stigma, *JC*, 4 Dec. 1914, pp.12–13 and 11 Dec. 1914, p.8; the *JC* commented that 'it would be futile to deny that the existence in certain regiments of anti-Jewish prejudice is too palpable to be mistaken'. See also, Mentor, 26 Nov. 1915, p.9 on discrimination and 'chipping'.

24. On the 'Derby Scheme' see Marwick, *The Duluge,* pp.76–85. For Derby's criticism, *JC*, 19 Nov. 1915, p.16; *The Times*, 8 Dec. quoted in *JC*, 17 Dec. 1915, p.7. Donald Maclean, MP, chairman of the House of Commons Tribunal also protested that Jews hadn't done enough, *JC*, 9 June 1916, p.5.

25. *JC*, 4 Sept. 1914, p.6 et seq. The 'Honour Roll' was closed after the introduction of conscription.

26. *JC*, 19 Nov. 1915, p.7, 21, 23; 12 Nov. 1915, p.13 on enlisting in Leeds; *JC*, 17 Dec. 1915, p.8 concerning recruitment in Manchester. Derby's official view on the matter was stated in a letter to Leopold de Rothschild, head of the Jewish Recruiting Committee in London, BOD, vol.17, 21 Nov. 1915.

27. *JC*, 19 Nov. 1915, pp.21, 23 on recruitment drives in London and Manchester.

28. On the issue of *cohanim*, see *JC*, 17 Mar. 1916, p.12; 24 Mar. 1916, pp.20–21; 23; 31 Mar. 1916, p.8. Russian Jews opposed to conscription sometimes disrupted the tribunals, JC, 14 Jan. 1916, p.7; Mentor, 7 Apr. 1916, p.11.

29. See speech of Lionel de Rothschild MP, House of Commons Debates, Fifth Series, vol.77, col.1026, (hereafter, 77 H.C. Deb. 5s 1026 etc.), 5 Jan. 1916; for the secular and spiritual points of view, *JC*, 28 Jan. 1916, p.11. The contrary opinion of Jewish pacifists was expressed in letters to *JC*, 21 Jan. 1916, p.16; 11 Feb. 1916, pp.18–20.

30. The clash between Hertz and the Leeds rabbis, can be tracked in the *JC*, beginning *JC*, 31 Mar. 1916, p.15, then 7 Apr. 1916, p.10, 14 Apr. 1916, p.18, 21 Apr. 1916, p.6. A similar controversy raged for months during the winter of 1917–1918 over the exemption of an alleged minister.

31. On various aspects the John Harris affair, see Evelyn Wilcock, 'Rev. John Harris: Issues in Anglo-Jewish Pacifism, 1914–1918', unpublished paper presented to the Jewish Historical Society of England, 14 Jan. 1988. It can be followed vividly through the pages of the *Jewish Chronicle* which may have been partial to Harris who had once been a regular contributor to its series 'Sermon of the Week'. Reportage of the affair begins, *JC*, 10 March 1916, p.7.

32. This is, of course, a complex issue and it is arguable that the Chief Rabbi at the time was correct in his ruling. As in many questions of Jewish theology and law, there is no clear cut answer and no unanimous rabbinical opinion.

33. Holmes, *Anti-Semitism in British Society*, pp.126–30; Bush, *Behind the Lines*, pp.181–86. Aspects are touched on in S. Kadish, 'Conscription or Deportation?:

Russian Jewish Aliens in England and the Question of Military Service in 1917',
unpublished paper, 1987.

34. Lucien Wolf, 'Memorandum', 20 June 1916, and 'Russian Jews and Military
Service', 15 Aug. 1916, File 87, Mowshowitch Papers, YIVO, New York, cited by
Kadish. Edward Sebag-Montefiore, chairman of the Jewish War Services Committee,
concurred in the need for complusion, communication, 25 Oct. 1916, HO45/10819/
157, cited by Kadish. Greenberg made his position clear in his leaders and articles
written as Mentor, JC, 26 May 1916, p.5; 9 June 1916, p.5; 16 June 1916, p.7; 23 June
1916, p.7.

35. JC, 14 Apr. 1916, p.9 for early misgivings; 7 July 1916, p.5; 14 July 1916, p.7. As
Mentor, he wrote a number of 'open letters' to the Home Secretary, Herbert Samuel,
reiterating his critique, JC 14 July 1916, pp.9–10; 21 July 1916, p.5.

36. The debate over enlistment or deportation is recorded in detail in the JC, 28 July 1916,
p.5, 4 Aug. 1916, p.5, 11 Aug. 1916, p.5, 18 Aug. 1916, p.5, 25 Aug. 1916, p.5. See
also, 84–85 HC Debs 5s, 11 July–22 Aug. 1916.

37. BOD, vol.17, 16 July 1916. For Greenberg's caustic remarks on Samuel's Jewishness,
see JC, 14 1916, pp.9–10. Samuel's Jewishness was taken up by the Liberal press,
too. The Nation, 5 July 1916, accused him of 'scourging his own race' and argued
that 'he is unfit to be the Home Secretary because he is not capable of being
just to the Jews'. It is perhaps significant that this episode is not mentioned in
Samuel's autobiography, Memoirs (London, 1945). Herbert Samuel, 1870–1963, b.
Liverpool; Liberal MP, 1902–18, 1929–35, Parliamentary Under-Secretary, Home
Office, 1905–09, Chancellor of the Duchy of Lancaster, 1909–10, Postmaster General,
1910–14, President of the Local Government Board, 1914–1915, Home Secretary,
1916–1917; first professing Jew in the Cabinet, first British High Commissioner for
Palestine 1920–1924.

38. The Chief Rabbi said in his Yom Kippur sermon that 'we grieve to think of the few
thousands among the hundreds of thousands constituting the Jewish citizenship of the
allied nations who desire to be exempted from the fulfillment of their elementary duty
of patriotism'. JC, 13 Oct. 1916, p.12.

39. JC, 6 Oct. 1916 pp.12–13 on East London press and 24 Nov. 1916, p.11. Comments
by Frederic Charrington on Stepney, JC, 22 Sept. 1916, p.7.

40. JC, 2 Mar. 1917, p.7.

41. JC, 9 Mar. 1917, p.7.

42. JC, 23 Mar. 1917, p.7.

43. JC, 13 Apr. 1917, p.5.

44. 93 H.C. Debs. 5s, 1562, 15 May 1917. JC, 18 May 1917, p.5.

45. JC, 22 June 1917, p.7.

46. JC, 27 July 1917, p.5; 24 Aug. 1917, p.9; 12 Apr. 1918, p.5. The author's grandfather
was exempted by an east London tribunal on medical grounds.

47. JC, 3 Aug. 1917, p.3.

48. JC, 24 Aug. 1917, p.3; 21 Sept. 1917, pp.5–6, 16 Nov. 1917, p.6 et seq. The matter
required a personal visit by Hertz and was not resolved until March 1918, JC, 1 Mar.
1918, p.6.

49. For 'No khaki . . .' see JC, 9 Mar. 1917, p.8; 30 Mar. 1917, pp.11–12. Concerning
dependants, JC, 21 Sept. 1917, p.5, 19 Sept. 1917, pp.5–6. Greenberg dubbed their
policy, 'a negation of all that the Board stands for', JC, 12 Oct. 1917, p.5.

50. JC, 28 Aug. 1914, p.11 for details of Webber's meeting, letter 9 Oct. 1914, p.19,
leader, 6 Nov. 1914, pp.5–6. For Adler's caveat, JC, 6 Nov. 1914, pp.5–6 and
Sebag-Montefiore's admonition, 13 Nov. 1914, pp.10–11.

51. JC, 27 Nov. 1914, p.5. Zionists like Greenberg also argued that a Jewish military
contribution to the allied cause would strengthen their claims to the victor's spoils
at the anticipated post-war peace conference.

52. JC, 11 Dec. 1914, pp.20–21; 8 Jan. 1915, p.7. Leonard Stein was later to claim that
Greenberg was one of the original proponents of the idea and that he acted from
Zionist motives, 'Eder as Zionist' in J. B. Hobman (ed.), David Eder. Memoirs of
a Modern Pioneer (London, 1945) p 135.

53. *JC,* 14 July 1916, pp.9–10; 25 Aug. 1916, pp.11–12; 1 Sept. 1916, pp.7–8.
54. *JC,* 30 June 1916, pp.15–16 and comment, p.7. On Jabotinsky's efforts, see Cohen, *English Zionists and British Jews,* pp.215–16 and 253–54; Vital, *Zionism: The Crucial Phase,* pp.228–29. Lucien Wolf made a similar proposal in the *Daily Chronicle,* 13 July 1916, reprinted, and commented on in *JC,* 8 Sept. 1916, pp.7, 17.
55. *JC,* 27 July 1917, p.5.
56. BOD, vol.17, 13 Aug. 1917.
57. *JC,* Mentor, 31 Aug. 1917, p.7.
58. *JC,* 7 Sept. 1917, p.5. See also the important account by the unit's first commanding officer, J. H. Patterson, *With The Judeans In The Palestine Campaign* (London, 1922) pp.18–29. Patterson ascribed the cleavage solely to anti-Zionism whereas it was more complex than that. At the Board of Deputies, Lord Rothschild, Dr Samuel Daiches and Nathan Laski who were sympathetic to Zionism opposed the Jewish Regiment on similar grounds to Greenberg.
59. *JC,* 3 Aug. 1917, p.3.
60. *JC,* 8 Feb. 1918, p.5.
61. Holmes, *Anti-Semitism in British Society,* p.136; Gilam, 'The Leeds Anti-Jewish Riots', p.34–35.
62. *JC,* 14 Aug. 1914, p.6 on discrimination in Leeds; 20 Nov. 1914, pp.7, 27 on Glasgow and east London; BOD, vol.16, 20 Dec. 1914, 16 Jan. 1915 and 18 Apr. 1915. See also the discussion in Bush, *Behind the Lines,* pp.168–169. The Jewish Board of Guardians resolved to intervene at a special meeting on 31 Aug. 1914, reported *JC,* 4 Sept. 1914.
63. On Belgian Jewish refugees, *JC,* 11 Sept. 1914, p.6; 16 Oct. 1914, p.5 et seq.
64. *46th Annual Report of the Board of Guardians for the Relief of the Jewish Poor* (London 1915), pp.16–28 (hereafter 46th BOGAR etc.). See also, 47th BOGAR, p.15 for 1915, 48th BOGAR, p.15. for 1916. See also, R. Samuel, *East End Underworld, Chapters in the Life of Arthur Harding* (London, 1981), pp.236–37.
65. *JC,* 23 July 1916, p.26; 4 Aug. 1916, p.10.
66. *JC,* 22 Sept. 1916, p.32 on Hackney; 1 Dec. 1916, p.25 on Petticoat Lane; 8 Dec. 1916, p.6 on Manchester; 15 Dec. 1916, p.8 on Leeds.
67. *JC,* 5 Jan. 1917, p.9 on Grimsby and Lincoln; 19 Jan. 1917, p.17 for Leeds and 26 Jan. 1917, p.11, 22 for Manchester; 11 May 1917, p.25 on the *East London Observer.*
68. R. Henriques, *Marcus Samuel: First Viscount Bearsted and the Founder of the Shell Transport and Trading Company, 1853–1927* (London, 1960) p.604; *JC,* 4 Jan. 1918, p.6 and 15 Mar. 1918, p.9. *JC,* 21 June 1918, p.5. There were also related disturbances at a by-election in East Finsbury, *JC,* 19 July 1918, p.5. For the boycott circular, see BOD, vol.17, 17 Feb. 1918: Percy Hurst, the author, was enlarging a private dispute with a Jewish furniture manufacturer.
69. *JC,* 22 Sept. 1916, p.7 for comments of Frederick Charrington on the East End; 27 July 1917, p.6 on the *Yorkshire Evening Post (YEP).*
70. The background on rationing can be gleaned from Marwick, *The Deluge,* pp.191–195 and Williams, *The Home Fronts,* pp.188–195 and 247–250. Also, Winter, *The Great War and the British People,* pp.215–229.
71. *JC,* 5 Jan. 1918, p.26.
72. *JC,* 8 Feb. 1918, p.20 on Newcastle; 15 Feb. 1918, p.18 on Leeds.
73. BOD, vol.17, 17 Mar. 1918, 21 Apr. 1918 and 26 May 1918; *JC,* 26 Apr. 1918, p.5; 14 June 1918, p.3.
74. *JC,* 28 Dec. 1917, p.22 on the East End; 8 Feb. 1918, p.20, for Leeds; 22 Feb. 1918, p.6, on claims of a 'ring' by a councillor for Borough in London; 15 June 1918, p.12.
75. See *JC,* 26 Apr. 1918, p.5 and 26 May 1918, p.8 on oil and fats; 19 Oct. 1917, p.6, 17 Feb. 1918, p.9 and 1 Mar. 1918, p.16 on Passover problems. A Food Committee was set up by the Board of Deputies to plead the Jewish case; see for example, BOD, vol.17, 17 Feb. 1918 on oil and fats.
76. For instance, *JC,* 9 Nov. 1917, p.16 in Glasgow; 14 Dec. 1917, p.26 in London and 16 Aug. 1918, p.5–6.
77. *JC,* 5 Oct. 1917, p.5, 18; 29 Mar. 1918, p.3; 19 Apr. 1918, p.6.

78. *JC,* 28 Sept. 1917, p.4; 1 Feb. 1918, p.12. See Bush, *Behind the Lines* p.181 and Marwick, *The Deluge,* pp.197–98 on general aspects of the bombing in 1917.
79. *JC,* 5 Oct. 1917, p.5, 18; *JC* sermon, 12 Oct. 1917, p.11; see also, *JC,* 29 Mar. 1918, p.3, 19 Apr. 1918, p.6.
80. *JC,* 5 Oct. 1917, p.5.
81. *JC,* 26 Apr. 1918, p.7; 3 May 1918, p.9 and 10 May 1918, p.7.
82. The accusation was first made by Maj. Tyron, 104 HC Debs. 5s, 1826–7, 12 Apr. 1918; it was taken up by Pemberton Billing, a notorious anti-alien and Jew-baiter, 105 HC Debs. 5s, 35, 15 April 1918; in a major railways debate, the claim was pressed by Mr Rawlinson, Maj. Tyron and won the support of William Joynson-Hicks, another bane of Jewish life in Britain, 106 HC Debs. 5s, 430, 434. *JC* comment, *JC,* 17 May 1918, p.3.
83. Marwick, *The Deluge,* p.195. See also the explanation by Sir Albert Stanley, President of the Board of Trade, 106 HC Debs. 5s, 390–393.
84. On the war record of Leeds Jewry, *YEP,* 14 Aug. 1914, reported in *JC,* 21 Aug. 1914, p.12; *Bradford Daily Argus,* 31 Aug. 1914, reported *JC,* 4 Sept. 1914, p.15; comments of the recruiting officer in Leeds, *JC,* 13 Aug. 1915, p.6. *JC,* 9 June 1916, p.6 on alleged disloyalty on Empire Day; 23 June 1916, p.15 on *YEP* comment concerning numbers of Jewish volunteers; 8 Dec. 1916, p.21 for councillor's comments; 15 Dec. 1916, p.23 on Sunday trading and butchers; 19 Jan. 1917, p.17 on Sunday trading; 26 Jan. 1917, p.11 prosecuted munitions worker.
85. Gilam, 'The Anti-Jewish riots in Leeds', p.34. Nor is it sufficient to refer simply to a vague 'tradition' of anti-Jewish feeling in such places; a more precise contextualisation is necessary and feasible. Cf. Holmes, *Anti-Semitism in British Society,* p.136.
86. See Cohen, *English Zionists and British Jews,* ch.7; S. Kadish, '"The Letter of the Ten" Bolsheviks and British Jews', in J. Frankel (ed.), *Studies in Contemporary Jewry.* vol.4, *The Jews and the European Crisis, 1914–21* (Oxford, 1988) pp.96–112; D. Cesarani, 'The Transformation of Communal Authority in Anglo-Jewry, 1914–1940' in D. Cesarani (ed.), *The Making of Modern Anglo-Jewry* (Oxford, 1989) forthcoming.
87. For a useful discussion of the extent and limitations of Englishness, see R. Colls and P. Dodd (eds.), *Englishness. Politics and Culture 1880–1920* (London, 1986).

The British Communist Party's National Jewish Committee and the Fight Against Anti-Semitism During The Second World War.

The Second World War saw an upsurge of anti-Semitic activity in Great Britain. This provided further opportunity for the Jewish Communist movement, centred mainly in London's East End, to assume a political and ideological presence within the Anglo-Jewish community. The Jewish Communists fought against the internment of Jewish aliens and charges that Jews controlled the black market. They organized demonstrations against the 1943 release from detention of Sir Oswald Mosley. The National Jewish Committee of the party developed theoretical positions on Jews and Fascism. This intense activity culminated in a number of electoral breakthroughs by the CPGB in Stepney in 1945–1946.

Nations at war often experience internal social and ethnic conflicts as well, with visible and exposed minority groups typically bearing the brunt of heightened tensions. Great Britain during the Second World War proved to be no exception to the rule. Although engaged in a struggle with an enemy, Nazi Germany, whose ideological underpinnings included a fanatical hatred of Jews, British society during this period itself experienced an upsurge in anti-Semitic activity.[1] This article will deal with the response of one sector of the Jewish population, centred around the Communist Party of Great Britain, to manifestations of anti-Semitism during the 1939–1945 period.

Stuart A. Cohen has referred to the 'wide spectrum' of Anglo-Jewish attitudes towards anti-Semitism, ranging from 'a tendency to ignore or excuse anti-Semitic phenomena' to 'a blatant and robust Jewish reaction to each and every perceived manifestation of prejudice.'[2] The Jewish Communists fell into the second category. While many of the traditional organizations in the community tended to shy away from confronting anti-Semitic groups, in the pre-1940 period the Jewish Communists in Stepney, along with Communist-influenced organizations such as the Jewish People's Council Against Fascism and Anti-Semitism, the Stepney Tenants' Defence League and the National Council for Civil Liberties, served as the main opposition to Sir Oswald Mosley's British Union of Fascists and other groups on the far right.

By contrast, the Board of Deputies of British Jews, the umbrella organization of the community, was reluctant to involve itself in direct confrontations with the Fascists. The Stepney Labour Party, which dominated the politics of the borough, was also strangely quiescent. Perhaps this reflected the dilemma faced by the party: an unstable coalition of Irish Catholics and Jews united around local 'bread and butter' issues and more concerned with the dispensation of patronage than with matters of ideology, it seemed unable to stand up to the challenge of the BUF. Many of its Irish members also proved sympathetic to Franco's Nationalists during the Spanish Civil War. The party was in consequence deserted by many Jews who were attracted by the CP's militancy.

As we shall see, the Communists continued to carry the anti-Fascist banner in wartime as well, keeping their verbal guns trained at the Fascists interned under Defence Regulation 18B, and remaining on guard for renewed Fascist activity in England, no matter what the guise or party label. Although the 1939 Hitler–Stalin pact did lead to some soul-searching, the CP did not experience a significant falling-off of Jewish support: the average working class Stepney resident was more immediately concerned with inadequate air raid precautions during the 'blitz' and the anti-Jewish paranoia of 1940 — problems which the Jewish Communist movement addressed forcefully.[3] And the party increasingly began to concern itself with the problem of anti-Semitism on a theoretical level. The National Jewish Committee of the CPGB, established in April 1943, came to provide the theoretical framework for the Communist Party's anti-Fascist analyses and activities.

By these actions, they earned the gratitude of a substantial number of Jews, especially in east London, the scene of so much pre-war turmoil. In the July 1945 general election, Phil Piratin, a Communist candidate, won election to the British Parliament from the Mile End division of Stepney. In addition to Piratin's seat, the Communist Party won all ten Stepney Borough Council seats which they contested that autumn, as well as Mile End's two London County Council seats the following spring.

Political Campaigns Against Domestic Fascists

Although the coming of war led to the imprisonment of hundreds of Fascist and the temporary suppression of many Fascist organizations, it also created new problems for the Jewish community. In the summer of 1940, Lord Rothermere's *Daily Mail* led a media campaign which hinted that Jews were likely to be 'Fifth Columnists'. Soon the wholesale round-ups began, and some 30,000 aliens — most of them Jewish — were interned, sometimes alongside Nazis.[4] *The Times* was moved to comment that 'the treatment of the refugees seems to be less favourable than that of prisoners of war',[5] while the *Jewish Chronicle*, the voice of Anglo-Jewry, said the round-ups had 'besmirched the fair name of this humane land'.[6]

'When the mass internments began, it was mainly the unionised

workers and Communists who opposed them.'[7] The *Daily Worker* of
26 July 1940, described in graphic detail the fear and paranoia in east
London's squalid back streets.[8] Why, asked another issue of the paper,
were the refugees forced to 'rot in concentration camps?'[9] As late as
1942, more than 2,000 Jews remained in camps, a source of constant
frustration for the Jewish community.[10]

Meanwhile, other forms of anti-Semitism were clearly visible in
Britain, a fact duly noted by observers as diverse as the writer George
Orwell; Sidney Salomon, secretary of the Defence Committee of the
Board of Deputies; and the Home Intelligence unit of the Ministry of
Information.[11] Indeed, Stepney Labour councillor Frank R. Lewey, who
was mayor during the 1940 'blitz', speculated that the Nazis may have
chosen to target London's East End in the hope that the local population,
conditioned by years of anti-Semitic agitation, would blame the Jews for
the ills and stage a revolt.[12]

One of the most persistent accusations made against the Jews during
this period was that they dominated the black market; the *Jewish
Chronicle* asserted in a leader that many people regarded this as 'almost
a Jewish monopoly'.[13] There were scarcely-veiled attacks upon Jews by
some Conservative MPs in Parliament, and some newspapers maintained
that not only individual Jews, but even synagogues, were involved.[14]

In January 1943, the Stepney Communist Party sponsored a mass
meeting at the Grand Palais against black marketeers;[15] however,
explained the editor of the *Daily Worker*, the solution was stricter
government surveillance, not anti-Jewish propaganda.[16] Willie Gallacher,
the Communist MP for West Fife, devoted three pages of his 1943
pamphlet, *Anti-Semitism: What it Means to You*, to refuting these
accusations. He pointed out that in Germany, where by 1943 Jews
were in no position to run anything, the black market flourished as
well.[17] A special meeting of the Stepney Borough Council urging the
government to make anti-Semitism a criminal offence was welcomed by
Communist councillor Phil Piratin, who announced he was 'concerned
about the growth of public activity by Fascist elements'.[18]

In late March, at its annual meeting, the National Council for Civil
Liberties, an organization in which Communists played a very active
role, also called for legislation which would make the dissemination
of anti-Semitic or Fascist propaganda a criminal offence. D.N. Pritt
described existing legislation as 'extremely obscure and insufficient
to deal with the evil as it exists at present'.[19] A few weeks later
the NCCL convened a London conference, attended by 450 delegates
and representing 273 organizations, to plan a nationwide campaign
against anti-Semitism.[20] It was a disturbing fact, said the NCCL, that
anti-Semitism should be on the increase in Britain 'at the very time when
we are fighting for our national existence against Fascism, which makes
the persecution of the Jews a cardinal point of its doctrines'. Julie Jacobs
of the London Trades Council warned that 'anti-Semitism is a knife at
the throat of Jew and non-Jew alike'.[21]

The Board of Deputies was not so eager for legislation against anti-Semitic propaganda. On 24 June 1943, representatives of the Board met with Jewish Members of Parliament to discuss the idea. It was decided that such legislation would be ineffective at best; at worst, it might result in court cases which would create bad publicity for the Jewish community.[22] In December, the Board's Committee on Community Libel argued that it would be difficult to secure passage through Parliament 'of so radical an alternation of the law as would enable civil proceedings to be brought for defamation of the Jews as a community'.[23] Even so moderate a periodical as the *Jewish Chronicle* was disgusted with the Board's reasoning.[24]

Even prior to the release of Mosley and other prominent Fascists in 1943–44, the CP was making political capital out of the resurgence of right-wing activity centred around W.H.S. Russell, the 12th Duke of Bedford, and his British National Party (successor to the pre-war British People's Party). Walter Holmes launched an attack in his *Daily Worker* column of 29 October 1942, noting that 'action against anti-Semitic propaganda ought to be taken here as it is under the law of the Soviet Union'.[25] The CPGB's general secretary, Harry Pollitt, vowed that the party would fight against 'every manifestation of race-hatred and Jew-baiting': he called on the Government to 'put under lock and key immediately' all purveyors of anti-Semitism.[26] Douglas Hyde, the *Daily Worker's* specialist on Fascist movements, kept the Soviet Embassy well-informed about the BNP's activities.[27]

On 23 February 1943, the CP called a meeting at Lincoln's Inn Fields. Among those scheduled to speak were the mayors of Stepney and Shoreditch; LCC councillor Maurice Orbach (a member of the Board of Deputies Trades Advisory Council) and Stepney councillor Piratin. 'To allow Fascism again to raise its head in Britain after we had thought it was suppressed, would be to run a grave danger', Piratin warned the crowd. The BNP's officials, he concluded, ought to be arrested. By 25 February the well-oiled Communist campaign had resulted in more than 300 organizations calling on Home Secretary Herbert Morrison to ban the party.[28] A few days later, the party's Political Bureau released a statement on anti-Semitism. Its proponents, it stated, were traitors 'doing Hitler's Fifth Column work'.[29]

The concern expressed by the Communists proved justified a few months later, when Morrison decided to release the Fascist leader, Sir Oswald Mosley, from the preventative detention in which he had been held since May 1940. The Communists were in a position to take full advantage of the political storm that erupted.

The National Council for Civil Liberties criticized the Government's decision in an emergency meeting held on 19 November.[30] Hundreds of telegrams and petitions poured into the Home Office[31] and mass protests were held. The CP's propaganda machine worked, 'all out'. In the *Daily Worker* of 19 November, Douglas Hyde published a profile of 'The British Hitler';[32] Walter Holmes remarked sarcastically that while the Russians were fighting the real Hitler inch by inch, the British people were given not a second front in Europe but Oswald Mosley.[33] In the next day's issue of the Communist paper, Harry Pollitt reminded readers that Mosley had participated in the 'Battle of Cable Street' in 1936; his release, according to Pollitt, was 'a betrayal of the anti-Fascist war'.[34] The CP also rushed into print an eight-page pamphlet, *Keep Mosley in Prison*, which described some of the protest meetings which had already taken place; these, it stated, were proof of the 'white-hot angry hatred of fascism' felt by the working class.[35]

Morrison assured the House of Commons on 23 November that, although the Government would continue to oppose the 'evil cancer' of Fascism, Mosley the man no longer posed 'any undue risk to national security'. His remarks did nothing to mollify Willie Gallacher, who demanded to know why, if Mosley was set free as a result of medical problems, the Indian leader Mahatma Gandhi remained in prison despite frail health.[36] Outside the House, 2,000 demonstrators from 300 war factories staged a protest, shouting 'Mosley in, Morrison out'.[37] A few days later the *Jewish Chronicle* asserted, in a leader entitled 'Morrison's Folly', that Mosley's release raised some doubt as to whether government leaders were 'really heart and soul in the war against the monstrosity Fascism'; the *Chronicle* dismissed the medical reasons given for the decision as 'preposterous'.[38] The *Daily Worker* wrote that the government had done more to harm national unity 'than Goebbels could ever have hoped to achieve'.[39] The CP put out an update of its earlier pamphlet, now retitled *Put Mosley Back in Prison*, which noted that William 'Lord Haw Haw' Joyce had broadcast his congratulations from Berlin upon hearing the news.[40]

The Communists linked the Mosley release to lagging anti-Fascist fervour on the part of Britain's rulers. R. Palme Dutt and Willie Gallacher saw in it a manifestation of pre-war Munichite tendencies; they both also reminded readers of Mosley's contacts in the 1930s with the Axis dictators, at the same time calling attention to Hitler's genocidal crimes in occupied Europe, some of which were already being discovered by advancing Soviet troops.[41]

In the working class neighbourhoods of Stepney, Mosley's release triggered widespread disapproval. On 24 November the borough council became the first municipal body in Great Britain to pass a resolution protesting the Government's action; the resolution, which was moved by M.H. Davis, the leader of the council, and seconded by W.J. Edwards, the MP for Whitechapel, pointed out that Stepney had suffered more from the activities of the BUF than had any other part of London.[42] At the urging of Phil Piratin and J.L. Fine, a Labour councillor and the secretary of the Mantle and Costume branch (largely Jewish in membership) of the National Union of Tailors and Garment Workers, a town meeting was called to demand that Oswald and Diana Mosley be re-interned and that Morrison be required to resign. Piratin, to the accompaniment of loud cheers, commended Dan Frankel and Edwards, two of Stepney's MPs, for speaking out against Mosley's release; Davis expressed shock that Clement Atlee, the member for Limehouse, who served also as deputy Prime Minister in Churchill's government, had refused to receive a deputation concerning the matter. Stepney Mayor Edward O'Brien criticized Morrison, while Fine promised that 'the protest is only just beginning'.[43] Thus the Stepney Labour Party, normally controlled by Irish members who were virulently anti-Communist, was pushed into an alliance with the local Communists as a result of the release of Mosley.

At the same time, the recently-formed National Jewish Committee of the CPGB saw in the Mosley imbroglio an opportunity to 'make of the Jewish people an active element of the Democratic life of the country' by encouraging them to participate in 'democratic and progressive action such as the demand for the re-internment of Mosley'.[44] One of the members of the Committee, Chimen Abramsky, castigated the Board of Deputies, in a letter to the *Jewish Chronicle*, for failing to protest against Mosley's release:

> This cowardice shames all Jews fighting heroically against Fascism.
> This backwardness, this lagging behind the democratic forces is a blot on our name. Let us Jews line ourselves up with all those who fight for real democracy.[45]

As if on cue, branches 3 and 9 of the Workers' Circle, a largely immigrant fraternal organization, took up Abramsky's challenge: when the circle met for its eleventh convention on 25–26 December, they introduced resolutions opposing the release of 'this Fascist and Anti-Semite'.[46]

But the release of Fascists — and the attendant protests — continued. Arnold Leese, a rabid anti-Semite, was freed in January 1944 for 'medical reasons'.[47] One of the last to emerge from prison, later in the same year, was Tory MP Archibald Ramsay, who in some ways personified the ties which prior to the war had linked some right-wing Tories with Fascism. In the House of Commons Willie Gallacher asked Morrison whether the mothers of Britain, whose sons were at war, were to be informed 'that their sacrifice has enabled him to release this unspeakable blackguard'. He added that 'anti-semitism is an incitement to murder'. Gallacher's speech received favourable comments from various Jewish quarters.[48]

The *Daily Worker* compared Ramsay's doctrines to 'those which terminated in the massacre [at the Maidanek concentration camp, Lublin] of more than 1,500,000 people';[49] the Communist paper spoke also of the 'Streicher-like obsession' of this, 'Britain's No.1 Jew baiter'.[50] The 'Daily Worker Defence League' issued an attack in the form of a pamphlet, *The Case of Captain Ramsay*.[51] The Central Committee of the Workers' Circle dispatched to Churchill a strongly worded resolution which deplored the release of this 'self-confessed anti-semite': 'We remind the people of Britain that Captain Ramsay has been described by a High Court Judge as a man whom Hitler could call friend.'[52] The Board of Deputies, however, once again remained silent, prompting Lazar Zaidman of the NJC to criticize its overall political strategy, including its negative attitude towards legislation that would make anti-Semitism a crime.[53]

Soon many of the newly released Fascists formed a group, the League of ex-Service Men and Women, which held its first meeting in Hyde Park on 5 November 1944; despite Home Secretary Morrison's stipulation that they refrain from political activity, they passed the day with anti-Semitic tirades.[54]

'The threatened renewal of large-scale activity by these reactionary elements is a reminder that we have a tough job ahead', warned the National Jewish Committee of the CP in February 1945.[55] 'Staggering as it may seem', wrote Douglas Hyde on the eve of victory in Europe, 'former Fascists are more active in Britain today than they have been for the last five years. They play an active part in newly created organisations and in old ones that are being resurrected'.[56]

The Jews of east London expressed their support for views such as these in a variety of ways. In May 1943, for example, when the east London sub-district of the CP was soliciting contributions for a campaign to ban all Fascist groups and to urge the invasion of western Europe, 37 out of 50 people in one Stepney factory promptly subscribed 17s. each; other workers throughout the borough and in neighbouring Hackney responded with similar generosity.[57]

Jews also made their position clear by flocking to rallies and meetings called by the east London branches of the CP. On 1 December 1943, for example, 1,300 people crowded into east London's largest theatre, the Hackney Empire, to attend a Communist rally. One month later, this attendance record was surpassed when 2,200 people were packed into the same hall for a New Year's Day Rally; 153 people signed up on the spot to become party members. The east London sub-district of the CP attributed these successes partly to good organization, partly to 'the political situation.'[58]

The National Jewish Committee and the Communist Approach to Anti-Semitism

Historically, the Communist Party had developed a rather mechanistic and reductionist analysis of anti-Semitism and Fascism; this was especially the case during the sectarian period of 1928–1935. A product of capitalist class conflict, argued the party, anti-Semitism served to divert workers, and movements such as the BUF were simply the tools of reactionary elements in the ruling class. Typical of this position was a Young Communist League pamphlet published during this period:

> Hitler grinds the working-class Jew together with the working-class Aryan, not because of nationality, race or religion, *but because*

of class. . . . On the other hand, Hitler, the leader of finance capitalism, allies himself with rich Jews. Why? Because their interests are the same.[59]

After 1935, the CP's popular front politics dictated a change in its strategy, even if that meant watering down the emphasis on the class nature of Fascism. Communists now sought support from Jews as an ethnic group, and not simply as members of the working class, and they helped organize groups such as the Jewish People's Council. The return to political isolationism in the 1939–1941 period put an end to such activities; the JPC, for instance, was disbanded in early 1940,[60] while the STDL was reduced to a Communist rump.[61] Randall Swingler, writing in the *Daily Worker* in 1940, could only react to a perceived increase in anti-Jewish incidents in London Underground stations by referring to anti-Semitism as a 'plague' spread by the ruling class to divide the British population.[62] The well-known biologist and Communist sympathizer, J. B. S. Haldane, even recommended that, in order to lessen attacks on themselves, Jews abandoned some of their 'racial distinctiveness'.[63]

Lukewarm sentiments such as these were less likely to surface after the German invasion of the Soviet Union, though some of the earlier attitudes about anti-Semitism persisted for a time. Willie Gallacher, in *Anti-Semitism: What it Means to You*, described anti-Semitism as 'a trick by which people are persuaded to tie the rope around their own neck . . . the trap whereby people voluntarily surrender themselves into slavery'.[64] John Gollan, then secretary of the party's Scottish Committee, discussed anti-Semitism, in an article in the *Labour Monthly*, in the context of a Fascist conspiracy which attacked an 'imaginary enemy' in order to distract the people from its real aim, the destruction of socialism.[65] And William Rust, editor of the *Daily Worker*, in the foreword to *13 Years of Anti-Fascist Struggle*, termed anti-Semitism 'a method of covering up foul and reactionary policies and setting the people against themselves'.[66]

As the war progressed, however, the CPGB's ideological response to anti-Semitism became more and more the domain of the Jewish Communists, after spring 1943 grouped around the National Jewish Committee. Admittedly, some of their early analyses were of a piece with that of non-Jewish Communists writing at the same time. In April 1942, Issie Panner, writing under the pseudonym 'I. Rennap', outlined the position of the party at that time in *Anti-Semitism and the Jewish Question*, which commenced with a short but comprehensive survey of Jewish history from antiquity to modern times. As a Communist, Panner stressed the 'universalistic' significance of what he described in one chapter heading as 'The Jewish Contribution to Human Progress'. Zionism was pronounced to be at odds with the 'rich, revolutionary tradition' of Jewish history admired by Marx and Lenin. In his analysis of anti-Semitism, Panner was particularly concerned to absolve workers of any responsibility for this 'diversionist weapon against the progressive forces in their struggle for a better and higher order of things'.[67] Anti-Semitism was explained, not as a deep-rooted conflict between cultures or religions, but as a deliberate tactic of Fascist politics. It followed that anti-Semitism was to be combatted by appealing to the pragmatic self-interest of the workers. 'To blame the Jews for the evils and discomforts created by war conditions and to accuse them of exploiting for profit the issues that are sore problems with the people', reasoned Panner, 'is to play Hitler's game here'. It was to be understood that 'the reactionaries in this country' who sought to exploit racial or religious prejudice were 'working against the interests of the British people and of democracy and freedom everywhere'.[68]

The CPGB none the less came to encourage a more explicitly Jewish campaign in the East End and other areas of Jewish population; one-time Stepney CP secretary Morry Lebow has recalled that this strategy was referred to as 'Jewish work'.[69] Perhaps the motives were not entirely the result of an ideological *volte-face*.

A letter from a Manchester Jew to Professor Selig Brodetsky, president of the Board of Deputies, dated 27 March 1942, described a meeting, closed to the press, between Harry Pollitt; Pat Devine, the CP District Secretary for Lancashire and Cheshire; and what the writer called a group of about 75 wealthy Jews. Pollitt recommended that Jews join the party in order to fight the growth of anti-Semitism in the country. It was Devine's speech which, according to the writer, 'revealed the true nature of the meeting — cash'. Devine announced that the CPGB was

> the only party solely connected with the fight against anti-Semitism. He inveigled the audience into believing that this was so and here is the result. The sum of no less than £1,059 was subscribed in hard cash. . . . Here were no heartbreaks in securing money — no covenants nor all the difficulties which are usually associated with efforts to persuade Jews to give money to worthy Jewish causes.

The writer informed Brodestky that the success of the gathering would no doubt result in further work by the CP among Jews.[70] The National Jewish Committee, a sub-committee of R. Palme Dutt's International Affairs Committee, was in fact established in April 1943 to study problems specific to the Jewish community; its members included Lazar Zaidman, Chimen Abramsky, Issie Pushkin, Alec Waterman, Alf Holland, Professor Hyman Levy, Mick Mindel, Alf Silverman, Peter Valentine and Harry Lubbock.[71] In 1944, Marx House published, as Leaflet No.8 in its 'Educational Commentary' series of 'Study and Discussion Notes', *Anti-Semitism — a Nazi Weapon*. The Board of Deputies and the CP made some gingerly attempts to co-operate with each other in the dissemination of pro-Jewish and anti-Fascist material, even though Sidney Salomon, secretary of the Board's defence committee, thought it might be going a little too far to employ speakers from Marx House, 'an organisation which is so notoriously Communist'.[72]

A weekend school for Jewish party members was held at Marx House on 22–23 April 1944; among the tutors were Maurice Essex and Hyman Levy.[73] The Jewish Communists went public with their programme at a conference of 450 people held on 9 May at Beaver Hall. The theme of the conference, which was organized by the east London district of the CP, was 'The Jewish Problem and the Role of the Communist Party'. In the opening address, Hyman Levy called for a Jewish Charter of Freedom in the spirit of the Atlantic Charter and the December 1943 Teheran agreements. Under such a charter, Jews could achieve equality of citizenship in every sphere of social and economic life; anti-Semitism would become a crime; and the Allied governments would take steps against racial discrimination in every country. 'Jewish progressives must serve their people', added Levy, by helping them to unite with the progressive forces everywhere. Bertha Sokoloff, who was to become branch secretary of the Stepney CP in the autumn of 1944, explained how 'politically proud' she was to be a Jew; another speaker, Alf Holland, urged Jewish Communists to study Jewish history, especially the role played by liberating heroes such as Bar Kochba. Asher Frucht of the Jewish Cultural Club and Alec Waterman both spoke of the need to persuade more Jews to become Communists; already, said Waterman, 'some of the best elements of Jewry have joined the CP'. The conference was concluded by a non-Jew, Willie Gallacher, who spoke on one of his favourite topics, the need for Jewish Communists to remain active in Jewish life. It was not enough, according to Gallacher, that they take part in trade union and working-class activities; they must also work as Jews so that all Jews, led by their Communist brothers, would support the working-class movement, which in turn would support freedom for the Jewish people.[74]

The party line was also made explicit in a 19 page pamphlet, *The Jewish Question: Statement by the National Jewish Committee of the Communist Party*, which appeared late in 1944. After pointing out that 'support for progressive Parties' was widespread among the Jewish people and asserting that the CP was 'in full sympathy with the Jewish people and their desire to be free from the scourge of anti-Semitism', this *Statement* reiterated Levy's demand for a 'Declaration of Jewish Freedom' which would be part of the worldwide post-war settlement and which would legally guarantee equality of civil rights for all Jews.[75]

After being approved by the executive committee of the CPGB, the *Statement* was presented at the NJC's third annual conference of Jewish Communists, on 13–14 January 1945. R. Palme Dutt, vice-chairman of the CP and head of the International Affairs Committee, opened the conference by noting that 'there has been a marked advance and development in the past year as a result of the work of the NJC and the Jewish comrades generally'. Dutt went so far as to regret that some Communists who were Jewish preferred to do general Party and trade union work, to the neglect of work in Jewish organizations. The NJC, according to Dutt, had been formed to combat this tendency without becoming too particularistic. During the discussion of 'The Jewish Question' which followed, various participants expressed the movement's intent 'to win all the most progressive, intelligent, and most active Jews to its ranks'.[76]

The 1945 General Election

One result of the conference was the drafting of yet another statement by the NJC, 'The Election Campaign & the Jewish People', which asserted that 'only a Labour and Progressive Government' would eliminate the underlying economic conditions which enabled anti-Semitism to flourish. The statement urged campaign workers to promise that 'care and attention' would be paid 'to the special cultural and communal needs of Jews in largely Jewish areas; it called for a 'fight to rally the Jewish people!'[77] Another position paper on 'Jews and the General Election' explained that, whereas the Tories had co-existed with Mosley and with Nazism in Europe, a Labour and progressive government would implement the February 1945 Yalta agreements and co-operate with Russia. 'If this is good for the people of Britain, as a whole, it is doubly good for the Jews of Britain. In such a situation Fascism and Anti-Semitism will be throttled.'[78]

As the election drew near, the Jewish Communists insisted all the more urgently that 'only a Labour and Progressive Government will enable us to wipe out the spreaders of race hatred, the enemies of the people'.[79] Lazar Zaidman wrote to a friend that the Jews, who held 'a key position in certain constituencies', would realize that it was in their own best interest to vote for the left in order to eliminate the social causes of anti-Semitism.[80] At the same time, the CP did its best to discredit the Tories. At the October 1944 CPGB national congress, Pollitt had indicated that Communist propaganda in the coming election would concentrate on linking Fascism and anti-Semitism to right-wing Toryism; this theme became a staple of CP literature.[81]

One pamphlet, entitled *Fascist Murderers: Pictures of the Concentration Camps You Must Never Forget*, interspersed gruesome stories and photographs of newly liberated camps such as Buchenwald with quotes from the Tory officials who had failed to take a strong stand against Hitler: 'When the General Election comes we must be sure that not one of these Tories who praised or appeased the fascists before the war, and so bear a responsibility for these crimes, will get back into Parliament.'[82] Another pamphlet, by R. Palme Dutt, linked the Tories with pro-German organizations such as the Anglo–German Fellowship; by means of extensive pre-war quotations, he demonstrated to his own satisfaction 'how Tories backed Hitler, Mussolini and Japan': 'every elector must feel a sacred duty to drive these Tory friends of Fascism from public life.'[83]

The *News Chronicle* noted that the election manifesto of the CP was very like that of Labour, although the Communists added two further proposals: that the voting age be lowered to 18 and that anti-Semitism be made a criminal offence.[84] In Stepney, the local CP also emphasized 'Jewish–Gentile unity' in the fight against anti-Semitism. Tom Rampling, who later became a borough councillor, wrote that 'every anti-Semite is a friend of the fascists; either as a fool or a knave he is keeping the people divided, so helping the Hitlerites and endangering the freedom of ordinary folk everywhere.'[85]

In May 1945, the *Jewish Forum* ran a feature on the resurgence of Fascist movements, which were said to be 'as active to-day as ever they were before'. 'Behind these little men are the Big Shots, the representatives of Big Business and Monopoly who backed Mosley and put Hitler into power. They are the men who determine Tory policy.' Jews had 'a fearful responsibility' to vote out the Tories: by doing so they would help to ensure that no one would 'revive the horrors of Belsen and Buchenwald'; but if they failed, it would be no more than a few months before Mosley and his thugs were 'terror-parading the streets again with anti-Jewish banners'.[86] Opinions such as these were not limited to the Communist press. In June 1945, *Di Tsayt,* the Yiddish daily, described the Tories as 'the traditional anti-alien party':

> In its ranks were to be found virulent anti-Semites. Many of its mem-bers, before the war, gave support to Hitler and Mussolini. They went to the Nazi rallies at Nuremberg, and were on intimate terms with Ribbentrop when he was the German ambassador here.[87]

Candidate Piratin made skillful use of such themes and sentiments. In his 'Appeal to the Jewish Electors', Piratin referred to himself as 'a good son of the Jewish people'; he termed the CP 'the champion of the freedom of the Jewish people'. From the ranks of the Tories, he asserted, had come the Captain Ramsays, the Anglo–German Fellowship and the 'Link'.[88] Piratin noted elsewhere that the Tories had never repudiated Ramsay; indeed, upon his release from prison and return to Parliament, Ramsay had been allowed to make a mockery of the democratic system by introducing a motion which would have revived a thirteenth century law requiring Jews to wear yellow badges.[89] One of Piratin's hand-outs featured the eye-catching announcement, 'British Fascists stage a return'; Piratin pledged as one of his 'immediate demands for Jewry' a law 'making anti-semitism and racial incitement illegal, as it is in Soviet Russia'.[90] His campaign literature linked the CP's opposition to Mosley and Ramsay with a long tradition of Communist agitation on behalf of 'full and equal rights for Jews'; in 1936, for example, at the 'Battle of Cable Street', while Labour and the Board of Deputies counselled passivity, the CP had 'made a stirring call to resist'.[91] Communist activists stressed that the Stepney party had 'led the agitation, led the propaganda, led the campaigning' against Fascist incursions such as those of Mosley's BUF.[92] In 1945, the reminder seemed a timely one to the Jews of east London.

HENRY SREBRNIK
Gettysburg College, Pennsylvania, USA

NOTES

1. The definitive treatment of this subject is Tony Kushner, *The Persistence of Prejudice: Antisemitism in Britain During the Second World War* (Manchester, 1989). For a brief overview, see Aaron Goldman, 'The Resurgence of Antisemitism in Britain during World War II, *Jewish Social Studies* 46 (Winter 1984) pp.37–50.
2. Stuart A. Cohen, 'Anglo-Jewish Responses to Antisemitism: Suggestions for a Framework of Analysis', in Jehuda Reinharz (ed.), *Living With Antisemitism: Modern Jewish Responses* (Hanover, N.H., 1987) p.85. It is of course also useful to remember that not every instance of hostility towards Jews is necessarily anti-Semitic. See Colin Holmes, 'Anti-Semitism and the BUF', in Kenneth Lunn and Richard C. Thurlow (eds.), *British Fascism: Essays on the Radical Right in Inter-War Britain* (London, 1980) pp.114–115.
3. See Henry F. Srebrnik, 'The Jewish Communist Movement in Stepney: Ideological Mobilization and Political Victories in an East London Borough, 1935–1945' (unpublished PhD thesis, University of Birmingham, 1984).
4. Andrew Sharf, *The British Press and Jews Under Nazi Rule* (London 1964) pp. 174–175; *Jewish Chronicle*, 28 Feb. 1941, p.19. See also Peter and Leni Gilman, *'Collar the Lot!': How Britain Interned and Expelled its Wartime Refugees* (London, 1980).
5. *The Times*, 16 Aug. 1940, p.2
6. *Jewish Chronicle (JC)*, 26 July 1940, p.10.
7. Michael Sayfert, '"His Majesty's Most Loyal Internees"', in Gerhard Hirschfeld (ed.), *Exile in Great Britain: Refugees from Hitler's Germany* (Leamington Spa, 1984) p.177.
8. *Daily Worker (DW)*, 26 July 1940, p.4
9. *DW*, 30 Nov. 1940, p.4.
10. *DW*, 15 May 1942, p.17.
11. George Orwell, 'War-time Diary, 1940', in Sonia Orwell and Ian Angus (eds.), *The Collected Essays, Journalism and Letters of George Orwell*, vol.2: *My Country Right or Left 1940–1943* (London, 1968; reprint edn, Harmondsworth 1970) p.428; Letter from Sidney Salomon to T.H. Hutchinson, 19 Dec. 1940, file C 15/3/19, Board of Deputies archives, London (BOD); Walter Laqueur, *The Terrible Secret: An Investigation into the Suppression of Information About Hitler's 'Final Solution'* (London, 1980) p.92.
12. Frank R. Lewey, *Cockney Campaign* (London, 1944) p.15.
13. *JC*, 13 Mar. 1942, p.10.
14. Ibid., 13 Mar. 1942, p.17; 17 July 1942, p.8.
15. *East London Advertiser*, 23 Jan. 1943, p.7.
16. William Rust, 'Foreword' to *13 Years of Anti-Fascist Struggle* (Manchester, 1943) p.1.
17. William Gallacher, *Anti-Semitism: What it Means to You* (London, April 1943) p.8.
18. Notice from J.E. Arnold James, town clerk, for an 'Extraordinary Meeting, Metropolitan Borough of Stepney', 23 Feb. 1943, file C 15/3/19, BOD; *Daily Worker*, 26 Feb. 1943, p.4.
19. *DW*, 29 Mar. 1943, p.3.
20. Elizabeth A. Allen, *It Shall Not Happen Here: Anti-Semitism, Fascists and Civil Liberty* (London, 1943) p.31.
21. *DW*, 19 Apr. 1943, pp.1, 4.
22. Transcript of the meeting, file C 10/2/8, BOD
23. 'Committee on Community Libel — 6 Dec. 1943', file C 4/1, BOD
24. *JC*, 31 Dec. 1943, p.8.
25. *DW*, 29 Oct. 1942, p.2.
26. Ibid., 12 Dec. 1942, p.2.
27. Douglas Hyde, *I Believed: The Autobiography of a Former British Communist* (London, 1952) p.168.
28. *DW*, 17 Feb. 1943, p.3; 19 Feb. 1943, p.3; 22 Feb. 1943, p.4; 25 Feb. 1943, p.3.

29. *Communist Policy: A Collection of the Principal Political Statements Issued by the Communist Party of Great Britain between June 1942 and April 1943* (London, 1943) pp.36–37.
30. 'The Release of Sir Oswald and Lady Mosley', *Civil Liberty* 4 (Dec. 1943) pp.1–2.
31. *DW*, 20 Nov. 1943, p.4.
32. Ibid., 19 Nov. 1943, p.2.
33. Ibid., 19 Nov. 1943, p.2.
34. Ibid., 20 Nov. 1943, p.4.
35. *Keep Mosley in Prison* (London, 1943) p.2.
36. *JC*, 26 Nov. 1943. p.6.
37. Ibid., 26 Nov. 1943, p.1.
38. Ibid., 26 Nov. 1943, p.10.
39. *DW*, 27 Nov. 1943, p.1.
40. *Put Mosley Back in Prison* (London, 1943) pp.3–4.
41. R. P. D[utt], 'Notes of the Month', *Labour Monthly* 25 (Dec. 1943) p.359; William Gallacher, 'Mosley and Morrison', *Labour Monthly* 26 (Jan. 1944) p.14.
42. *East London Advertiser*, 26 Nov. 1943, p.1.
43. *DW*, 7 Dec. 1943, p.4; *East London Advertiser*, 10 Dec 1943, p.4.
44. 'Party Work Amongst the Jews in Britain', typescript, National Jewish Committee, Communist Party, 8 Dec. 1943; the Lazar Zaidman collection (University of Sheffield) (ZC).
45. Letter to the editor from C[himen] Abramsky, *JC*, 24 Dec. 1943, p.15.
46. 'The Eleventh Convention', the *Circle* 11 (Apr. 1945) p.4.
47. *JC*, 21 Jan. 1944, p.5.
48. *DW*, 27 Sept. 1944, pp.1, 4; 29 Sept. 1944, p.1; 2 Oct. 1944, p.2; *JC*, 29 Sept. 1944, p.5.
49. *DW*, 27 Sept. 1944, p.1.
50. Ibid., 27 Sept. 1944, p.4, and 28 Sept. 1944, p.2.
51. *The Case of Captain Ramsay* (London, 1944).
52. Central committee minutes, Workers' Circle, 1 Oct. 1944, ZC.
53. L[azar] Zeidman [sic], 'Jewish Board of Deputies in London Discusses Post-War Policy', *The Review: A Jewish Monthly* (February 1945), p.12.
54. *DW*, 6 Nov. 1944, p.1; *JC*, 10 Nov. 1944, p.16.
55. 'Commentary', *Jewish Opinion* (Feb. 1945), p.9.
56. *DW*, 5 May 1945, p.2.
57. 'Finance as a Weapon', *Organising for Victory in 1943* (London, May 1943) pp.18–19.
58. L. Gollhard, 'How East London Organised a Record Rally', *Tune Up Our Organisation* (London, Jan. 1944) p.3.
59. *10 Points Against Fascism* (London, c. 1934) p.11. Emphasis in original.
60. *JC*, 12 Jan. 1940 p.21.
61. K. Brill 'The World His Parish', in Kenneth Brill (ed.), *John Groser, East London Priest* (London, 1971) pp.103–104; St. John B. Groser *Politics and Persons* (London, 1949) p.71. Father Groser, then vicar of Christ Church, Stepney, was president of the STDL until his resignation in February 1940.
62. *DW*, 14 Oct. 1940, p.5.
63. *JC*, 7 Nov., 1941, p.1.
64. William Gallacher, *Anti-Semitism: What it Means to You*, p.17.
65. John Gollan, 'Anti-Semitism', *Labour Monthly* 25 (June 1943) p.179.
66. *13 Years of Anti-Fascist Struggle*, p.1.
67. Issie Panner ['I. Rennap'] *Anti-Semitism and the Jewish Question* (London, 1942) p.114.
68. Ibid, p.116.
69. Interview, Morry Lebow, London, 21 Nov. 1978.
70. L. Harris to Selig Brodetsky, 27 Mar. 1942, file B 4/RV12, BOD. Devine had been an anti-Fascist organiser in east London in the 1930s. Both his widow and cousin called him a 'brilliant fund raiser' who was 'very good at getting money from Jewish businessmen'. Interviews, Gloria Devine Findlay and Charles Findlay, London, 15 Sept. 1987.

71. For the founding of the National Jewish Committee, see the 'Report of National Jewish Committee to International Affairs Committee'; TS in ZC.

72. Sidney Salomon to Frank Renton, 28 July 1944; file C 15/3/9, BOD. See also, in the same file, the exchange of letters between Salomon and J.W. Morgan, librarian of Marx House; and between Salomon and Jack Knife, secretary of Marx House.

73. 'Details of the Week-End School for Jewish Party Members To Be Held at Marx House, 1 Doughty St., W.C. 1 on 22nd. & 23rd. April 1944'; TS in ZC.

74. The transcript of this meeting, in TS, is in ZC; see also the summary in the *DW*, 12 May 1944, p.2.

75. *The Jewish Question: Statement by the National Jewish Committee of the Communist Party* (London, 1944) pp.6, 13, 17–18.

76. 'The Communist Party. National Jewish Committee. Third Annual Enlarged Meeting. 13, 14 Jan. 1945'; TS, pp.1, 4, ZC.

77. 'The Election Campaign & the Jewish People. Statement by the National Jewish Committee'; TS, pp.1, 3–4 ZC.

78. 'Jews and the General Election'; draft TS [1945], ZC.

79. 'Commentary', *Jewish Forum* (May–June 1945) p.12.

80. 'Letter from Lazar Zaidman to Isaac Gust', London, 31 May, 1945, ZC.

81. *Victory. Peace. Security. Report of the 17th National Congress of the Communist Party Shoreditch Town Hall London E.C.1. October 28–30 1944* (London, 1944) p.24.

82. *Fascist Murderers: Pictures of the Concentration Camps You Must Never Forget* (London, April 1945) p.8.

83. R. Palme Dutt, *Truth About the Tories* (London, June 1945) pp.11–14.

84. *News Chronicle*, 9 June 1945, p.4.

85. *A Stepney to Be Proud of: Plan and Proposals*, (London, [winter 1944–1945]), p.5.

86. 'Commentary', *Jewish Forum* (May–June 1945) pp.11–12.

87. 'Yidn Un Di Vahlen' ['Jews and the Elections'], *Di Tsayt*, 29 June 1945, p.2.

88. Phil Piratin, 'Appeal to the Jewish Electors'; TS ZC.

89. Phil Piratin, 'The Communist Party and the Jewish People. Every Jew Must Vote Progressive!', *Jewish Forum* (May-June 1945) p.1; Ramsay's motion got no seconder. See also the flyer, *Mile End Election Special! Vote Piratin*, p.2. The *Daily Worker* claimed that 'Captain Ramsay has never been repudiated by the Conservative Central Office'. *Daily Worker*, 1 June 1945, p.4.

90. *Vote for Piratin. A Fighter Against Fascism*; ZC.

91. 'Notes for Canvassers and Speakers: The Communist Party and the Jewish People': undated mimeo, ZC.

92. Interview, Solly Kaye, London, 31 Oct. 1978. An east London Communist Party official, Kaye served as a CP borough councillor in Stepney (later Tower Hamlets) from 1956 to 1971.

The Impact of Hostility on Germans in Britain, 1914–1918

How Germans in Britain became a public scapegoat has been discussed in studies of the social and political history of the First World War, but the effect on the Germans themselves and how they reacted is rarely examined. This essay attempts to redress the balance by looking at the question principally from the point of view of Germans who lived through the experience.

I

The First World War was a period when xenophobia against an 'alien' people was given every opportunity to flourish. Almost every section of society and institution sympathised with anti-German sentiments, if not condoning their violent manifestations. Pre-war xenophobia, primarily directed against Russian Jews, appears to have widened its scope to include Germans for the duration of the war.

The main focus of this essay is on the Germans themselves and demonstrates that they were not simply the helpless victims of government restrictions and public hostility, but were able to organise themselves, sometimes with the assistance of their few British sympathisers, to provide financial and moral support for those particularly badly affected.

According to the 1911 census, there were 58,326 Germans in Britain, as well as another 6,500 who had become naturalised British citizens. Germans formed the second largest group of foreign residents after Russians. Germans had come to Britain for a number of reasons, including its more liberal political climate and to take advantage of economic opportunities. They mostly settled in large towns — over 50 per cent in London — and worked in a narrow range of urban trades and services. Finance and commerce occupied a significant minority. Substantial numbers worked as waiters, hairdressers, butchers, bakers, tailors and domestic servants.[1]

Numerous organisations catered to their needs, including philanthropic institutions, churches, a hospital and social and cultural organisations. Many were founded and supported by a wealthy élite. At the other end of the scale were working men's clubs, often associated with socialist politics.[2] Germans did not form a homogeneous community, but were divided by social and political differences, as well as by religion. The majority were Protestant, but there were some Catholics and a sizeable proportion of Jews.

Compared with other immigrant groups, there was a lack of major religious, racial or cultural barriers between German residents and the British population. There was a high rate of intermarriage between the two groups. The influx of Russian Jews, who were also much more concentrated in one geographical area of London, probably diverted attention away from German immigrants. The almost total lack of interest shown by the Royal Commission on Alien Immigration in 1903 seems to indicate that they were not thought of at that time as part of the 'alien problem'.[3]

In the years leading to the outbreak of war, it appears that increasing hostility to Germany and its ambitions started to cause some resentment against Germans in Britain, particularly against their economic influence. Suspicions grew, encouraged by the popular press, that people of German origin were working against Britain, as spies disguised as waiters or barbers or, as the *National Review* suggested, manipulators of the press and financial affairs.[4]

On the outbreak of war, resentment against German immigrants and their influence rapidly turned to open hostility. Propaganda, both official and unofficial, played a large part as it helped transform the war into a struggle between good and evil.[5] Not only the German government and military authorities but the entire German people were held responsible for methods of warfare regarded as barbaric. From there it was a short step to transferring the blame to Germans living in Britain.

Much of the agitation against Germans was based on the claim that they posed a threat to national security. However, this often cloaked resentment of their economic influence. The war appeared an opportunity to rid the country of not only economic interests controlled from Germany itself, but those of German residents in Britain. The Anti-German League, founded in September 1915, combined protectionism with agitation to amend immigration and naturalisation laws and stirring up hatred. It was superseded by the British Empire Union, which promoted a similar programme.[6]

The wealthier nationalised Germans, who were not interned and were allowed to carry on their businesses, were a particular target. It was alleged that they had a secret influence controlling events — the 'Hidden Hand'. This theme echoed traditional anti-Semitic stereotypes and many of their targets were Jewish.[7] There was also agitation for the sacking of German workers, for example, in hotels and restaurants where their influence was particularly visible.[8]

Public vigilance, encouraged by the Northcliffe press, ensured that the enemy aliens question was a significant issue for successive wartime administrations. Within a few days of the outbreak of war, the Home Secretary, McKenna, introduced the Aliens Restrictions Act (ARA). It gave the Home Secretary powers to exclude or deport aliens without appeal; to prevent their landing in the country; to require them to register with the police; to prohibit their residence in certain areas; and to prohibit travel beyond a five mile radius without a permit.[9]

The ARA was based on the recommendations of a sub-committee of the Committee of Imperial Defence, asked by the Cabinet in 1909 to investigate the question of aliens in wartime. Concern was prompted by fears, which the War Office believed realistic, of collusion in an invasion by German spies. The war provided an opportunity to put contentious measures, like registration, into effect, for which the Government felt there would not be public support in peacetime. The ARA was passed almost without protest from Liberal MPs.[10]

The enemy alien question continued to be a major political issue over the next nine months. Government policy on internment appeared confused, as orders to start and stop arrests and make releases were made and countermanded due to the different approaches of the Home Office and the War Office. A section of Unionist MPs and the right-wing press used demands for a firmer policy to attack the Government without appearing unpatriotic.[11]

Asquith avoided acceding to hard-liners' demands for general internment fearing — perhaps mistakenly — opposition within his party, until finally forced to take action by anti-German riots and demonstrations following the sinking of the *Lusitania* in May 1915. On 13 May he announced that all enemy alien males of military age were to be interned. Men over military age, women and children were to be repatriated, except in special circumstances. An advisory body, judicial in nature, was to be set up to consider exemptions. Again there was almost no opposition from Liberal MPs.[12]

But neither this victory, nor the formation soon afterwards of a coalition government with Unionist participation, satisfied the die-hard Unionist MPs and the Northcliffe press. They pressed the Government to stop all exemptions from internment, repatriation and removal from the prohibited areas. The Lloyd George government formed in December 1916 did not substantially alter policy towards enemy aliens. The campaign to 'intern them all' reached a new height in spring and summer 1918. In July, the Government agreed to some new restrictions on enemy aliens.[13] The Allied breakthrough on the western front towards the end of summer meant the issue lost much of its public significance. But it was by no means dead. Enemy aliens were a major issue of the 1918 election and the focus on post-war reconstruction directed attention to the whole question of aliens in Britain.[14]

II

The Government's measures and public hostility had a dramatic impact on the lives of Germans in England. In addition to the disruption caused by internment and repatriation, other regulations under the ARA, the Defence of the Realm Act (DORA) and other emergency legislation restricted the rights of enemy aliens. Different sections of the German population were affected differently, depending on age, sex and national status. Nationality was to some extent related to class, since only the more prosperous Germans had been able to afford naturalisation papers. Naturalised British subjects and German women who had acquired British citizenship by marriage were exempt from restrictions, although they could be detained without normal legal procedures under 14B of DORA.[15]

The most immediate effects of the War were felt by the poorer Germans. Large numbers of employees were sacked, or lost their jobs when German business houses closed. Waiters and servants were the chief victims, but clerks, governesses, teachers and hairdressers were also affected.[16] Unemployed Germans could not turn at first for help to the Labour Exchanges, which had been instructed on the outbreak of war not to place enemy aliens in employment, although they were later allowed to place them in jobs for which no British workmen could be found.[17]

Also facing immediate destitution were wives who were unable to receive pay from husbands who had returned to Germany.[18] Many Germans were turned out of their lodgings. Many enemy aliens had to leave their homes or livelihoods in the prohibited areas, which included most of the east coast and several large towns.[19] Many came to London, increasing the burden on the philanthropic societies. It was reported that over 500 foreigners besieged the offices of the German Benevolent Society one day soon after the outbreak of war. Hundreds of poor Germans waited outside the United States Embassy, which had charge of the interests of Germans and Austro-Hungarians, in the hope of receiving aid.[20]

The British and German governments both acted to establish a system of relief. The Home Office set up a Destitute Aliens Committee on 20 August and the Treasury made funds available to the Local Government Board to relieve the strain on the Poor Law authorities. From 19 November British-born wives and children of interned aliens received an allowance from the Local Government Board. Funds were provided, via the United States Embassy, for the enemy alien wives of interned or combatant Germans, Austrians or Hungarians and this was soon extended to wives born in neutral and allied countries. However, the allowance paid by the British government — kept much lower than the separation allowance paid to soldiers' wives — was inadequate to pay for more than the bare necessities of food and lodging. The maximum allowance was payable only when the husband had been fully employed when interned, so many did not receive the full amount. Many of the women, it was reported, came from the better class of working people, who were not accustomed to manage with so little.[21]

In any case, many women, such as the wives of men who had been dismissed but not interned, were not eligible for allowances. Although the German government grants were more generous than the British, the German government withdrew them from some families as the war progressed; for example, from families where the husband had applied for naturalisation after the outbreak of war, or where nationality had been lost, or where a son was serving in the British army, even as a conscript.[22]

Men were not eligible for allowances and, if able-bodied, would find it very difficult to get charitable help for themselves. For many the only alternative in the early months of the War was to give themselves up for internment. At first the Home Office saw internment as a remedy to the problem of destitution. The Destitute Aliens Committee envisaged that only the really dangerous enemy aliens would be detained by the military authorities. Other institutions — similar to workhouses, but with a security guard — would accommodate the destitute. Negotiations were begun with charitable bodies to set up such institutions, but were overtaken by the decision to impose mass internment in May 1915.[23]

Germans were also affected by riots and other violent incidents. According to official statements, 257 people were injured in the *Lusitania* riots, 107 of whom were police or special constables, and only one person was seriously injured.[24] However, Sylvia Pankhurst believed that many victims did not report their wounds. The Friends' Emergency Committee for the Relief of Germans, Austrians and Hungarians, which sheltered many during the riots, also thought it saw many tragedies not reported in the press.[25] 1,950 claims to about the value of £195,000 were made for damages to property, payable by local police authorities. Not all of this damage, however, was to German- or Austrian-owned property. *The Times* reported that some aliens were too afraid to give evidence in court.[26] There were many other incidences of threatened or actual violence.[27]

The imposition of mass internment and repatriation resulted in the break-up of family life for thousands. By 22 November 1915, when the compulsory repatriation of men over military age, women and children was virtually complete, about 9,500 people had left the country.[28] Although British-born wives and the mothers of children born in Britain were not normally repatriated, this measure caused great hardship, particularly to those who had lived here for many years and had few remaining links with Germany. In one case, a man poisoned himself and tried to poison his wife and family rather than let them all be repatriated. The number of Germans interned rose to about 26,500 in the same period.[29]

Wives left behind had to cope with practical problems and the strain of separation in the face of social ostracism, unable to turn to neighbours, friends and even family, as British women whose husbands were away in the forces could do. It was reported in April 1916 that there were alarming changes in the mental, psychological and physical condition of the wives of interned aliens, attributed to separation, poverty and isolation.[30]

The situation was made worse because many of the institutions which had provided support or social facilities were forced to close down or restrict their activities. The German Hospital lost much of its usual source of income as a large proportion of Germans in London was dispersed.[31] This must have affected other institutions as well. Some organisations closed voluntarily, such as the German Athenaeum club, which had catered for an exclusive social elite, in October 1914. Other German clubs and restaurants were shut down and their members or patrons interned on security grounds, particularly in the later stages of the War when the Government took new powers. The socialist clubs were particular victims, although in reality least likely to be pro-Kaiser.[32] The German Gymnasium was sold in June 1916.[33]

The German churches were affected by the prevailing hostility and were one of the targets of the Anti-German League. Some people were afraid to remain members of the German church. Services were reduced or the church might shut altogether.[34] The Government took powers to stop the circulation of newspapers in the language of an enemy state in September 1914 and the three main London German language papers all ceased publication.[35] The situation in the provinces was even more isolated than in London, where the German population, helped by a stream of arrivals from the provinces, remained at a level of about 9,000 adults (not including British-born wives). In Liverpool, however, the adult German population was reduced to 174 by July 1916 and in Manchester to 274.[36]

Despite the closure of cultural and social institutions, the German benevolent organisations in London were able to continue their existence, partly as they were useful to the Government, and partly because their wealthy and influential patrons adopted successful tactics to allow them to survive in a hostile environment. The wartime work of these organisations is also evidence that many of the better-off naturalised Germans were willing to identify themselves with their former compatriots sufficiently to continue their involvement with German institutions, despite outside pressures.

The Society of Friends of Foreigners in Distress (SFFD), a German-run organisation, carried out an adroit manoeuvre to avoid being identified as an 'enemy' organisation. It called together all the foreign benevolent societies, including those of allied and neutral countries, to form a Central Council of United Alien Relief Societies (CCUARS). Appeals for funds for the CCUARS were then made in the name of all aliens, regardless of creed, nationality or sex, but in reality the CCUARS was little more than the SFFD under another guise. Each constituent relief organisation dealt with its own nationality, leaving the CCUARS itself to deal with enemy aliens, together with the societies specifically for Germans and Austrians, such as the German Benevolent Society, Sir Ernest Cassel's King Edward VII British German Foundation and the Franz Joseph Institute.[37]

The CCUARS' desire to disassociate itself from any taint of the Hun can be seen in its resolution on the sinking of the *Lusitania*. Expressing its 'abhorrence of the wanton destruction of women and children', it decided to refuse relief to Germans of military age not already known to it and to restrict relief to those known to it only until the Government should intern them.[38]

The Destitute Aliens Committee at the Home Office approved its scheme of working and was represented on the Council. The relationship worked to the benefit of both parties. The CCUARS was able to announce that it worked under the supervision of the Home Office and was 'in constant communication with the police' over doubtful cases.[39] The Destitute Aliens Committee, for its part, believed the foreigners' benevolent societies had sufficient funds to alleviate a considerable burden falling on the local Poor Law authorities and on the State generally and so decided to 'assist, advise and control' agencies that welcomed their interest.[40] The Home Office used the CCUARS as its agent to make arrangements for compulsory repatriation. The CCUARS believed that this enabled it to use its influence with the Home Office to give consideration to special cases of hardship.[41]

In the six and half years of its existence, the CCUARS raised £154,000 — a small sum compared with mainstream war charities. A vast proportion was given by five major donors, all of German origin: Sir Otto Beit, Herman Kleinwort, Sir Ernest Cassel, Sir Edgar Speyer and Baron Bruno von Schröder. Von Schröder alone contributed over £92,000 and donated a home for the children of destitute enemy aliens.[42] There are numerous other examples of naturalised Germans giving donations or other help to poorer Germans and internees. Sir Ernest Schuster, a prominent barrister, gave advice to Germans on legal problems.[43] Prosperous naturalised Germans in Manchester and Bradford organised committees to provide relief for distressed enemy aliens.[44] Dr Karl Markel, who had had an important role in the chemical industry, set up a committee to visit men in the internment camps and provide them with books. The notoriety this brought him shows the risks accompanying such activity.[45]

Baron von Schröder, a Prussian aristocrat and banker, continued as before the War to be the most prominent benefactor of German organisations. But he seems to have decided it wiser to maintain scrupulous impartiality, sending a gift of 9d to both prisoners and guards at internment and prison-of-war camps at Christmas, and a substantial sum to British prisoners in Germany. The committee of the German Hospital, in which he was very influential, followed a similar policy. The committee added extra beds (paid for by von Schröder), and put 50 beds and its convalescent home at the disposal of the War Office. This did not prevent his remaining one of the die-hard anti-Germans' favourite targets, particularly because his son was fighting in the German army. The fact that he quickly obtained naturalisation within the first days of the War seemed to substantiate the view that the rich got special treatment.[46]

Giving money to war charities seems to have been a means for naturalised Germans to demonstrate their loyalty to Britain. Sir Ernest Cassel gave massive donations to non-German charities throughout the War. Another of the CCUARS' patrons, the catering firm owner, Appenrodt, subscribed £3,000 to war charities in the first month of war and promised to donate 25 per cent of his takings for the duration of the War.[47]

Many naturalised Germans seem to have thought at first that keeping a low profile would save them from trouble. The intensified attack on enemy aliens in May 1915, however, led to a number of public declarations of patriotism. Memorials protesting the loyalty of naturalised Germans were sent to the Lord Mayor of London. Deputations visited the Mayors of Nottingham and Bradford, although the Bradford deputation did not want their names known for fear of repercussions for relatives in Germany.[48] A committee of naturalised British subjects of German and Austro–Hungarian birth was formed and quickly organised a patriotic meeting.[49]

Another of these gestures was the so-called 'loyalty letters'. These were public protestations of loyalty to Britain and condemnations of German methods of warfare, sent to *The Times* by both prominent naturalised Germans and scores of more obscure individuals. The idea was not initiated by naturalised Germans but a response to a suggestion by Sir Arthur Pinero. He said that they should do so in their own interest, as silence laid them open to the supposition that they were sitting on the fence.[50]

An undertone of resentment can be detected in some of the letters that doubt should have been cast on the loyalty of naturalised subjects. Sir Felix Semon, former surgeon to Edward VII, who had previously refused to sign a statement condemning Germany in the *Evening News*, agreed with great reluctance to Pinero's suggestion. He had felt silence was his best policy. However, he now felt that this could only be interpreted either as pro-German sentiment or as fear to compromise himself in the eyes of Germany, although he was afraid his decision might affect relations in Germany.[51]

The 'loyalty letters' episode has perhaps tended to give the misleading impression that naturalised Germans wished to sever all links with their former country of origin in their eagerness to prove their patriotism. It was a great risk, particularly for a person of German origin, to show friendship towards German enemy aliens as it would be interpreted by many as disloyalty. However, the involvement of naturalised Germans in charitable activities on behalf of other Germans shows that there were people willing to preserve links with their former compatriots despite the undoubted pressures to minimise contact.[52] Sir Ernest Schuster and Sir Ernest Cassel are both examples of people who signed loyalty letters and also gave significant charitable help to German enemy aliens.

The wealthier naturalised Germans were not the only section of the German population to organise itself in the face of hardship. At the other end of the social and political scale, a kitchen was set up on the outbreak of war at the headquarters of the Amalgamated Union of Hotel, Club and Restaurant Workers, with the help of members from the anarchist and Communist movement, to provide meals for German waiters thrown out of work. The Union also offered advice on how to obtain naturalisation papers. Rudolf Rocker, the German anarcho-syndicalist, set up a communal kitchen in the East End. He and others also set up a relief committee for interned comrades.[53] Rocker and the majority of his associates opposed the War and their activities led to internment on security grounds.

Apart from these examples of how Germans organised relief themselves — and there may well be others where records have not been kept — outside organisations also provided help. These included the American YMCA, which worked in the internment camps, and a committee set up by the International Women's Suffrage Alliance to help stranded women in the early months of the War.[54] Of most significant impact was the Friends' Emergency Committee for the Assistance of Germans, Austrians and Hungarians in Distress (FEC). Assisting enemy aliens was one way for the Society of Friends, which convened the FEC, to continue to work positively for peace and reconciliation, despite the failure for their hopes and ideals demonstrated by the outbreak of war.[55]

The FEC decided to work solely with aliens identified as 'enemies'. As this principle was directly opposed to that of the CCUARS, formal links between the two were limited, although in practice they co-operated considerably.[56] Despite its more radical philosophical position, the FEC, similar to the CCUARS, worked in co-operation with the Home Office and the police. It did not criticise government measures directly: this policy was probably essential for it to be allowed to continue its work.[57] The CCUARS and the FEC helped provide a safety net for many poorer Germans and Austrians, especially women. They supplemented inadequate allowances with clothing and boots and helped in times of illness and childbirth. The CCUARS also provided regular relief to people not eligible for various reasons for allowances from either the German or British governments.[58]

It is difficult to know what proportion of the enemy alien population was reached by their work. It was inadvisable for the FEC and CCUARS to publicise their work widely through conventional means. Many Germans now in financial difficulties did not come from a class which usually needed to rely on charity, and were probably not as well attuned to finding out where help could be found as some sections of the working class. The CCUARS' constituent societies, such as the SFFD and the German Benevolent Society, were already widely known among the German population in London, where its work was predominantly carried out. In 1916, it had five salaried staff and 38 voluntary workers. It did not work in internment camps.[59]

The FEC, in 1918, had files on 6,000 cases and 175 visitors in London, as well as an extensive network of contacts in the provinces who could reach isolated districts where only a few Germans lived. Provincial committees of the FEC were set up, and worked with local prosperous German residents. The FEC tried in particular to lessen the social isolation and bitterness felt by enemy aliens. It arranged visits to homes of internees' wives and organised parties and social gatherings. Its provincial contacts made work in the internment camps, scattered around the country, more feasible.[60]

It is impossible to do justice here to the subject of internment, but a brief consideration is worthwhile, in particular as some interesting issues about political and class divisions between internees are raised in reports of the camps. However the camps were not a microcosm of German society in Britain: internees were not a representative sample of Germans living in Britain, as there was a lower proportion of settled and established German immigrants. This was because older immigrants (over 55) were not interned, nor were those exempt on the grounds of very strong connections with Britain or whose occupation or business was essential to the war effort.[61] Naturalised Germans were not interned either. Instead, there was a relatively large number of transients, including sailors captured on merchant ships and men captured while returning from overseas voluntarily to join the German army.

Reports of US Embassy officials present a picture of fairly decent conditions, despite the need for minor improvements.[62] FEC reports give a similar impression.[63] The reports of representatives of Switzerland and Sweden, which became the protecting powers for enemy subjects in British camps after US entry into the War, are rather less favourable. This probably reflects the food shortages of the latter part of the War and damage to morale from long-term confinement.[64]

If for the most part the Government seems to have kept to the Hague Conventions of 1899 and 1907, which laid down the conditions under which civilian and military prisoners-of-war were to be kept, some examples of irregularities are related by contemporaries. Sylvia Pankhurst quotes a letter from a woman whose husband was struck on the head by a bayonet; the commandant refused to hold an inquiry.[65] Richard Noschke, interned at Stratford camp, describes mistreatment by British soldiers.[66] According to Rudolf Rocker, men at Olympia were forced to break stones, contrary to the Hague Convention. He also relates that at Alexandra Palace, to which he was later moved, a notorious sergeant assaulted a man, although the internees successfully campaigned to have him transferred.[67] Another internee, however, Cohen-Portheim, could recall no cases of mistreatment.[68] Noschke and Rocker both record that complaining to US officials achieved little.[69] One of the most severe incidents was a riot at Douglas camp on the Isle of Man in November 1914, during which six internees were shot and killed by military guards. It appears poor conditions and food provoked the disturbance. The political nature, if any, of the riot is unclear.[70]

Leaving the physical conditions in the camp aside, reports from many different sources indicate that the chief evil of the camps was the psychological effects of imprisonment. Anxiety about their families and frustration at their inability to help them, feelings of injustice at being imprisoned without having committed a crime and lack of privacy are all pointed to as causes of stress.[71] In the belief that work would cure the prisoners' mental ills the FEC helped set up handicraft activities. Internees also set up activities on their own initiative. A US Embassy report from March 1916 depicts bustling communities with numerous educational classes, dramatic clubs, orchestras and sports facilities, especially in the larger camps.[72] Despite these activities, the evidence suggests that the mental health of prisoners deteriorated and a mental condition known as 'barbed wire fever' was even identified.[73]

Another significant feature of camp life was class division. It was War Office policy to segregate internees on the basis of status. Two 'gentlemen's camps' were set up for those willing to pay extra for better conditions while there were separate sections for those who wished to pay for the privilege in other camps. Poorer prisoners carried out camp fatigues for paying prisoners and provided personal services as stewards, barbers, tailors and launderers.[74]

These distinctions were not only the product of War Office policy. According to Cohen-Portheim, distinctions existed even within the gentlemen's camp at Wakefield. One section was very Prussian in tone and prided itself on its nationalistic spirit. The aristocrats maintained the social exclusivity which had marked aristocratic life in Germany, and several chose to live in a hut together known as *die Grafenhütte*. Cohen-Portheim's own section, mostly composed of businessmen and commercial clerks, had its own recognised social distinctions. Bank clerks were regarded as superior to other clerks and had their own *Bankbeamtenhütte*.[75] According to Rocker the initiative to separate the classes on the prison ship, the *Royal Edward,* came from a group of internees themselves. Baron von Nettelheim, the leader of this group, which included many army reserve officers, negotiated with the ship's captain to pay for better accommodation, food, service and exercise area. Although they claimed to be great German patriots, they showed no solidarity other than that of class and used British soldiers to throw poorer internees out of some coveted cabins.[76]

At both Wakefield and on the *Royal Edward,* the national solidarity that camp life might be expected to produce did not overcome the class divisions that the men brought with them. It is difficult to say whether these divisions reflect the structure of the society formed by Germans living in Britain, of German society or even of British society, as internment camp society consisted of a complex mix of the three: 'real Germans' and 'Anglo' Germans made to live together, under the external control of the British army.

The internal administration of the camps was run by 'captains', internees in some camps elected by the prisoners themselves, in others, chosen by the Commandant. It is unclear how the system of captains relates to class differences, although in one case at Alexandra Palace (to which the men on the *Royal Edward* were transferred) a Swabian nobleman was unsuccessfully put up for election by the German patriot group.[77] Noschke relates how 'regular workmen' accused an elected committee of swindling and succeeded in getting rid of it.[78]

It might be expected that the experience of internment would have an effect on the views of Germans settled in Britain about their adopted country. For many, it would be their first experience of an all-German environment for many years. The Aliens Committee of the Ministry of Reconstruction believed that the German environment in the camps had redeveloped German national feeling, but this view conveniently justified its decision to recommend repatriation of internees.[79] Rocker found hysterical patriotism at Olympia among internees who had lived a long time in Britain. He thought that, as they were being punished as Germans, they had to justify themselves as Germans. An anti-patriot himself, he interpreted their patriotism as a way of asserting their human dignity and pride against the humiliations to which they were subjected.[80]

Cohen-Portheim's analysis is perhaps more objective. He thought that men who had lived in England a long time obviously wished to return to their families and businesses, and therefore did not wish to be hostile to Britain. However, as they were suspected of a lukewarm patriotism, they had to show they were as patriotic as the nationalistic elements, who generally had few British connections. Cohen-Portheim thought that the generally expressed hatred of the British was of the same nature as British hatred of Germans, that is, that the pressure of public opinion enforced conformity.[81]

The reactions of Germans both inside and outside the camps to the situation in which they found themselves were complex and varied. They reflected both differences in individual circumstances, such as length of residence in Britain, their reasons for coming to the country and whether they intended to try and re-establish their life here after the War. They also reflected the fact that the Germans did not constitute a homogeneous community. The multiplicity of German organisations that existed before the War, which might appear to indicate a flourishing communal life, catered in many cases to sectional interests — to particular social, political or religious groups within the German population. The charitable activities of some of the richer naturalised Germans indicate that they felt some responsibility towards and common interest with Germans who, unlike them, were subject to the ARA. Many also felt that, in their insecure position, they needed to demonstrate publicly their loyalty to Britain. The motivation of those with relatives left in Germany was further complicated by fears that pro-British actions might have repercussions for them.

Life in the internment camps reflected to some extent the divisions within German society in Britain. However, the influence of the relatively high proportion of Germans without substantial British connections and the abnormal environment of camp life makes the internment camps a more complex social and political mix.

III

The Government had been considering how to deal with enemy aliens remaining in the country after the end of the War since June 1916 when an Enemy Aliens Sub-Committee of the Reconstruction Committee was set up. In January 1917, its terms of reference were extended to an examination of the alien question generally.[82]

The committee, renamed the Aliens Committee of the Ministry of Reconstruction, concluded in January 1918 that the Aliens Act of 1905 was ineffective against all but the poorest aliens and recommended that the more stringent wartime measures be retained. In the 1919 Aliens Restriction Act, the Government took the power to continue the 1914 Aliens Restriction Act for two years. Subsequently extended, it provides the principles on which current legislation is based.[83] Wartime Germanophobia therefore had a lasting impact in creating the conditions in which the 1914 and 1919 Acts were passed, although it can be argued that it was not only a specific reaction to Germans, but evidence of a much wider and more deep-rooted xenophobia. Not only enemy aliens, but the whole question of aliens in British society were brought into the debate of 1918–19.

The committee also recommended that the great majority of internees be repatriated at the end of the War. Several thousand internees over 45 or in poor health had already been released and sent to live in Holland by agreement with Germany. At the Armistice there were still 24,450 enemy aliens interned. Another 21,000 remained at liberty.[84]

A total of 3,250 Germans applied for exemption from repatriation (more may have been deterred from applying by the further period of internment necessary while the application was considered) and 3,050 were allowed to stay. The majority had British wives or children or long residence in Britain.[85]

Repatriation meant the separation of many families was continued. On their release from internment those not repatriated had to find work in a hostile climate. Maintenance grants from the British government ceased on release. But the claim of the Aliens Committee that there would be 'a social and commercial boycott' of Germans does not seem to have been carried out fully. The CCUARS reported that, although prospects had looked hopeless, in most cases former internees succeeded in finding work. Some employers appealed to the appropriate committee for their former employees to be exempt from repatriation, ostensibly on the grounds of national interest.[86]

German life in Britain never returned to the pre-war situation. By

1921, the German population was reduced to 12,358, less than a quarter of its pre-war level, and Germans were not allowed to apply for naturalisation until 1931.[87] Whether Germans would have retained their own national character or been largely absorbed into the general population had the War not intervened can only be a matter for speculation. The arrival of a stream of refugees in the 1930s again completely changed the character of German settlement in Britain.

STELLA YARROW
London

NOTES

HO   Home Office Files, Public Records Office
HC   House of Commons Debates, Fifth Series (Hansard)
IWM, WWC   Imperial War Museum, Women's Work Collection

1. Census of England and Wales, 1911, vol.IX, Birthplaces . . . Ages and Occupations of Foreigners Cd 7017, 1xxvii, 1 (hereafter Cd 7017). Population figures given do not include 5,447 German women who had acquired British nationality by marriage; Hermann Kellenbenz, 'German immigrants in England' in C. Holmes (ed.), *Immigrants and Minorities in British Society* (London, 1978), p.75; H. Oliver, *The International Anarchist Movement in Late Victorian London* (London, 1983), pp.5–7; Henry Semon and Thomas McIntyre (eds.), *The Autobiography of Sir Felix Semon* (London, 1926) pp.60, 140; Francis Oppenheimer, *Stranger Within. Autobiographical Pages by Sir Frances Oppenheimer KCMG* (London, 1960) pp.21, 30; Colin Holmes 'Germans in Britain' in J. Schneider et al. (eds.), *Wirtschaftskräfte und Wirtschaftswëge — Festschrift für Hermann Kellenbenz* (Nuremberg, 1978) pp.581–593; Gregory Anderson, 'German clerks in England 1870–1914. Another Aspect of the Great Depression Debate' in K. Lunn (ed.), *Hosts, Immigrants and Minorities. Historical Responses to Newcomers in English Society 1870–1914* (Folkestone, 1980), pp.201–221.
2. L Katscher, 'German life in London', *The Nineteenth Century*, 21 (1887) pp.726–36; Maureen Neumann, *An Account of the German Hospital in London from 1848 to 1948* (London, 1971); Rudolf Rocker, *The London Years* (London, 1956) pp.66–9, 139; Oliver, op.cit., pp.5–7, 17–19; Semon and McIntyre, op. cit., pp.109, 126.
3. Over 60 per cent of German men who were married had British wives. Cd 7017; HO11522/287235; Ministry of Reconstruction. Report of the Aliens Committee. (Appendix. Census of Aliens 1 July 1917) 1918 Cmd 8916 (hereafter Cmd 8916); Royal Commission on Alien Immigration, II, Evidence, (1903) Cd 1742 ix 6.
4. Holmes, op.cit., pp.383–4; Anderson, op.cit., pp.201–221; David French, 'Spy Fever in Britain, 1900–1915', *The Historical Journal*, 21,2 (1978) pp.355–70; Colin Holmes, *Anti-Semitism in British Society 1876–1939* (London, 1979) pp.71–83.
5. Cate Haste, *Keep the Homes Fires Burning. Propaganda in the First World War* (London, 1977) pp.78–105.
6. Haste, op.cit., pp.128–30; *The Times*, 12 May 1915, 13 May 1915. See also Panikos Panayi's contribution in this volume.
7. Gisela Lebzelter; 'Anti-Semitism — A Focal Point for the British Radical Right' in Paul Kennedy and Anthony Nicholls (eds.), *Nationalist and Racialist Movements in Britain and Germany before 1914* (Oxford, 1981) p.96; HC LXXII, 1330, 24 June 1915.
8. *The Restaurant and Hotel Review*, Sept. 1914, Oct. 1914, Mar. 1915; *The Times*, 16 Jan. 1915.

9. The term 'enemy alien' covered citizens of Germany, Austro–Hungary, Turkey and Bulgaria. Government measures applied to all of these, although Austro-Hungarians consistently received better treatment than Germans, in recognition of the greater public odium attached to Germans. 'Subject races' such as Czechs and Poles were recognised, for the most part, by the Government as 'friendly aliens'.

10. French, op.cit., pp.358–360.

11. Ibid., pp.367–9; HC LXVI, 226–268, 28 Aug. 1914, LXVI, 583–604, 9 Sept. 1914, LXVIII, 79–123, 12 Nov.1914, LXVIII, 1361–1405, 26 Nov. 1914, LXX, 833–916, 3 Mar. 1915; J.C.Bird, 'Control of Enemy Alien Civilians in Great Britain 1914–1916' (unpublished PhD thesis, University of London, 1981) pp.54, 65–6.

12. French, op.cit., p.369; HC LXXI, 1842–78, 13 May 1915.

13. Bird, op.cit., pp.119–30; Haste, op.cit., pp.134–8; HC LXXXIII, 1047–92, 29 June 1916.

14. Haste, op.cit., pp.138–9, Kenneth Morgan, *Consensus and Disunity: The Lloyd George Coalition Government 1918–1922* (Oxford, 1979) pp.39–42.

15. Bird, op.cit., pp.200–232, 242.

16. IWM WWC Relief II 5/1, 5/2.

17. The First World War Memoirs of Richard Noschke (Unpublished manuscript in the Imperial War Museum Collection, hereafter Noschke); Bird, op.cit., p.272.

18. IWM WWC Suffrage and Politics II 10/1; *The Friend*, 14 Aug. 1914.

19. HO45 10734/258157; IWM WWC Relief II 5/2, 5/4. 6/3.

20. *The Friend*, 28 Aug. 1914; *The Times*, 25 Nov. 1914; IWM WWC Relief II 5/2, 5/4, 6/3; HO45 11005/26025.

21. *The Friend*, 13 Aug. 1915; 21 Apr. 1916; IWM WWC Relief II 5/4, 5/5, 5/6, 6/2.

22. IWM WWC Relief II 5/2, 6/1, 6/3; *The Times*, 13 May 1915.

23. IWM WWC Relief II 5/2, 6/2; HO45 11005/260251, HC LXXX, 911, 29 Feb. 1916.

24. HC LXXXI, 1970, 17 May 1916.

25. Sylvia Pankhurst, *The Home Front. A Mirror to Life in England during the World War* (London, 1932) pp.170–1; *The Friend*, 21 May 1915.

26. HO45 10787/298199. The figure refers to Metropolitan Police District only; *The Times*, 14 May 1915.

27. In *The Log Boys*, by 'Mrs W' (London, 1916) a British-born wife gives examples from her experience. See IWM WWC Relief II 5/34.

28. HC LXVI, 313, 24 Nov. 1915.

29. HC LXXXI, 1793, 13 May 1915; LXVI, 313, 24 Nov. 1915;

30. *The Friend*, 21 Apr. 1916.

31. Neumann, op.cit. p.81

32. *The Times*, 26 Oct. 1914, 28 Jan. 1915; HC XC, 1672, 26 Feb. 1917, HC XCV, 1686, 9 July 1917; Rocker, op.cit., p.243; Bird, op.cit., p.229–30

33. *The Times*, 30 June 1916.

34. Ibid. 3 Sept. 1915, 27 Sept. 1915; *The Friend*, 19 Mar. 1915; HC LXXXII, 106, 4 May 1915.

35. *Illustrated Press Directory* (London, 1914); Bird, op.cit., p.230.

36. PRO CAB 126/7; HO45 11522/287235.

37. IWM WWC Relief II 6/3, 6/4.

38. IWM WWC Relief II 6/3.

39. IWM WWC Relief II 6/10.

40. HO45 11005/260251.

41. IWM WWC Relief II 6/1.

42. Ibid.

43. HO45 10734/238157.

44. *The Friend*, 24 Mar. 1916.

45. J.M. Cohen, *The Life of Ludwig Mond* (London, 1956), p.161; IWM WWC Relief II 5/3; *The Friend*, 2 July 1915; HC LXXXIII, 1060, 1084, 29 June 1916; LXXXIV, 609, 17 July 1916, 1347, 24 July 1916, XCVIII, 2161–2, Nov.7 1917.

46. HC LXVIII 1391, 1531 26 Nov. 1914, LXXXI 2360 13 May 1915, LXXII 870, 1380 24 June 1915, C 69, 3 Dec. 1917; Neumann, op.cit., p.79

47. Brian Connell, *Manifest Destiny. A Study in Five Profiles of the Rise and Influence of the Mountbatten family* (London, 1953) p.69; *The Restaurant and Hotel Review*, Sept. 1915.
48. *The Times*, 15 May 1915, 18 May 1915.
49. Ibid. 18 May 1915, 28 May 1915.
50. Ibid., 11 May 1915.
51. Semon and McIntyre, op.cit., pp.298–308. Sir Edgar Speyer refused to sign a loyalty letter and eventually left for the United States. See C.C. Aronsfeld 'Jewish enemy aliens in England during the First World War', *Jewish Social Studies*, 18 (1956) pp.275–83.
52. Semon and McIntyre, op.cit., p.313.
53. *The Catering Worker*, Sept. 1914; Rocker, op.cit., p.243.
54. Noschke op.cit.; *The Friend*, 24 May 1916, IWM WWC Relief II 10/1, HC LXXXI, 1178, 5 Apr. 1916.
55. *The Friend*, 14. Aug. 1914, 28 Aug. 1914, 4 Sept. 1914, 8 Dec. 1914; IWM WWC Relief II 5/26.
56. *The Friend*, 24 Mar. 1916; IWM WWC Relief II 6/3.
57. *The Friend*, 4 Dec. 1914; IWM WWC Relief II 5/1, 5/2, 5/3.
58. IWM WWC Relief II 6/2.
59. IWM WWC Relief II 6/1, 6/2.
60. IWM WWC Relief II 5/2, 5/4; *The Friend*, 22 Jan. 1915, 21 May 1915, 24 Mar. 1916, 21 Apr. 1916.
61. HO45 10756/267450, HO45 11522/287235.
62. Reports of Visits of Inspection made by Officials of the United States Embassy to Various Internment Camps in the United Kingdom 1916 Cd 8324 xv (hereafter Cd 8324).
63. *The Friend*, 4 Dec. 1914, 1 Jan. 1915, 8 Jan. 1915, 8 June 1915.
64. Bird, op.cit. pp.162–64.
65. Pankhurst, op.cit., pp.386–7.
66. Noschke, op.cit.
67. Rocker, op.cit., pp.245, 340–43.
68. Cohen–Portheim op.cit., p.70.
69. Noschke op.cit.; Rocker, op.cit., p.315.
70. *The Times*, 23 Nov. 1914, 28 Nov. 1914, 16 Dec. 1914, 17 Dec. 1914, 30 Dec. 1914.
71. Cohen–Portheim, op.cit., pp.88–9, 119; Rocker, op.cit., p.258, 317, *The Friend*, 18 June 1916, 24 Mar. 1916, 6 Oct. 1916; Noschke; IMW WWC Relief II 5/2.
72. Cd 8324.
73. Bird, op.cit., pp.162, 164.
74. HO45 10760/269116; Cd 8324; Bird, op.cit., p.151; Cohen–Portheim, op.cit., pp.65–6, 99.
75. Cohen–Portheim, op.cit., pp.100–9.
76. Rocker, op.cit., pp.259–78.
77. Ibid., pp.288–289; HO45 10760/269116.
78. Noschke, op. cit.
79. Cmd 8916.
80. Rocker, op.cit., p.258.
81. Cohen-Portheim, op.cit., pp.87, 107–8.
82. Cmd 8916.
83. Bernard Gainer, *Alien Invasion. The Origins of the Aliens Act of 1905* (London, 1972) pp.208–9.
84. Cmd 8916; IWM WWC Relief II 5/4; Report of Committee Appointed to Consider Applications for Exemption from Compulsory Repatriation submitted by Interned Enemy Aliens 1919 Cmd 383 x 125 (hereafter Cmd 383).
85. Cmd 383.
86. Cmd 8916; Cmd 383; IWM WWC Relief II 6/1.
87. Census of England and Wales 1921 Preliminary Report 1921 Cmd 1485 xvi 257; Bird, op.cit., p.252.

The British Empire Union in the First World War

The question of the British Radical Right before 1914 and after 1918 has received much attention from a wide range of historians. The influence of this political grouping during the First World War has, however, been largely ignored. This article attempts to fill this gap with specific reference to one particular pressure group — the British Empire Union. The piece pays attention to the organization's ideology and shows how this was put into action, before attempting to assess its influence.

The British Empire Union came into existence in April 1915 under its original name of the Anti-German Union (AGU). The latter title was in fact only kept for about a year but it suggests the main preoccupation of the organization throughout the War. During the 1920s and 1930s it devoted most of its attention to fighting Communism and spreading propaganda about Empire.[1] It continued to exist after the Second World War and in 1960 became the British Commonwealth Union.[2] Its objectives had changed very little, as revealed by the *Annual Report* of 1963 which stated that it aimed to counter 'all false doctrines and fallacies of Socialism and Communism' and 'to give our people knowledge of the Commonwealth and its vast undeveloped resources whilst refuting the many false conceptions which have grown up with regard to its past history'. The organization continued to produce publications during the 1960s[3] but ceased to have any political importance by 1975 when it came under the control of a group of directors who used its name for purely business purposes. Throughout its history, the BEU has been connected with political figures of some importance, including Lord Leith of Fyvie, Lord Charles Beresford, William Joynson-Hicks, Lord Carson, the Earl of Derby, Lord Croft and Sir John Biggs-Davison. From December 1916 until Summer 1952 it published a journal on a regular basis.[4]

As has been indicated, the British Empire Union displayed particular concern about the threat of Germans, particularly those in Britain during the First World War (one of the peaks of its importance). Before 1914, hostility towards German aliens had shown itself on various occasions in the form of 'spy-fever' and the development of ideas about German/Jewish domination put forward by Leo Maxse and his *National Review*. Germanophobia became far more widespread during the Great War and it is for this reason that the BEU became important. The organization apparently came into existence following the appearance of an article by E. B. Osborn 'in one of our great daily newspapers' dealing with 'the menace of the alien enemy amongst us'. As a result of this, Osborn allegedly received a flood of letters and money on the following morning. Out of 'this invaluable chaos' the Anti-German Union 'came into being' with Sir George Makgill as organizer and secretary.[5]

These events probably happened, if at all, in April 1915, (as subsequent publications gave this as the foundation date of the Union).[6] The first mention of the organization in a major newspaper came in an article in the *Glasgow Herald* of 13 May 1915, which pointed out its aims. This is a significant date, just six days after the sinking of the *Lusitania,* an event which resulted in a peak of hate propaganda against Germany, leading, in turn, to widespread attacks upon German property in Britain.[7] These events almost certainly gave the AGU a boost. During the following month it held its first major meeting in the Aeolian Hall in London when Leo Maxse spoke about 'the German blight' affecting Britain.[8]

The organization aimed, above all, at 'the Extirpation — Root and Branch and Seed — of German Control and Influence from the British Empire'.[9] One method it used to justify this policy was to rewrite British history in order to show that Britain had been under German influence before but had managed to overcome it. More specifically, it accepted the ideas of the conspiracy theorist Ian Colvin, who claimed that during the Middle Ages the Hanseatic League had set up a colony in England and other European states, with a view to German 'world dominion'. They acted as 'advance agents' for Germany, preparing the way 'for conquest by peaceful methods — bribery, spying, and juggling with the law'. When Queen Elizabeth came to power, the German, 'was making the bid for mastery over us, then as now — and not the Spaniard'. However, Queen Elizabeth acted decisively to rid Britain of the Germans.[10]

The present government should behave similarly, argued the BEU because a 'Mysterious Hand' of influence affected all aspects of British life and hindered the war effort.[11] Makgill claimed that during the Edwardian years vast numbers of Germans of military age had entered Britain in order to prepare the way for an invasion. Now, during the War, German settlers and colonies could be found throughout the country, usually near important seaports, naval bases, and 'certain well-recognized lines of defence or important railway lines'. Makgill drew no distinction between Germans who had retained their nationality and those who had become naturalized British subjects because '[i]f a man were a German agent, one of the first things he would do would be to pay the few guineas necessary to get the magic "scrap of paper" which, in the view of our lawyer politicians, creates in a German a clean heart and a British soul'.[12]

The BEU claimed that naturalized Germans had infiltrated the political scene in Britain. 'Germans and British-born pro-Germans still sat in our Privy Council and in our House of Commons; they had wealth and influence quite out of proportion to their numbers.' In December 1917 Ellis Powell, the editor of the *Financial News* who did much to arouse publicity over the pre-war Marconi scandal, addressed a meeting at which he told his audience: 'With these influences at work did they wonder that they had got into the third year of the War. If these influences were allowed to continue, they would get into the sixth year of the War.' On another occasion, Captain E. Parsons, who became a prominent BEU publicist at the end of the War, claimed that before 1914 Germany had 'put a millionaire on each side in politics in every country of the World' and had penetrated the British legislature and press.[13]

Much attention also went towards the question of people 'of German extraction', 'who continued to be employed in our Government Offices', particularly the Foreign Office.[14] The 'Hidden Hand' of German influence had also penetrated British business, commerce and finance.

> Time was when the British merchant and manufacturer cheerfully welcomed into their houses and their workshops the German "volunteer" who, in order to master effectually the secrets of British business, gladly gave their services for nothing, and then took their departure for the Fatherland, fully prepared to use against the Briton, in every part of the world, the knowledge and experience they had gained in British offices and factories.

During the War, 'the German's hold upon the small trader and the average citizen in his various occupations is still maintained — he throttles great and small alike'. Germans were particularly important as bakers, miners, barbers, and waiters. They consequently, according to the BEU, filled their 'pockets with the wages that should be paid to our own folk'. And, in order to keep their custom, they changed the names above their shops to English ones.[15]

The BEU paid particular attention to the question of German banks in London, despite the fact that, under licences issued by the Home Secretary in August 1914, they could only complete transactions which they had entered into before the War.[16] Lord Leith of Fyvie, the President of the BEU from 1916, stated that,

> These German banks differ entirely from English banks. The latter are purely organized to do a banking business, the primary purpose of German banks is to develop the commerce of the German Empire by insidious penetration, at all times by the advice and direction of their secret service and spy departments.[17]

The BEU certainly took steps to 'eradicate the curse of Germanism, and pro-Germanism, and naturalized Germanism'.[18] It used the law courts, held both peaceful and violent meetings, and generally publicized its ideas. As the AGU it first attracted public attention in June 1915 when Makgill brought a case against two prominent naturalized Germans in the High Court asking by what authority they claimed to be Privy Councillors. The two individuals concerned were the financiers Sir Edgar Speyer and Sir Ernest Cassel. Makgill's action proved unsuccessful because in December the judges who heard the case decided that both Speyer and Cassel could keep their positions, regardless of their alien birth.[19] But despite his failure Makgill claimed to have at least made public 'the serious need for drastic reform of our naturalization laws' and during 1917–19 the BEU put forward various proposals in this direction in order 'to preserve effectually the heritage of British blood' from any 'foreign tramp who asks for it at the Home Office'. The question of naturalization lay 'at the bottom of plans for purging our national life of German taint for the future'.[20]

In May 1917 a meeting of the Walthamstow branch of the Union demanded that 'no German shall be naturalized for a period of 21 years after the War' and that 'all naturalization papers taken out during a period of 21 years prior to the War shall be cancelled'. A leaflet printed by the national organization laid down seven preconditions which should be met before any alien received British citizenship in future. These included a full disclosure by the applicant of his previous history and business and a public notice of application with advertisement in the local papers.[21] When the Government did introduce a Bill in July 1918 an article in the *Monthly Record* attacked it because the Home Secretary did not receive strong enough powers to revoke certificates. The piece suggested that all subjects of enemy origin naturalized since 1870 should revert to their former nationality. Meanwhile, another article put forward the idea that everyone of enemy origin should be disenfranchised.[22] In addition, there were constant calls for measures to disqualify naturalized aliens from membership of the Privy Council or either House of Parliament or from holding any other public office.[23]

Throughout the War, the BEU campaigned for the closure of all remaining German institutions, often using forceful methods. In the summer of 1915, for instance, when a German Church in Forest Hill, south London attracted the attention of the AGU, it began to hold demonstrations outside the building while services proceeded. Scuffles broke out at a meeting on 5 September which led to the closure of the building by the police. One of the Union speakers, Lindsay Johnson, had claimed that the Church lay in an 'important strategic position on the London and Brighton line'. He believed that 'when the foundation was laid in 1882 it was with a view to the future'.[24]

At the same time as these events took place the Union also drew attention to a German Farm Colony in Great Munden, Hertfordshire. The Government had actually turned this into an internment camp for old and invalid alien enemies but Richard Glover, a leading light in the Union, arranged a meeting nearby on 18 September at which he proposed a resolution demanding the 'immediate shutting up of the German Army base camp at Great Munden, and the internment of W. Muller, its commandant, and the Germans garrisoned there under his command'. Those present at the meeting carried the motion unanimously.[25] The Union organized further meetings during the course of the following weeks. On 2 October Glover delivered another speech at which he asked 'everyone of my Countrymen to have that dirty Huns Nest *smoked out* which is 6¾ miles from where you are now. (Loud applause)' [sic].[26] Glover's call did have some effect because the camp came under attack. This local hostility worried the Army Council (involved in the administration of the building), which suggested that 'the place should be closed and these aliens interned in one of the existing "camps"'. The Home Office rejected this suggestion, however, and Libury Hall, Great Munden, retained its inhabitants until the end of the War.[27]

In the summer of 1916 the BEU devoted attention to German restaurants which remained open in London. Makgill took a report about one of them, Voight's, to Scotland Yard. The account claimed that those in the building knew beforehand of Zeppelin attacks, which had occurred during the previous September. After one of these, 'They were mocking the English, who, as they said, fled in panic at Zeppelin raids'. William Joynson-Hicks raised this topic in the House of Commons and, as a result of the pressure, the restaurant received orders to close. The Union also managed to secure the closure of at least one other German eating establishment in London, again with the help of Joynson-Hicks.[28]

The BEU had a further success in May 1917; this time with a German religious meeting in Walthamstow. On 27 May J. F. Graves, the local branch secretary, together with several of his supporters, entered a Church Hall in Walthamstow High Street and asked for Pastor John Kiel to stop his service because he prayed 'for the Kaiser and the Fatherland'. The minister refused and sent for the police who took down the names of the intruders and, at the request of Graves, the Germans present. Graves and his followers then left 'under protest' and held a demonstration nearby in which speakers from BEU branches throughout London participated. Graves announced that another meeting would be held on the following Sunday. However, this did not take place because the Deacons of the Marsh Street Congregational Church, responsible for the Hall, informed 'local Germans that they must forthwith cease to hold their service' in the building.[29]

These few examples serve to illustrate the action which the BEU undertook in its attempts to close German establishments. In addition, the organization held numerous, and larger, meetings throughout the War demanding a stricter government internment policy. This question had attracted the attention of the Right from the start of the War and continued to do so even after the introduction of wholesale internment for male alien enemies of military age in May 1915. The BEU's demands in this direction were certainly not unique. The organization often called meetings at times of peak anti-German and anti-alien feeling.

One of these peaks came in June 1916 following the death of Kitchener; an event blamed on spies and leading to attacks on German property in Islington, north London.[30] The Union called an 'Intern-all-Germans demonstration in Hyde Park' for 13 June which was attended by about 1,000 people who 'enthusiastically adopted' a resolution demanding the internment of naturalized as well as unnaturalized Germans. In addition to this meeting the BEU also held three others in Hyde Park during the course of June and July and a total of about 50 throughout the country for the whole of 1916.[31]

The following summer witnessed further activity by the organization. On 8 June, for instance, the Putney and Wandsworth branch of the Union held a gathering at a local hall. The speakers included A. D. Dawnay, the Mayor of Wandsworth and a very active anti-German, and George Curnock, of the *Daily Mail*. Dawnay called for sweeping action. He asserted that, 'The word "alien" covered a variety of people who, they considered, had no right here, and he was not disposed to trust one more than another. The only way to do away with the danger was to insist on doing away with the whole alien fraternity'. Curnock, meanwhile, claimed that among the 20,000 Germans and Austrians still at liberty 'were some of the most dangerous people on earth'.[32]

Curnock also appealed for canvassers to help with a petition demanding wholesale internment. The branch eventually obtained 43,000 signatures which it presented to the Home Secretary, Sir George Cave, in December 1917.[33] The Oxford branch had less success with its own canvassing. The local secretary, Mrs E. M. Jee, collected just 26 signatures which she sent to her MP, J. A. R. Marriot, for transmission to the Home Secretary.[34]

The BEU reached a peak of activity during the summer of 1918. This was a time of intense anti-alien feeling throughout the country brought on by a combination of factors, particularly the real possibility of military defeat following the German spring offensive.[35] The Union held weekly meetings in Hyde Park which began to attract national attention from late July.[36] The largest anti-alien demonstration of the War took place on 24 August. As on previous occasions, this received advanced publicity in the press.[37] Although the National Party actually organized the event, the BEU played a major part in the proceedings. At 2.30 pm crowds gathered in Hyde Park to hear speeches from five different platforms. Supporters of the BEU assembled at the third where they listened to, among others, Arnold White and Ellis Powell. Shortly after 3 pm a procession formed in order to take a petition, demanding the interment of all alien enemies, to Downing Street. About 1,250,000 people had signed the petition which ran to over two miles in length.

In the marching ranks were members of the Provisional Grand Council of the National Party, thousands of discharged soldiers and sailors, branches of the British Empire Union, deputations from the Committees of Public Safety formed in various cities and towns of the country, Dominion soldiers, trades unions, and a great many of the general public, men and women, which included many representative City men of the Baltic and the Stock Exchange.[38] This was the last major war meeting demanding wholesale internment, although during 1919 the BEU continued its anti-alien campaign by playing a role in the fight for the Aliens Act.[39]

The BEU also endeavoured to promote British business in place of German, both at home and abroad. This meant, in the first place, a demand for the closure of all German firms remaining in Britain, particularly the banks. These received regular criticism, culminating in a meeting at the Cannon Street Hotel on 21 March 1917 where the speakers included Ellis Powell, Leith of Fyvie, and Ronald MacNeill, Unionist MP and a Vice-President of the BEU.[40]

From its days as the AGU the organization called for a boycott of German products and employees. It asked British shopkeepers to display posters which declared, 'No German Goods Sold', 'No German Labour Employed', 'No Germans Served'.[41] In 1917 the BEU drew up a 'Consumer's Pledge' to be widely circulated:

> We pledge ourselves not to deal with any firm which to our knowledge is German controlled, has Germans in its employ, or knowingly deals in German goods; and will give our custom to those firms which undertake to give preference to the employment of British subjects and the purchasing of British goods.
>
> In short, we will be anti-German, not only in sentiment, but also in practice.[42]

The Union appealed directly to women as purchasers:

> If you buy German goods, you are sending money to Germany; you are helping her to prepare new armaments for another War. Remember the men who have fought to protect you; remember what they deserve — good wages, full employment — and buy British Goods.[43]

In July 1918 the BEU adopted the boycott proposed by the Merchant Seamen's League which involved a refusal to employ Germans 'in any capacity on land or sea' and a pledge 'not to purchase or use, or cause to be used, any goods of German origin'. This boycott would continue for at least six years after the end of the War.[44]

Support for British products went together with opposition to those from Germany. In May 1917 the Belfast branch of the Union held a 'British Empire Union Week' during which local firms agreed to use window displays to draw attention to the 'importance of supporting British manufactures as against those of Teutonic origin'.[45] After the War the BEU aimed at securing employment and 'good wages' for British workers by manufacturing 'as much as we possibly can at home'. It wanted the imposition of 'heavy and almost prohibitory duties on all imports' from Germany and other hostile nations. Tariffs should be lower for products from allied and neutral countries and lowest of all for products from the Empire.[46]

In addition to opposing Germans in Britain, the BEU also attacked pacifists and socialists because these also appeared a threat to the war effort. In the first group it included all organizations which did not support a crushing defeat of Germany. Thus, an AGU leaflet warned the public to beware of the Union of Democratic Control, the Stop the War Committee, the Fellowship of Reconciliation, the No-Conscription Fellowship, and 'other Political and Sentimental Peace-mongers'. All these bodies allegedly had one aim in mind: 'to injure their own country'. Their leaders consequently deserved the labels of 'traitors' and 'enemies of the State'. In this way they shared certain similarities with alien enemies.[47] A major article in the *Monthly Record* described them as 'insidious persons at work in our midst who are using their intelligence, and their undoubted powers of organization, to minimise all our efforts and nullify the result of our victories'.[48]

During 1917 the Union's journal ran a series called 'Pacifist Portraits'. The first feature looked at Sir John Simon, who had resigned from the Cabinet because of the introduction of conscription, and stated that he 'will assuredly be remembered in English history as the principal patron of shirkers and skulkers in the dark days of the Great War'. Another article in this series accused Ramsay MacDonald of having 'anti-British' and 'pro-German proclivities'. Bertrand Russell, meanwhile, was said to 'have done more to sow the seeds of treachery at home and injure our cause abroad than any of the politicians of Parliamentary rank'. He had made Cambridge 'the scene of the most insidious plot for propagating the Anti-British principles of the Union of Democratic Control'. He had 'corrupted the minds of young people without a knowledge of the realities of life' and would not object 'if his country were trodden into blood and mire by the Prussian jack-boot so long as his *à priori* principles of non-resistance and the superiority of German culture were conceded and applied'.[49]

The British Empire Union went to any lengths to prevent pacifist meetings from taking place, including the use of violence if all else failed. However, other methods did sometimes prevail. In December 1916, for instance, the Union managed to stop Emily Hobhouse, of the Women's International League, from taking part in an exhibition arranged by Sylvia Pankhurst's organization, the Worker's Suffrage Federation. The BEU called the attention of Westminster City Council, responsible for the administration of the hall where the meeting took place, to this fact. The Council thus obtained an undertaking from the Worker's Suffrage Federation that Hobhouse would play no part in the proceedings.[50]

The AGU kept 'a perfectly well-known band of bullies for the purpose of breaking up meetings and wrecking halls' and made use of 'anonymous leaflets, threats over the telephone and forged tickets for the same purposes'.[51] These 'bullies' went into operation in January 1916 in an attempt to prevent the Society of Friends from holding 'Educational and Constructive Meetings on Peace' in their Meeting House in Bishopsgate. This series of gatherings had actually begun in October 1915 and none of the subsequent Monday afternoon meetings faced any interruption until 10 January when C. R. Buxton of the Union of Democratic Control was engaged to speak. However, as he rose to make his address, Richard Glover shouted: 'You're trying to preach pro-Germanism under the cloak of religion. You're a traitor and you ought to be hung by the neck.' Glover's supporters, 'who were evidently present in force', cheered loudly. During the course of the meeting Buxton repeatedly had the charge of 'pro-German' hurled at him and 'was unable to utter two consecutive sentences without interruption'.[52]

Buxton again failed to give his speech planned for the following Monday because his opponents outnumbered his supporters. The meeting degenerated into total pandemonium with the rival factions trying to shout each other down. On 24 January AGU members began to cheer for Kitchener ten minutes before Buxton had even appeared although in the end Buxton did receive some attention when answering questions. The Anti-German Union foiled another attempted meeting on 31 January. Before it began Lindsay Johnson proposed a resolution, 'That we make no terms of peace whatever until Prussian militarism is absolutely and irrevocably crushed'.[53]

At the beginning of February the Society of Friends Peace Committee invited representatives of the AGU to a conference 'with a view to the removal of misunderstanding of the purpose of those Monday afternoon meetings'. But the Union officials refused on the ground that the Society had connections with the Union of Democratic Control. The Quakers held a discussion among themselves at which they agreed to ask the AGU 'to repudiate a threat said to have been made at last Monday's meeting, that a continuance of the gatherings will be prevented by physical force'. The Union seems to have ignored the appeal because the gatherings continued to face opposition. The Society of Friends therefore eventually abandoned the meetings on 13 March.[54]

At the end of 1916 the BEU took part in one of the most violent anti-pacifist demonstrations of the War. The National Council for Civil Liberties planned to hold a conference in Cardiff on 11 November with the aim of discussing industrial conscription, civil liberty and peace negotiations. In early October news of this reached Captain Atherley Jones, the Organizing Secretary of the Welsh Branch of the BEU. During the course of the following month Jones made every effort to prevent the meeting from taking place. He appealed to the local Chief Constable, the 'Competent Military Authority for Cardiff' and the Home Office, but none of these would take any action. Jones also contacted the trustees of the Cory Hall, where the planned meeting would take place, but had no success.

Jones's committee therefore decided to hold two counter-demonstrations: the first in the Wood Street Congregational Church on Friday 10 November and the second in the open air on the following day at the same time as the National Council for Civil Liberties conference. This caused some apprehension to the Chief Constable of Cardiff who contacted the Home Office with a view to cancelling the conference. The latter took no action, however. The Friday evening meeting went ahead as planned. The speakers included C. B. Stanton MP, of the British Workers League, which had also played a part in organizing these events. Stanton declared that he would do all in his power to prevent the Cory Hall conference from taking place. Another MP, Major-General Sir Ivor Herbert, read a letter of support from Lloyd George.

On Saturday morning the Home Office received a telegram from the National Union of Seamen which warned that its members would stop the Cory Hall meeting. Marchers from the Cathays Park counter-demonstration went straight towards the Cory Hall and, led by Stanton and Captain Tupper of the Seamen's Union, forced their way in to join many sympathizers who had earlier entered by simply paying at the door. The National Council for Civil Liberties speakers, who included James Winstone, President of the South Wales Miners' Federation, and Ramsay MacDonald, could not make themselves heard. After destroying the furniture, the invaders took control of the meeting, which concluded with a resolution 'calling on the Government to use all the resources of the nation in a relentless prosecution of the War'. The Chief Constable of Cardiff estimated that about 1,500 people had participated in these events.[55]

In January 1917 members of the BEU played a prominent part in breaking up a meeting in Walthamstow, where the planned speakers included Ramsay MacDonald and Mrs Philip Snowden. As soon as the Chairman began to speak, J. F. Graves, the Secretary of the Walthamstow branch of the BEU, interrupted to declare that the holding of the meeting was 'a disgrace to Walthamstow'. When Mrs Snowden started her own oration the heckling became more general. The proceedings degenerated into chaos with the entry into the hall of a group of Canadian soldiers who took over the platform while fighting broke out elsewhere in the building. Subsequently, all the speakers were forcibly ejected and the opponents of the meeting took it over and made pro-War and anti-pacifist speeches.[56]

The BEU also played a role in the fierce rioting at the meeting held in the Southgate Brotherhood Church in Hoxton on 28 July 1917, an event made famous by Bertrand Russell. The gathering 'was preceded by the posting of notices in local public houses inciting the violence'. It is not possible to say whether the Union printed or distributed these but a local policeman pointed out that opposition to the meeting was aroused 'through the activities of the British Workers National League and the British Empire Union, who have been systematically inciting persons against the Workmens' and Soldiers Council' which had organized the meeting. The policeman concerned also stated that the hostile feeling 'was doubtless accentuated by articles which have recently appeared' in the *Daily Express*, the *Daily Mail* and the *Morning Post*.[57] This whole series of examples shows that the anti-pacifist riots of the war years always had some sort of organization behind them and did not arise spontaneously — an impression given by many contemporary accounts.[58]

The BEU often attacked pacifists in the same breath as 'socialists'; an understandable fact as many of the most prominent peace protestors also played a major part in the Labour movement. Leith of Fyvie wrote that 'there is a mixed body of Pacifists, Socialists, Internationalists, Revolutionists and others, bound together under the ILP and the UDC'. Another senior member of the BEU, F. E. Culling Carr, claimed that individuals such as MacDonald and Snowden might 'pose as Pacifists and Conscientious Objectors, but their main objective is *Revolution*'.[59]

The Union also directed propaganda against 'socialist' ideology and practice in its own right. The idea of industrial action in wartime aroused particular indignation. Robert Blatchford, in an article reprinted in the

Monthly Record, stated that this 'would be an act of treachery, a crime'. He then asserted that workers on the home front faced far more favourable conditions than soldiers on the battlefield.[60] The BEU further attacked the Independent Labour Party for being '"intellectual" in the sense that the vast majority of its prominent members have never done a stroke of manual work in their lives. It is an amalgam of all the foolish, futile 'ics and 'isms which aim at the preventing of an understanding between Capital and Labour, so that talking delegates may fish up something for themselves in troubled waters'.[61]

Captain Parsons compared the ILP with the Russian Communists. In the first place he believed that the Germans controlled both groups. He spoke of 'the Bolshevist principles with which Germany is innoculating the different nations of the earth with whom she is at War'. In this way she had produced 'a simmering state of civil strife' in each power which brought about 'a state of affairs favourable to German domination, German peace, and finally German world power, as in Russia'.

Parsons warned against voting for any of the Labour candidates whom Arthur Henderson proposed to field at a future election because 'the unspeakable hell created by Bolshevik principles in Russia . . . might easily be created here'. He stated that Henderson 'proceeds to propose the suicide of the State by the extinction of that private enterprise upon which our existence, as an economic and military power, is based . . . Russia has done as Mr Henderson wishes on a large scale, and suicide is the result'.[62] But, despite these views, hostility to socialism played only a secondary role in BEU propaganda during the War. Not until the 1920s did it become a primary consideration.[63]

More important at this stage was the Union's desire to see 'a vigorous prosecution of the War'. This meant, for instance, a call for the full use of Britain's sea power. A 'more effectual blockade' should be enforced and British merchant ships should be armed to enable them to 'defend themselves against piratical attacks'. William Le Queux, the popular spy novelist, wrote in the *Monthly Record* that the Government should place enemy aliens upon merchants vessels so that if the German Navy attacked it would injure its own countrymen.[64]

BEU propagandists also wanted air raids on both military and civilian targets. Lord Charles Beresford, at a City meeting in December 1916, said that Zeebrugge, a German submarine base, should come under fire a thousand times 'day and night'. 'We should give our young men the machines they wanted, and tell them to pulverise Zeebrugge. The commonsense man did not pursue hornets with a net, but attacked the nest.' Joynson-Hicks, meanwhile, called for the destruction of 'such places as Frankfurt or Cologne'. At the same time, a Congregational minister supported air reprisals 'not as a measure of vindictiveness, but as a defence; not to inflict suffering on women and children in Germany, but to defend the women and children of England'.[65]

The Union demanded that the Government should not start peace negotiations 'until military defeat had compelled Germany to sue for terms of peace'. MacNeill declared that Britain had to smash the 'brutal bully of Europe upon the blood-stained anvil that he himself has forged'. Only a decisive defeat could prevent another war 'within the passage of a generation' because Germany viewed the present conflict as a 'stepping stone' to obtaining 'finally the Empire of the world'. Furthermore, following the conclusion of peace, 'Germany should, for a period of years, be ostracised, be set outside the pale. Neither in trade nor in social life should we be called upon to meet this generation which William Hohenzollern has set up'. The 'German nation must do penance, and, if possible be purified'.[66]

Ultimately, the British Empire Union wanted to establish:

> a Union of men and women not only in Great Britain but in every portion of the Empire; to foster actively and pursue Imperial ideals; to promote a closer Union, a freer intercourse between all parts of the Empire; to initiate, encourage, and support measures calculated to solidify and strengthen the Empire, and to oppose vigorously all measures antagonistic to these principles.

Furthermore, the BEU desired to see a move away 'from the old habit of merely working for one party or another'. This should be replaced by co-operation 'for one subject — the welfare of the Empire'. But, as with anti-Communism, imperial unity only became a major objective of the organization after 1918.[67]

It is difficult to estimate the importance of the Union during the War. One approach is to examine the number of branches and members it had and to assess the significance of its ideology. During 1917 and 1918 over 50 branches existed nationwide. The most active included Belfast, Farnham, Islington, Oxford and Wandsworth. A majority were situated in middle-class districts. Typical examples include Brighton, Cheltenham, Harrogate, Hastings, Kingston, Reigate, Stroud and Wimbledon. Nevertheless, local organizations could also be found in places such as Glasgow, Islington and Walthamstow. The BEU even had offshoots in other parts of the Empire. In Canada, for instance, Toronto, Montreal, Ottowa, Winnipeg and Calgary all counted members. Furthermore, supporters existed in Hong Kong and Shanghai, while the Bahamas had a membership of 59.[68]

The available evidence does not provide an accurate picture of the overall number of BEU members. Some of the more active branches did have a substantial membership: for instance, in 1917 Belfast's totalled about 300, Glasgow had 400 members and, in the same year, Farnham boasted 300; Brighton claimed 1,300 as early as 1916;[69] and by 1918 the figures had reached 655 in Farnham, 505 in Hampstead, 300 in Croydon, 360 in Southsea, 550 in Edinburgh and 1,000 in Belfast. If we add these together we arrive at a total figure for 1918, from these branches alone, of 3,370. Remembering that over 50 branches existed, we might guess at a substantial national membership of 10,000.[70]

John MacKenzie, referring to the BEU during the 1920s and 1930s, states that 'it was no fringe group' because it counted many establishment figures among its senior members. This was also the case in 1918 when its Vice-Presidents included 25 peers or their wives. Among these we can find the Earl and Countess of Bathurst, Lady Glanusk, the Earl of Harewood and Lord Napier. Furthermore, the Prime Ministers of Australia, New Zealand and Newfoundland acted as patrons.[71]

If one returns to its ideology, it can be seen that the BEU put forward nothing uniquely its own. Colvin's ideas about German domination in the past, for instance, were formulated quite independently from the Union. The question of the 'Hidden Hand' also received attention outside the BEU. The books of Colvin and White on the subject had no connection with the organization. On the question of spreading anti-Germanism, Fleet Street played a more important role than an organization the size of the BEU could. The peak of anti-alien activity in the summer of 1918 would not have been reached without the Northcliffe papers. On 8 July, for instance, the *Evening News* declared on its front page that, 'This is Enemy Alien Week'. At the same time, the press also played a major part in whipping up feeling against pacifists. Furthermore, the BEU's ideas about imperial unity came from the Tariff Reformers. The organization can therefore be seen as a pressure group which unified many of the ideas of the Radical Right during the First World War. Its intense activities certainly played an important cumulative role in stimulating and popularizing anti-German sentiment in Britain. Moreover, its most important activists could certainly be included in any analysis of the Radical Right: Leith of Fyvie, Beresford, Joynson-Hicks and MacNeill.

Such individuals played a major part in propagating Germanophobia to such an extent that it probably affected Britain more than any other form of hostility towards aliens in the country's recent history. During the Great War, British society *en masse* became intolerant towards anything which it believed had the taint of Germany. On a minor level this led to a boycott of German music and art. Worse, naturalized Germans who had spent most of their lives in Britain faced social boycott and constant criticism in the press. Large numbers of poorer Germans, meanwhile, lost their jobs and came under physical attack. The riots against the German community following the sinking of the *Lusitania* developed into a pogrom: they were an attempt to clear out the German community and had the support of establishment figures such as Lord Derby.

Furthermore, the intense feeling created by the First World War meant that any group opposed to the conflict suffered as we have seen with regard to pacifists. Unlike some periods in modern British history, when it played a secondary or more subtle and covert part, intolerance became dominant and blatant between 1914 and 1918, as British society as a whole moulded closer together under the threat of possible military defeat. We can see the foundation of the BEU as an embodiment of this process. Yet it was only one example, and perhaps not the most important, of such a body. Among others we can include the National Party, the British Workers League and the Vigilantes. In fact, we can see the First World War as the high point of the influence of the Radical Right. Despite the attention which this group's activities have attracted during the Edwardian and inter-war years, at neither time did it have a great influence upon government policy. The situation in the Great War was quite different. In the area of enemy aliens legislation, for instance, the Radical Right played a major role. It forced those in authority to introduce wholesale internment and repatriation, to pass vindictive legislation controlling the lives of Germans within Britain, and to confiscate all German property in Britain. As we have indicated, the importance of the Radical Right is part of the same process which led to the growth of intolerance during the Great War. The reason for these developments seems obvious: Britain was under threat. If political extremism grows from economic or political instability, the First World War provided the perfect soil from which it could grow. At various stages during the conflict, Britain was close to defeat. Such instability has rarely occurred in twentieth century British history . Perhaps this best explains why the extreme right became so important during the Great War.

PANIKOS PANAYI
University of Keele

NOTES

I would like to thank Arnd Bauerkämper, Tony Kushner and Kenneth Lunn, who commented upon an earlier version of this article.

1. Robert Benewick, *The Fascist Movement in Britain* (London 1972) pp.39–40; John MacKenzie, *Propaganda and Empire* (Manchester, 1984) pp.156–7.
2. Mackenzie, ibid., p.171, n.16.
3. See, for instance, Alan Gray, *What Price Sanctions Against South Africa?* (London, 1966).
4. Originally entitled the *British Empire Union Monthly Record* (henceforth *Monthly Record*) it became the *Empire Record* in February 1921.
5. *Forest Hill, Sydenham and Penge Examiner*, 16 July 1915. For details of pre-war spy scares see Christopher Andrew, *Secret Service* (London, 1985) pp.34–49. For Maxse see Colin Holmes, *Anti-Semitism in British Society 1876–1939* (London, 1979) pp.71–2.
6. See, for instance, *Monthly Record*, Mar. 1918, p.ii.
7. See Panikos Panayi, 'The Lancashire Anti-German Riots of May 1915', *Manchester Region History Review*, vol.II (1988).
8. *The Times*, 19 June 1915.
9. Imperial War Museum (henceforth IWM), British Empire Union Leaflet, no.23.
10. *Forest Hill, Sydenham and Penge Examiner*, 20, 29 Aug. 1915.
11. *Monthly Record*, May 1917, p.49.
12. Sir George Makgill, 'The War of Liberation: The German Invasion', *English Review*, vol.10 (1915) pp.482–4, 488.
13. *Monthly Record*, Aug. 1917, p.91, Feb. 1918, p.35; *Hampshire Observer*, 9 Feb. 1918.
14. *Monthly Record*, May 1917, p.53, June 1918, p.80.
15. Ibid., July 1917, p.73; *Forest Hill, Sydenham and Penge Examiner*, 13 Aug. 1915.
16. PRO HO45 10765/272100/6.
17. British Empire Union, *Close the German Banks* (London, 1917) p.2.
18. Ibid., p.12.
19. *The Times*, 24 June, 15, 23 July, 17, 18, 19 Nov., 18 Dec. 1915; *Forest Hill, Sydenham and Penge Examiner*, 6 Aug. 1918.

20. *Monthly Record*, Feb. 1917, p.25, Feb. 1918, p.31.
21. *Walthamstow, Leyton and Chingford Guardian*, 4 May 1917; IWM, British Empire Union Leaflet, no.23.
22. *Monthly Record*, July 1918, p.90, Sept. 1918, p.iii
23. Ibid., Feb. 1918, p.31; IWM, British Empire Union Leaflet, no.23.
24. *Sydenham, Forest Hill and Penge Gazette*, 10, 17 Sept., 8 Oct. 1915; *Forest Hill, Sydenham and Penge Examiner*, 24 Sept. 1915; *The Times*, 13 Sept. 1915.
25. *Forest Hill, Sydenham and Penge Examiner*, 8 Oct., 1915.
26. PRO HO45 11006/264762/38.
27. PRO HO45 11006/264762/37.
28. *Hansard* (Commons), 5th ser. LXXXIII, 1054–7, 29 June 1916; IWM, British Empire Union Leaflet, no.13; *Monthly Record*, Dec. 1916, p.2, July 1917, p.72.
29. *Walthamstow, Leyton and Chingford Guardian*, 1 June 1917.
30. *John Bull*, 17 June 1916; Cate Haste, *Keep the Home Fires Burning* (London, 1977) p.129.
31. *Evening News*, 7, 12 June 1916; *The Times*, 14 June 1916; *Monthly Record*, July 1917, p.75.
32. *Putney News-Letter*, 8 June 1917.
33. Ibid.; *The Times*, 14 Dec. 1917.
34. PRO HO45 10756/267450/721.
35. A. J. P. Taylor, *English History 1914–45* (Harmondsworth, 1985 reprint) pp.143–4.
36. *The Times*, 22 July 1918; *Monthly Record*, Aug. 1918, p.108, Sept. 1918, p.120.
37. See, for instance, *Evening News*, 24 Aug. 1918.
38. *The Times*, 26 Aug. 1918; *Evening News*, 24 Aug. 1918; *Monthly Record*, Sept. 1918, p.120. Lloyd George, who was absent when the petition arrived in Downing Street, quickly disposed of it. See Michael MacDonagh, *In London During the Great War* (London, 1935) pp.309–11.
39. See, for instance, *Monthly Record*, Nov. 1918, p.144, Mar, 1919, p.53, June 1919, p.93.
40. The entire proceedings of this meeting are covered by the British Empire Union publication entitled *Close the German Banks*.
41. IWM, Anti-German Union Leaflet, 'Beware'.
42. *Monthly Record*, Feb. 1917, p.24.
43. IWM, British Empire Union Leaflet, no.12.
44. *Monthly Record*, Aug. 1918, p.98.
45. *Belfast News-Letter*, 1 May 1917.
46. *Monthly Record*, Oct. 1917, pp.113, 114. Imperial free trade was 'at present unobtainable'.
47. IWM, Anti-German Union Leaflet, 'Beware'; IWM, British Empire Union Leaflet, no.20; *Forest Hill, Sydenham and Penge Examiner*, 3 Sept. 1915; *Monthly Record*, Jan. 1918, p.iii.
48. *Monthly Record*, June 1917, p.65.
49. Ibid., Jan. 1917, p.16, Feb. 1917, p.28, Apr. 1917, p.46.
50. Ibid., Jan. 1917, p.10.
51. Jo Vellacott, *Bertrand Russell and the Pacifists in the First World War* (Brighton, 1980) p.170.
52. *Standard*, 11 Jan. 1916; *The Times*, 11 Jan. 1916; *Friend*, 17 Mar. 1916.
53. *The Times*, 18, 25 Jan., 1 Feb. 1916; *Christian World*, 27 Jan. 1916.
54. *The Times*, 11, 15 Feb., 7, 14 Mar. 1916; *Friend*, 17 Mar. 1916.
55. PRO HO45 10810/311932/19 and 20.
56. *Monthly Record*, Feb. 1917, p.30; *Walthamstow, Leyton and Chingford Guardian*, 12 Jan. 1917.
57. Vellacott, op. cit., p.170; *Hackney and Kingsland Gazette*, 30 July 1917; *Monthly Record*, Mar. 1918, p.iii; PRO MEPO 3/150.
58. See, for example, the report about the Southgate Brotherhood Church riot in *Hackney and Kingsland Gazette*, 30 July 1917.
59. *Monthly Record*, June 1917, p.65, Mar. 1918, p.43.

60. Ibid., Oct. 1917, p.112.
61. *Monthly Record*, Feb. 1917, p.28.
62. British Empire Union, *No.1. Aims of Labour. By Arthur Henderson. ('Our External and Internal Peril'.) A Reply by Capt. Parsons* (London, 1918) p.5; British Empire Union, *Aims of Labour Series (Reply No.2). The Sovereignty of the World. A Fight for Life or the Peace of Death* (London, 1918) pp.10, 13.
63. See, for instance, British Empire Union, *Danger Ahead* (London, 1922).
64. *Monthly Record*, Jan. 1917, p.14, Apr. 1917, p.47, May 1917, p.52, Mar. 1918, supplement.
65. *Monthly Record*, Jan. 1917, p.14; *Evening News and Southern Daily Mail*, 30 June 1917.
66. *Monthly Record*, July 1917, p.74, Aug. 1917, pp.86–90, May 1918, p.67.
67. IWM, British Empire Union Leaflet, no.15. For the Union's Imperial objectives after the Great War see MacKenzie, op. cit., pp.156–7, 232, 234. See also the numerous publications of James Stanley Little, including, for instance, *The Empire: Folly to Reason* (Bournemouth, 1932).
68. *Monthly Record*, Mar. 1917, June 1917, p.66, Oct. 1917, pp.ii, iii.
69. Ibid., Dec. 1916, p.6, Apr. 1917; *Belfast News-Letter*, 1 May 1917; *Glasgow Herald*, 28 Nov. 1917.
70. *Monthly Record*, Mar. 1918, p.iii, Oct. 1918, p.132; *Belfast News-Letter*, 1 May 1918.
71. MacKenzie, op. cit., p.157; *Monthly Record*, Mar. 1918, p.ii.

III RACISM AND REVISION

Hilaire Belloc and the 'Marconi Scandal' 1900–1914: A Reassessment of the Interactionist Model of Racial Hatred

This study begins by examining, in some detail, the assumptions which lie behind an 'interactionist' model of racial hatred. To date, this theory — with specific regard to recent histories of anti-Semitism and Fascism in Britain — has been largely unchallenged as a self-proclaimed 'revisionist' orthodoxy. The second half of this paper takes the 'Marconi Scandal' (1911–1914), which has often been read in 'interactionist' terms, and offers an alternative reading of this event. In particular, the fiction of Hilaire Belloc, one of the main protagonists of the 'Marconi Scandal', will show how Jews were constructed in ways that anticipated the 'scandal' and supplied an interpretative framework for 'understanding' it in racial terms.

I

In a recent volume of essays, interactionism has been described as a 'revisionist approach to the question of British racism and fascism'.[1] Briefly put, an 'interactionist' or 'convergence' theory of racial conflict derives mainly from sociological theories of 'middleman minorities'. The most influential sociologist in this regard is Edna Bonacich whose work emphasizes that racial hostility can be understood rationally as a 'conflict between the middleman and the host society'.[2] This approach is especially contrasted with psychological theories of scapegoating, where the subject of racial hatred is viewed merely as a projection of the irrational psyche of a prejudiced personality.[3] Interactionists have largely rejected a scapegoat theory of prejudice because, according to this understanding of scapegoating, the 'recipients of hostility' are 'essentially irrelevant to an understanding' of racial conflict.[4] Historians and social scientists who lay claims to 'historical truth', avoid 'moral sentiment' and seek an objective 'analysis' of racism and anti-Semitism, adopt an interactionist model because, in Bonacich's words, they are then able to examine the '"reasonable" point of view' of 'each party to the conflict'.[5] In terms of this model, both the victims and the purveyors of racism are treated as having a 'reasonable' perspective that must be examined in a balanced fashion by the dispassionate historian or social scientist.[6] The rational basis of racial hostility is, therefore, at

the centre of interactionist theory, which concentrates, above all, on
certain objective factors causing minority groups to be the subject of
racial hatred.[7] With regard to anti-Jewish racism, for instance, the
interactionist position can be briefly summarized with the belief that
'we cannot ignore the role of the Jews in the creation of antisemitism'.[8]
A full-length study of British anti-Semitism along interactionist lines,
therefore, points to 'an irreducible core of Jewish involvement' in certain
'Jewish' financial scandals and 'special characteristics' that made Jews
'visible' in the context of specific 'conflict situations'.[9] Elaborating on
this question of 'visibility', it is stated that:

> . . . the tendency displayed by some sections of Jewish communities
> in the Diaspora to retain their own distinctive culture and forms
> of social organization has served at times as a magnetizing factor
> in attracting the attention of nationalistic groups and created
> complications for some sections of Jews in terms of ultimate
> loyalty.[10]

The slippage here from sociological theories of 'middleman minorities'
to the 'distinctive' nature of ethnic 'culture and forms of organization'
demonstrates the ill-defined characterization of the factors which are said
to cause 'irreducible irritations' and result in racial conflict.[11] By claiming
both specific historical events and ethnic 'visibility' as elements in an
interactionist model of social conflict, convergence theorists confuse
the contextualization of anti-Semitism with a coercively assimilationist
construction of racism which argues that ethnic minorities should adopt
the dominant culture to avoid race-hatred.[12]

II

The confusion of ethnic 'visibility' with wider historical processes is
especially apparent in the debate concerning the 'turn to antisemitism'[13]
of the British Union of Fascists (BUF) in the 1930s. Within the last
decade, this debate has been one of the key sites for the promotion of
interactionism.[14] In particular, the economic depression of the 1930s has
been said to have 'heightened the visibility of the Jewish community in
the eyes of their East End opponents'. It is the 'economic, geographical
and cultural separation' of the East End Jewish community that is,
once again, constructed as a factor which, in the context of economic
depression, brought about hostility towards Jews.[15] Yet, as a recent
comparative study of modern anti-Semitism has argued, there is no
direct link between the strength of Jewish communal particularism and
the level of political anti-Semitism.[16] The dangers of the interactionist
model in this regard is that it can easily slip into a theory of 'well-earned'
anti-Semitism where the lack of Jewish assimilation is deemed to be the
reason for racial attacks on Jews.[17] According to this common-sense

argument, anti-Semitism is essentially a 'Jewish problem' which can be eradicated by Jews changing their patterns of behaviour.[18] Taken to its extreme, the interactionist search for 'rational' factors which cause anti-Semitism is not dissimilar from the Mosleyite position which argues that the BUF attacked Jews not on 'account of race or religion' but for 'clearly discernible reasons'.[19] These 'reasons' vary from the role of 'Jewish anti-fascists', who opposed the BUF, to the conspiratorial belief in a Jewish 'drive' to bring about the Second World War.[20] Mosley's biographer, who has adopted an interactionist position, echoes these sentiments and emphasizes that 'there is no doubt that some local Jewish communists were more violent than anything produced by East London or any other branch of British fascism' and that 'a Jewish malaise of [the 1930s] was to be obsessed with fascism'.[21] These are hardly 'objective' statements, but point to a special 'Jewish' propensity for violence and 'obsession' with Nazi Germany which more overt apologists for Mosley have echoed.[22] Most important, just as Mosley claimed that the BUF's anti-Semitism was caused by Jewish anti-Fascists, anti-Semites, in general, have pointed to 'actual' Jewish behaviour as the 'reason' for their hostility to Jews.[23] Thus, a recent familiar defence of Mosley argues that because 'Jews were numerous not only in the Communist Party but in the international banking community', Mosley attacked Jewish Communists and Jewish capitalists on 'political' and not 'racial' grounds.[24] Such casuistry has been repeated by more 'objective' historians.[25]

III

What, however, differentiates a crude interactionism from its more sophisticated counterparts is the construction of a racial 'tradition of hostility' which anti-Semites and other racists can draw upon and which 'transcends' the particular 'reasons' for racial conflict.[26] Sophisticated interactionists postulate this 'tradition' to avoid a crude causal connection between Jewish behaviour and 'host' reaction. Nevertheless, the inter-actionist belief in the 'rational' basis of racial intolerance in any particular circumstance entails a problematized notion of a 'tradition of hostility' within British society. Thus, according to a sophisticated interactionist, anti-Jewish racism occurs 'within a social context in which images of Jews had already been constructed *as a result of previous and, in some cases, ongoing social conflict*'[27] (my emphasis). In these terms, Judeophobia, even though it may transcend a particular 'social conflict', is still related to specific Jewish behaviour; that is, within these terms of 'analysis', Jews remain timeless 'agents within the conflict situation'.[28] An inevitable corollory to the foregrounding of the 'conflict situation' within interactionism is that, for 'convergence' theorists, a tradition of racial hostility is necessarily a secondary, non-determining 'subordinate ideology'.[29] It is a paradox, therefore, that interactionist histories of anti-Semitism both demonstrate the prevalence of the most extreme forms of Judeophobia in British society and yet, at the same time, marginalize this 'tradition' and oppose it to a 'tolerant' liberal state.[30] But this is the logic of a construction of racism based on over-determined 'conflict situations' which, by definition, denies the prevalence of a racial discourse within the state, major political parties and British liberal culture.[31] Because of this paradox, interactionists, therefore, 'debate' the so-called 'turn to antisemitism' of the BUF in the mid-1930s as if British Fascism were not already suffused with race-thinking.[32]

IV

It is worth briefly comparing an interactionist 'tradition of hostility' with the more productive construction of racial discourse in Edward Said's work on Orientalism.[33] Influenced especially by Michel Foucault, Said differs markedly from 'convergence' theorists by emphasizing that racial discourse is, essentially, a series of 'representations', not '"natural" depictions of the Orient'. Said's analysis, therefore, emphasizes '*not* the correctness of [Orientalist] representation' but the determining power of these representations to create the 'Orient' in the consciousness and institutions of the west.[34] It is, in particular, the dimension of power between minority and majority groups in a 'conflict situation' that is missing from interactionist theories. Moreover, in naturalizing racial discourse as a 'reasonable' perspective, interactionism fails to take account of racism as, above all, a social construction and not a 'natural depiction' of minority groups. With these strictures in mind, I now want to make out a case for the determining imprint of racial discourse within British society which was, above all, responsible for the anti-Semitic interpretation of the 'Marconi Scandal' (1911–1914). This, as we have seen, has been represented by interactionists as a 'Jewish' financial scandal with an 'irreducible core of Jewish involvement'.[35] What I want to show is that the 'Marconi Scandal' was, in fact, already 'written' and a part of British racial discourse long before it actually 'happened'. I will make out this case with specific reference to the fiction of Hilaire Belloc, one of the main protagonists of the 'Marconi Scandal'. In these terms, it was not the 'core of Jewish involvement' that 'created' the 'Marconi Scandal' but the racial representations of Jewish financiers already prevalent in British society.

V

The novels of Hilaire Belloc have been described extravagantly as the 'best guide' to an understanding of 'Edwardian politics'.[36] Reinforcing this point, the literary critic, William Empson, has argued that: 'An early stage in the revolt against Parliamentary democracy can be seen in the comic novels of Belloc, written around 1910, largely inspired by the Marconi Scandal'.[37] The comic novels to which Empson refers are *Emmanuel Burden* (1904), *Mr Clutterbuck's Election* (1908), *A Change in the Cabinet* (1909) and *Pongo and the Bull* (1910), even though the 'Marconi Scandal' took place between 1911 and 1914 and thus can hardly be said to have been their source of 'inspiration'. Empson, however, can be forgiven for muddling his chronology when we note the remarkable similarity between Belloc's fictional financial scandals and the 'Marconi Scandal'. Significantly, *Emmanuel Burden*, the first novel in this series, appeared anonymously in instalments from April 1900 onwards, a full decade before the 'Marconi Scandal'.[38] By the turn of the century, Belloc was convinced that a 'small group of Jewish financiers' were masterminding the demand for the retrial of Captain Dreyfus in France and that the Boer War (1899–1902) — rather like the French 'Panama Scandal' (1892–93) — was caused largely by a 'clique of mainly Jewish cosmopolitan' plutocrats.[39] Belloc was, in fact, steeped in French political anti-Semitism which he imported to England with, at first, little success.[40] His 'strident exotic antisemitism' isolated him at Oxford during his student days and made the publisher, A. P. Watt and Son, wary of publishing a novel that could be accused of 'Jew-baiting'.[41] Belloc, therefore, carefully 'revised certain objectionable sections of the novel' and rewrote *Emmanuel Burden* in a tone of almost blanket irony.[42] However, having said that, all of Belloc's main political concerns, which were to preoccupy him throughout his life, are present in this novel. The central figure in *Emmanuel Burden*, for instance, is Mr I.Z. Barnett, a German-Jew who grows in power and influence throughout Belloc's next three novels. By the time of *Pongo and the Bull* (1910), Barnett is the immensely powerful Duke of Battersea, friend, confidante and financial advisor to the Prime Minister of England. And, just as the 'Marconi Scandal' was connected with the Imperial Conference of 1911 — which approved plans for the building of state-owned radio stations throughout the British Empire — the M'Korio Delta scandal in *Emmanuel Burden* was concerned with England's imperial interests in Africa. Both 'affairs' are constructed around the conspiratorial buying of shares by Cabinet Ministers in companies which profit from Britain's imperial expansion. At the centre of Belloc's fictional conspiracy, however, is the dark hand of 'Cosmopolitan Finance' (p.89) which corrupts Emmanuel Burden — an 'honest Englishman and good man' (p.312) — who is the symbol of an innocent Old England. Barnett, by contrast, is 'in some inscrutable way linked with the Fate of England' (pp.66–7) and is one of the 'forces of the modern world' (p.21) which eventually overcomes Burden. That Barnett is 'linked with the fate of England' has the 'force of prophecy' (p.67) for the novel's narrator. Belloc, too, articulated this dark prophetic vision when, as a Liberal Member of Parliament from 1906–1910, he characterized the House of Lords as 'a body which stood as a Committee for the protection of the interests of the modern Anglo-Judaic plutocracy under which they lived'.[43] This belief was confirmed by the ending of *Emmanuel Burden* which sees a triumphant Barnett, now Lord Lambeth, achieving 'more than fortune — true political power, a thing to him worth all the effort of a life' (p.287). It is, in particular, the dire consequences of an all-powerful 'Anglo-Judaic plutocracy' dominating the British political system that is the subject matter of Belloc's next three novels. Stemming directly from Belloc's experiences as a Member of Parliament, these are the novels, presumably, that indicate Belloc's profound 'understanding' of Edwardian politics.

With the publication of *Mr Clutterbuck's Election* (1908), Belloc repeats many of the themes in his earlier novel. The naive Englishman, Mr Clutterbuck, is once again corrupted by the increasingly influential Barnett who, as the aging Duke of Battersea, and President of 'Barnett and Sons' Bank', has the power to 'launch' Clutterbuck 'upon public life' as a Member of Parliament (pp.56–7). As in *Emmanuel Burden*, a financial scandal is at the centre of Belloc's novel. In fact, the 'Anapootra Ruby Mines Scandal' (p.218) eventually makes Clutterbuck see the error of his ways, but not before the 'Peabody Yid' (p.64), as he is known throughout this novel, increases his political power.[44] Where *Mr Clutterbuck's Election* particularly differs from *Emmanuel Burden* is in the introduction of Mr Bailey, an attractive bluff Englishman who, like Belloc, was a one-time rebellious Independent Liberal Member of Parliament. Bailey, in fact, was anticipated in Belloc's previous novel by Mr Abbott, who had correctly unmasked 'conspiracies upon every side'.[45] Bailey, however, has 'gone mad upon the Hebrew race' (p.170) and, more specifically, points to Jewish conspiracies 'upon every side'. He even anticipates the *New Witness* group which 'campaigned' against the 'Marconi Scandal' by organizing meetings of 'protest' about the 'Anapootra Ruby Mines Scandal'. Given that there were a number of prominent members of the *New Witness* circle who had 'gone mad upon the Hebrew race', it is interesting, in this light, to examine Belloc's characterization of the avowedly anti-Semitic Bailey. As David Lodge has argued, Bailey is not simply 'a caricature of the antisemite, put into counterbalance, for the sake of fairness, the portrait of Barnett'.[46] In fact, an example of Bailey's anti-Semitism ironically demonstrates its similarity to Belloc's own beliefs:

> . . . all the great family of Arnold were Jews; half the English aristocracy had Jewish blood . . . every widespread influence, from Freemasonry to the international finance of Europe, was Israelite in his eyes; while our colonial policy, and especially the gigantic and successful struggle in South Africa, he twisted into a sort of petty huckstering, dependent upon Park Lane (pp.179–180).

Two years after this was published, Belloc was to argue in a letter to Oswald John Simon that:

> The existence of the Anglo-Judaic plutocracy seems to me a fact as obvious as the existence of the French Army, or of the House of Commons, or of St. Paul's Cathedral. . . . [T]he command of European finances is mainly in the power of a race alien to Europeans . . .[47]

Belloc's pro-Boer anti-Semitism is well known and he, like Bailey, also Judaized 'the great family Arnold'.[48] Nevertheless, Belloc was to differentiate himself from his fictional character in terms of Bailey's 'fanatical' anti-Semitism. Just as Mosley was to distance himself from the many 'pathological' anti-Semites outside the BUF and base his own attack on Jews on supposedly 'reasonable' 'political' grounds, Belloc was similarly to argue that Jews must be opposed because of the destructive power of 'Jewish Finance' and not merely because of an abhorrence of Jewishness *per se*.[49] Thus, Belloc was to state in an interview in the *Jewish Chronicle* that 'no-one can say with truth that I have ever objected to the practice of Judaism, but I do object most strongly to Jewish cosmopolitan financial influence'.[50] Belloc used this logic to try and control the more 'fanatical' anti-Semites in the *New Witness* circle, such as F. Hugh O'Donnell and Cecil Chesterton:

> . . . It is legitimate to point out . . . the fact that Jewish financial power has prevented people from knowing the truth about the most famous foreign trials where Jews were concerned. But just because these matters so nearly verge upon violent emotion, it is essential to avoid anything like the suspicion of fanaticism. It destroys all one's case and weakens all one's efforts.[51]

Therefore, like Mosley, Belloc was an extreme interactionist who reacted to certain 'facts' about 'Jewish financial power' in a supposedly 'rational' non-fanatical manner. Belloc, moreover, was to articulate some of the main tenets of 'convergence' theory in his book on *The Jews* published in 1922 but largely written over a decade before this.[52] The central theme in this book is that an 'alien' Jewish presence in European culture was a major cause of 'friction' (or anti-Semitism) in Europe because of the antagonistic 'interests of the two races'.[53] This argument, I would suggest, is similar in its logic to 'convergence' theorists who postulate an inevitable conflict of interests between 'visible' ethnic communities and the 'host' community. However, Belloc can undoubtedly be distinguished from post-war interactionism in that he consistently went beyond the logic of a theory of 'well-earned' anti-Semitism and promoted a wide range of Jewish conspiracy theories. Throughout his life, for instance, he believed that, because of the Dreyfus Affair, Jews helped weaken France before the First World War.[54] Like Mosley, who argued that there was a Jewish 'drive' to bring about the Second World War, Belloc's 'emotions' could not be contained by his own 'rational' perspective on 'the Jews'. This can be seen especially in *Pongo and the Bull* (1910), which was published a year before the 'Marconi Scandal'.

Interestingly, *Pongo and the Bull* eschews the ironic tone of Belloc's previous novels. Set in a degenerative future, the novel constructs a world where the Duke of Battersea is 'the very centre' of British political life, largely because his 'name alone could support the credit of the country' (p.18). Relying on Battersea, the Government needs to raise an enormous loan to stem an uprising in India. Battersea is in a strong position to negotiate as he points to the difficulty of the Government's position with 'one allusion after another to the gradual decline of the borrowing power of the government . . .' — a decline, it is implied, which Battersea helped to create (p.70). In a clear reference to the House of Rothschild, as well as anticipating Marconi, Battersea wants to include various relations in the loan: 'There iss my brother Chames . . . You know Chames . . . and sohn also. Well! Each most know!' (p.70). For the first time, the alien 'racial' nature of Battersea's 'old usurer's heart' (p.74) is articulated by Belloc without an 'antisemitic' intermediary:

> . . . the Duke of Battersea . . . lay in Battersea House not yet asleep. He was feeding internally and nourishing his soul upon Dolly [The Prime Minister] and the Indian Loan. He held Dolly between his spatulated forefinger and his gross thumb. But then he did not understand blood which was not his own, nor what sympathies might arise between men of one race and one society. (p.90).

The vampire imagery of the parasitic Battersea 'feeding internally' on the British government is reinforced by Belloc's reference to Battersea as of another 'blood'. In an article on the 'Jewish Question', written in *The Eye Witness* in 1911, Belloc again expresses such imagery: '. . . it is an unfortunate but unquestionable fact that everywhere a sort of Jew presents himself to the public view, not only as an oppressor of the poor, but an alien oppressor — an oppressor incapable of understanding the feelings of those he oppresses.'[55] Significantly, the plot of *A Change in the Cabinet* was predicated on a Cabinet Minister 'of English lineage' being turned insane at the 'immoral' way in which he makes money out of politics.[56] For Belloc, therefore, the worst aspects of plutocratic power were represented by a dominant racial 'alien oppressor . . . incapable of understanding the feelings of those he oppresses'.

VI

By 1910, figures such as Mr Barnett were, for the first time, Cabinet Ministers in a Government that was considered 'the most corrupt in British history' well '*before* the so-called Marconi Scandal broke'.[57] As Ken Lunn has demonstrated:

. . . the scandal was only part of a much wider campaign [in the *Witness*] against Jews, and, in particular, against Jewish wealth and power. In this context, it might be added that attacks on Rufus Isaacs, Herbert Samuel and other Jewish politicians whose names became linked with financial scandals, had begun long before rumours of corruption in connection with the Marconi contract became widespread.[58]

As both the editor of *The Eye Witness* and as a novelist, Belloc clearly contributed to these 'rumours of corruption' and a common belief in 'alien' Jews undermining British political life. For Belloc, to say the least, there was a large element of self-fulfilment in these racial constructions which, as Lunn has argued, 'helped to create the Marconi Scandal'.[59] Interactionism, by concentrating on the particular 'conflict situations', fails to take account of the fact that these representations of Jews saturated all aspects of British society long before they were institutionalized by particular 'antisemitic' groups or individuals. As I have shown, the logic of 'convergence', in its most extreme form, inevitably leads to a theory of 'well-earned' anti-Semitism where racial hostility is constructed purely as a reaction to 'minority' behaviour.[60] Instead of blaming the victim, however, I would suggest an alternative perspective which concentrates on a racial discourse which is not confined to extremist groups or individuals but is a part of the 'social, political and economic contexts' of British culture as a whole.[61] It was, above all, the determining imprint of this discourse that 'caused' the anti-Semitic interpretation of the 'Marconi Scandal' and not the 'irreducible core of Jewish involvement'. In other words, the 'Marconi Scandal' was constructed out of a racial discourse that was already in place and which could be drawn upon by all sections of British society. It was this discourse that was able to 'explain' Asquith's administration as the apotheosis of 'corruption'. For some, such as the *New Witness* group, the racial otherness of the Jewish Cabinet Ministers in this administration also 'explained' Asquith's inability to deal with the very real problems besetting Imperial Britain in the years leading up to the First World War.

BRYAN CHEYETTE
University of Leeds

NOTES

I would like to thank David Cesarani and Tony Kushner for their invaluable help during the writing of this paper. As is usual, the author takes full responsibility for its contents.

1. Kenneth Lunn and Richard C.Thurlow (eds.), *British Fascism* (London, 1980) p.15 and 'Introduction' passim.
2. Edna Bonacich, 'A Theory of Middleman Minorities', *American Sociological Review*, vol.38 (1973) pp.589, 583–594. See also Bonachich's, 'A Theory of Ethnic Antagonism: the Split Labour Market', *American Sociological Review*, vol.37 (1972) pp.547–59.
3. Bonacich, 'A Theory of Middleman Minorities', op. cit., p.589.
4. Colin Holmes, *Anti-Semitism in British Society 1876–1939* (London, 1979) p.31. For a repetition of these views see Robert Skidelsky, 'Reflections on Mosley and British Fascism' in Lunn and Thurlow (eds.), op. cit. p.84.
5. Bonacich, 'A Theory of Middleman Minorities', op. cit. p.589. See also Skidelsky, op. cit., p.79, and Holmes, op. cit., pp.1, 227.
6. Colin Holmes's 'Anti-Semitism and the BUF' in Lunn and Thurlow, (eds.), op. cit., p.120 echoes Bonacich when he argues that anti-Semitism 'arose out of . . . a conflict of interests, when each side believed it had a reasonable point of view'.
7. Holmes 'Anti-Semitism and the BUF', op. cit., p.130 and passim.
8. Ibid., p.128
9. Holmes, *Anti-Semitism in British Society*, op. cit., pp.81, 100–101.
10. Ibid., p.186.
11. The phrase 'irreducible irritations' is taken from J. Higham, 'Antisemitism in the Gilded Age', *Mississippi Valley Historical Review* vol.43 (1956–7) p.566 and qualified by Holmes in his *John Bull's Island: Immigration and British Society 1871–1971* (London, 1988) p.301. For a comparison with the strident interactionism of Holmes's previous work see *Anti-Semitism in British Society*, op. cit., p.231.
12. For a study of coercive assimilationism in a Jewish context see Bill Williams, 'The Anti-Semitism of Tolerance: Middle-Class Manchester and the Jews 1870–1900' in A.J. Kidd and K.W. Roberts (eds.), *City, Class and Culture: Studies of Social Policy and Cultural Production in Victorian Manchester* (Manchester, 1985) pp.74–102.
13. Richard Thurlow, *Fascism in Britain* (Oxford, 1987) p.104.
14. Lunn and Thurlow, op. cit., ch.1 and 5–9.
15. Holmes, 'Anti-Semitism and the BUF', op. cit., p.120.
16. Todd Endelman, 'Comparative Perspectives on Modern Anti-Semitism in the West' in D. Berger (ed.), *History and Hate: The Dimensions of Anti-Semitism* (Philadelphia, 1986) pp.111–12. For a recent debate along these lines see Jacob Katz 'Misreadings of Anti-Semitism', *Commentary*, vol.76 (July 1983) pp.39–44 and vol.76 (Dec. 1983) pp.30, and 32–33.
17. For this argument see Tony Kushner, *The Persistence of Prejudice: Anti-Semitism in British Society During the Second World War* (Manchester, 1989) p.5 and 'Introduction' passim.
18. Ibid., p.92.
19. Oswald Mosley, *My Life* (London, 1968) pp.336–7.
20. Ibid., pp.338–9 and ch.18 passim. Mosley argues in this chapter that 'there was no shadow of suspicion that we were an anti-semitic movement when Jews attacked our Olympia meeting . . .' (p.338) and that, quoting one of his contemporary speeches, 'the organised power of Jewry, in a racial interest, has consistently striven for the last eighteen months and more to foster the policy of war . . .' (p.339).
21. Robert Skidelsky, *Oswald Mosley*, (London, 1975) pp.380, 397.
22. See, for instance, Diana Mosley, *Loved Ones: Pen Portraits by Diana Mosley* (London, 1985) p.186, and Mosley op. cit. p.338. Interestingly, Diana Mosley includes the Jewish artist, Mark Gertler, in the pantheon of extremely 'violent' Jews in *Loved Ones*, p.22.
23. Mosley, op. cit., p.338. Skidelsky in his *Oswald Mosley*, op. cit., p.381 echoes the Mosleyite position when he argues that the BUF became anti-Semitic in the 1930s because of 'the attitude of Jews themselves, and they must take a large share of the blame for what subsequently happened'. This position is slightly qualified in his 'Reflections on Mosley and British Fascism', op. cit., pp.78–99.

24. Jonathan Guinness, *The House of Mitford*, (London, 1984) p.336. Guinness's mother is Diana Mosley.
25. Skidelsky in his 'Reflections on Mosley and British Fascism', op. cit., p.86 distinguishes between 'political' and 'biological or religious' anti-Semitism and associates Mosley with the former.
26. Holmes, *Anti-Semitism in British Society*, op. cit., pp.136, 190.
27. Ibid., p.231.
28. Ibid.
29. Holmes, 'Anti-Semitism and the BUF', op. cit., p.127.
30. Holmes, *Anti-Semitism in British Society*, op. cit., pp.104–5, 226.
31. For a critique along these lines see Williams, 'The Anti-Semitism of Tolerance', op. cit., passim, D. Cesarani, 'Anti-Alienism in England after the First World War', *Immigrants and Minorities*, vol.6 (Mar.,1987) pp.22–3, Kushner, *The Persistence of Prejudice*, ch.5 and my 'Jewish Stereotyping in English Literature 1875–1920: Towards a Political Analysis' in T. Kushner and K. Lunn (eds.), *Traditions of Intolerance: Historical Perspectives on Fascism and Race Discourse in British Society* (Manchester, 1989) pp.12–32.
32. Thurlow, op. cit., pp.104–111 writes explicitly from a 'convergence' perspective on this matter and distinguishes between the BUF's 'anti-Jewish sentiments' and 'full-scale political anti-semitism' (pp.105, 107). John Vincent convincingly argues that there was nothing new in Mosley's anti-Semitic appeal in the 1930s, *Times Literary Supplement*, 4 Apr. 1975, p.351.
33. Edward Said, *Orientalism* (London, 1978).
34. Ibid., pp.21, 1–28 passim.
35. Holmes, *Anti-Semitism in Britain Society*, op. cit., p.81. Holmes also points to the 'identifiable core of grievances' which the BUF had against 'certain Jewish interests in the East End', idem., p.190.
36. A.J.P. Taylor, 'Introduction', Donald Read (ed.), *Edwardian England* (London, 1982) p.12.
37. 'Introduction' in John Harrison, *The Reactionaries: A Study of the Anti-Democratic Intelligentsia* (New York, 1966) p.9. All quotations from Hilaire Belloc's fiction are taken from the original London editions and cited within the text.
38. Robert Speaight, *The Life of Hilaire Belloc* (London, 1957) p.151.
39. Jay P. Corrin, *G.K. Chesterton and Hilaire Belloc: The Battle Against Modernity* (London, 1981) pp.14, 23. This is by far the best book on Belloc's politics.
40. Speaight, op. cit., pp.97, 120–121, 184 and Corrin, op. cit., pp.215, 218–219 has evidence of Belloc's involvement with and influence by Paul Deroulede's *Ligure des Patriotes*, Charles Maurras's *Action Française* and Eduard Drumont, the author of *La France Juive: Essai d'Histoire contemporaine* (1886).
41. Speaight, op. cit., p.97 and Corrin op. cit., p.24.
42. Corrin, op. cit., p.24 and Speaight, op. cit., pp.181–182.
43. Quoted in *The Times*, 23 Feb. 1910 and the *Jewish Chronicle*, 11 Mar. 1910, p.14.
44. The term 'Peabody Yid' derives from the four per cent model dwellings which Lord Rothschild constructed in London. For this see Hilaire Belloc, *Pongo and the Bull* (London, 1910) p.18 and Jerry White, *Rothschild Buildings* (London, 1981).
45. *Emmanuel Burden* (London, 1904) p.89.
46. David Lodge, 'The Chesterbelloc and the Jews' in his *The Novelist at the Crossroads* (London, 1971) p.151.
47. Letter to Oswald John Simon, 2 Mar. 1910 cited in the *Jewish Chronicle*, 11 Mar. 1910, p.14.
48. Lodge, op. cit., pp.150, 156.
49. For Mosley's relationship to extreme anti-Semitism see Richard Thurlow, *Fascism in Britain*, op. cit., ch.4. The comparison between Belloc and Mosley is worth exploring further, especially given the rapprochement between Belloc's 'Distributism' and the BUF in the 1930s.
50. *Jewish Chronicle*, 'The Jewish Question: Interview with Hilaire Belloc, MP', 12 Aug. 1910, p.14.

51. Letter to Maurice Baring, 27 Aug. 1913. Cited in Speaight, op. cit., p.362. For
     O'Donnell's relations with Belloc see Kenneth Lunn, 'The Marconi Scandal and
     Related Aspects of British Anti-Semitism, 1911–1914' (unpublished PhD thesis,
     University of Sheffield, 1978) ch.5 and 6. Lunn's thesis is by far the best account
     of the 'Marconi Scandal'.
52. Kenneth Lunn, 'Political Anti-Semitism Before 1914: Fascism's Heritage?', in Lunn
     and Thurlow (eds.), op. cit., p.28, makes out a case for 'the pattern of thought' of
     Belloc's post-war writings on 'the Jews' being 'clearly established by 1911'. Belloc
     himself confirms this argument by declaring as early as 1910 that 'he has taken an
     increasing interest in the Jewish question, and that he proposes to write a book on
     it', *Jewish Chronicle*, 25 Feb. 1910, p.8.
53. *Jewish Chronicle*, 'Interview', op. cit., p.14 and Hilaire Belloc, *The Jews* (London,
     1922) p.3 and ch.4–6. Belloc idem., p.159 summarizes his extreme interactionism:
     'The Anti-Semitic movement is essentially a reaction against the abnormal growth
     in Jewish power, and the new strength of Anti-Semitism is largely due to the Jews
     themselves'.
54. Corrin, op. cit., p.14. Interestingly, both biographers of Belloc take an interactionist
     position when discussing Belloc's anti-Semitism. Speaight, op. cit., p.184 argues
     that 'Jewish financial power did, very often, cut a repellent figure' and that Jewish
     plutocrats engaged in 'irresponsible speculations'. A.N. Wilson, *Hilaire Belloc*
     (London, 1984) pp.195–200, argues in similar terms to Belloc that the 'Marconi
     Scandal' 'stinks' and that Cecil Chesterton failed 'to check his facts, or to investigate
     the villainous five with sufficient rigour' (p.197). Instead he 'phrases his accusations in
     hysterical anti-Jewish language; [and] spoilt, forever, an investigation which needed
     making and which could, with more subtlety, have toppled his enemies' (p.199).
55. *The Eye Witness*, 31 Aug. 1911. Cited in Lunn, op. cit., unpublished PhD thesis,
     p.185.
56. In *Mr Clutterbuck's Election* (London, 1908) p.202, Belloc argues that 'the occasions
     on which it is possible to bring against a man *of English lineage* the grave accusation
     of hampering with political morals are very rare . . .' (my emphasis).
57. G.R. Searle, 'Critics of Edwardian Society: The Case of the Radical Right',
     in Alan O'Day (ed.), *The Edwardian Age* (London, 1978) p.91. Significantly,
     G.K. Chesterton continued to believe this throughout his life. See, for example,
     G.K. Chesterton, *Autobiography* (London, 1936) p.202.
58. Lunn, op. cit., unpublished PhD thesis, p.200.
59. Lunn, 'Political Anti-Semitism Before 1914', in Lunn and Thurlow op. cit., p.23.
60. The absence of any detailed analysis of the Jewish community in Colin Holmes's
     Anti-Semitism in British Society, op. cit., accounts for what has been called the
     'uneasy balance' in this book which is 'devoted in the main to anti-semites and
     their arguments'. For these comments, see the review of Holmes's work by Ken
     Lunn in *Social History* vol.6. (May 1981) pp.257–259. This 'imbalance' has been
     somewhat rectified by Holmes in his recently published *John Bull's Island*, op. cit.,
     pp.275–317.
61. Todd Endelman, 'Comparative perspectives on Modern Anti-Semitism in the West',
     p.112. For a broad analysis of racial discourse in British culture see my *Jewish
     Representations in English Literature and Society 1875–1925: A Study in Semitism*
     (forthcoming).

Beyond the Pale? British Reactions to Nazi Anti-Semitism, 1933–39

The reactions of the British people to the persecution of the Jews in Nazi Europe have received scant attention. The little that has been written has stressed the sympathy generated by the atrocities at the cost of disguising the complexity of the responses that emerged before 1939. In contrast this article suggests that anti-Semitism of a liberal and conservative variety helped to shape reactions in Britain. Moreover it argues that liberal attitudes towards Jews determined both refugee policy and the treatment of refugees in Britain and ultimately caused government and public alike to misinterpret the full horror and significance of the holocaust.

'Englishmen of all classes and of all parties were offended by the Nazi treatment of the Jews . . . [It] did more than anything else to turn English moral feeling against Germany, and this moral feeling in turn made English people less reluctant to go to war.' Here A.J.P. Taylor provides a classic liberal analysis of British reactions to Nazi anti-Semitism during the 1930s. Taylor does not ignore the existence of hostility to Jews in Britain — indeed, he believes 'there was a good deal of quiet anti-semitism in England'. Nevertheless such antipathy, he argues, did not affect the revulsion of the British public to Nazi anti-Semitic barbarity. Moreover Taylor believes that Nazi persecution of Jews helped remove native anti-Semitism, even if somewhat reluctantly: 'some English people were no doubt . . . annoyed at having to repudiate the anti-semitism which they had secretly cherished'.[1] This essay will seek to qualify Taylor's assumptions. First it will suggest that, while there was widespread disgust at Nazi treatment of Jews, British reactions were far more complex than Taylor leads us to believe. Furthermore these reactions can only be understood in terms of a specifically British discourse which included anti-Semitism of a liberal and conservative nature. Second it will argue that British anti-Semitism was more tenacious than Taylor and others have allowed for. It must be emphasized that these issues are not simply of theoretical concern — a detailed examination of them enables a sophisticated analysis of British responses to the Jewish catastrophe. In addition it calls into question the common assumption that the holocaust destroyed British anti-Semitism or at least pushed it beyond the pale of respectability.[2]

It is vital, therefore, before examining the specific reactions and responses to the Jewish plight in the 1930s, to analyse briefly the nature of British anti-Semitism. Until recently, few historians took the existence of modern hostility to Jews in Britain seriously. Since the late 1970s, however, several monographs and articles have been devoted to the subject. How have these writings affected the perception of British anti-Semitism? Have we moved, to paraphrase Jonathan Sarna, 'from the myth that Britain is different to the myth that Britain is not different at all'?[3] On one level — that of the existence of an anti-Semitic tradition in Britain — no clear consensus exists. Bill Williams, Colin Holmes and, in a much more limited and narrow way, Gisela Lebzelter, have argued for such a tradition.[4] Geoffrey Field and, to a lesser extent, Lloyd Gartner and Todd Endelman take a different line, suggesting that it is wrong to waste too much time in trying to trace what they perceive as a weak and subterranean theme in British history — one that they suggest has made no political impact whatsoever.[5] On another level — that of the *nature* of British anti-Semitism — there is greater agreement among these scholars. To Field it is 'a particular form of anti-Semitism, a vague expression of national and class fears, allied to strong ethnocentric feeling in general'. Holmes also sees it as a vague and 'amorphous antipathy'. In similar fashion Endelman has emphasized the unsystematic and apolitical nature of British anti-Semitism throughout the nineteenth and twentieth centuries. Field in particular contrasts the 'less ideological and less political' English style with Continental anti-Semitism which could lead to either mass anti-Semitic parties in Germany or the Dreyfus case in France. 'There was nothing equivalent in England' concludes Field.[6]

This approach, which emphasizes the lack of an *illiberal* tradition of anti-Semitism in Britain has been challenged by a more radical group of historians of Anglo-Jewry. In particular Bill Williams has argued that the driving force of British anti-Semitism, and racism in general, is to be found within the dominant liberal culture. Williams identifies a pressure on Jews to conform which he labels 'the antisemitism of tolerance'. He describes the workings of this process on late Victorian Manchester, and how in practice it acted to control the lives of both Anglicized middle-class and immigrant working-class Jews in this great northern town. Similarly, at the level of the liberal state, David Cesarani has illustrated how the Home Office imposed an immigration policy in the 1920s aimed particularly at Jewish aliens. Through the 1919 Aliens Act the British government succeeded in deporting hundreds of 'subversive' Jews. Cesarani thus questions Field's assumption that 'only the periphery of politics was ever affected by anti-Semitism'. Bryan Cheyette also questions the nature of British tolerance and identifies a fundamental ambivalence towards Jews within British culture, clearly evident in mainstream English literature.[7] In the works of the popular socialist author H.G. Wells, Cheyette sees the liberal 'antisemitism of tolerance' philosophy in operation. Indeed Wells' reaction to the holocaust is most revealing in this context and will be examined later.[8]

In my own work, while making necessary allowance for the confusing evidence that the historian of anti-Semitism in Britain often has to face, I have emphasized the *ideological* nature of this most persistent of British prejudices.[9] This was most clearly evident in its organized forms, such as the 'Chesterbelloc' school or the British Union of Fascists in the 1930s. This tradition of extremist anti-Semitism has been well-documented, but its relationship to mainstream culture is left relatively unexplored.[10] Belloc and Mosley adhered to an exclusionist, or what I will call conservative analysis of the Jewish question — that the Jews were a powerful, dangerous and alien force in British society. Belloc's solution was apartheid, Mosley's expulsion. For either, to be both British and Jewish was a contradiction in terms. Neither Belloc nor Mosley found much *active* popular support for their anti-Semitism. Nevertheless the contemporary literature and social surveys of the 1930s and 40s do suggest that most people in Britain saw the Jews, even British-born Jews as somehow foreign.[11] Moreover many (on the left as well as the right) believed that Jews exercized inordinate power in society.[12] Such anti-Semitism did not find its outlet in the form of a mass political party but it did lead to Jews being excluded from many sections of British society in the inter-war period, and on a state level to a highly selective immigration policy with regard to possible Jewish entrants.[13] This 'conservative' anti-Semitism was rarely justified using purely racist language. It was, as Field suggests, less precise tending towards ethnocentricity. It does *not* follow that it was therefore non-ideological. Certainly its impact on Anglo-Jewry in terms of exclusion could be quite profound.[14]

This, however, represented only one aspect of the hostility that Jews in Britain had to face. Indeed, more dominant in that pressure was a liberal discourse demanding that the Jew should assimilate totally into British society.[15] The theory was that of an unwritten emancipation contract which could be summarized as follows: Britain was a tolerant society and was thus opposed to the *intolerance* of anti-Semitism. The Jew, in return for his total acceptance in Britain, would remove any distinctiveness. The corollary of this, however, was that if anti-Semitism persisted after emancipation then it was the Jew's own responsibility. This philosophy, which ultimately blamed Jewish behaviour for the existence of anti-Semitism, I will call here liberal or assimilationist anti-Semitism. Few would articulate its logic as clearly as did H.G. Wells in his belief that the concept of the 'Chosen People' provoked anti-Semitism, but many (in fact a large majority according to Mass Observation) were convinced by Wells' arguments.[16] In short, what is being suggested is that there was a theoretical framework from which the British public would evaluate the events that took place in Nazi Europe. Only by referring to these ideological traditions can one understand the complicated and, on the surface, often contradictory reactions to the persecution of the Jews in the 1930s.[17]

Without such an analytical device, generalizations in this important subject are made almost impossible. One is left only with the confusion that emerges from the study of the reactions of diverse individuals —

an approach that tends to emphasize only psychological quirks, rather than meaningful trends.[18] Indeed, as Martin Gilbert and others have indicated, there was no *clear* link between personal relationships with Jews in Britain and attitudes to the Nazi persecution of the Jews of Europe.[19] Within the individual there was often a contradictory impulse that both demanded of the Jew that he keep apart from Gentile society yet also perceived that the solution to the 'Jewish question' was for the Jew to move closer and remove his alleged exclusivity.

The duality is neatly illustrated by the case of Sir Horace Rumbold, British Ambassador to Berlin, 1928–1933. There is no doubting Rumbold's profound xenophobia — a distrust of foreigners that contained a specific anti-Semitic element. On a social level he disliked Jews and he also accused the Jews in Europe of intrigue, profiteering and spreading the plague of Bolshevism.[20] Rumbold, despite his world travels, disdained foreigners and, ultimately, to him, Jews were an irritant and 'an alien race'. Berlin, wrote Rumbold in 1928, was a fine city but 'the only fly in the ointment is the number of Jews in the place. One cannot get away from them'.[21] With this attitude, and his admiration of the nationalist aspects of the Nazi programme, it might be assumed that Rumbold would have been an admirer of Hitler's movement. In fact his biographer, Martin Gilbert, suggests that he was appalled by its anti-Semitism and 'never deflected from his view that Nazism was evil'.[22]

This was reflected in two important memoranda sent to Sir John Simon, the Foreign Secretary, in late March and early April 1933, where Rumbold revealed a profound understanding of Nazi anti-Semitism. As he wrote on 28 March 1933: 'The Jewish community in [Germany] are faced with a much more serious danger than mere bodily maltreatment or petty persecution'.[23] The two dispatches do, however, also indicate the complexity of Rumbold's views on 'The Jewish problem'. In explaining the Nazi regime's anti-Semitism, Rumbold emphasized two factors. First he stressed Jewish behaviour in pre-Nazi Europe: Rumbold believed that the Jews held a monopoly over many of the professions, as well as controlling the finance, arts and newspapers of the country.[24] It is vital, nevertheless, to recognize that Rumbold did not provide a blanket criticism of pre-1933 Jewish activities. Rumbold was at pains to differentiate *types* of Jews and his strongest language was reserved for the post-war Jewish immigrant to Germany — 'a most undesirable type of Hebrew reached the larger cities'. It was these Russian and Galician Jews with their profiteering and Bolshevism that *created* so much anti-Semitism in Germany during the 1920s, according to Rumbold. What he then perceived in 1933 was that 'the best elements in the Jewish community will now have to suffer and are suffering for the sins of the worst'.[25]

Rumbold, perhaps more aware than any other leading British civil servant of the extent and true nature of Nazi anti-Semitism in 1933, still adhered to a liberal critique of Jewish behaviour. 'Bad' Jews, by remaining apart from the German people, and exploiting 'their racial superiority', had created anti-Semitism in a post-emancipation society.[26] Yet Rumbold, who shared Hitler's disgust at the East European Jew and who harboured fears of Jewish power, could not accept the validity of Nazi anti-Semitism. This brings us to the second factor in Rumbold's account of the persecution of the Jews — Hitler's *obsession* with the Jewish peril.

From studying the speeches of the Fuhrer and a close reading of *Mein Kampf*, Rumbold was aware that Hitler subscribed 'to the most violent anti-Semitic principles' and that his hatred of Jews went beyond rationality. *Mein Kampf* 'teem[ed] with contradictions and misconceptions'.[27] He realized that Hitler's anti-Semitism represented a total world view and was thus unacceptable to Rumbold. Rumbold was certainly not above making powerful racial categorizations, but he objected to the all-encompassing racism of Hitler. Indeed Rumbold was one of the first to grasp the essential nature Nazi anti-Semitism, that its objection to the Jew was racial and not religious in origin.[28] The Ambassador believed that through a breakdown in German society, due primarily to the economic crisis, Hitler was able to translate the latent anti-Semitism of the German populace into a political programme. At first Rumbold's two explanations appear contradictory but, within his own ideology, the two could be harmonized. The Jews, or more specifically 'a comparatively limited number of persons, mostly immigrants', had acted as an irritant and made the whole German Jewish community unpopular. Many Jews were, however, good Germans who were 'industrious and valuable' in Rumbold's words. A good German was, of course, inferior to the Englishman, who 'always has a better sense of fair play than a foreigner'.[29] But a bad alien Jew in Germany was beyond the pale; his behaviour could be said to be simply un-English. The same, however, could be said of Nazi anti-Semitism — it was wrong, unfair and unsporting because it was totally indiscriminate. As he wrote to his son in May 1933, he could not accept Nazism because he was 'a convinced believer in the liberty of the subject'.[30] The apparent paradox of Rumbold's attitudes is thus explained, as is his persistent intolerance of alleged Jewish misbehaviour. Rumbold was capable of seeing the implications of Nazi anti-Semitism, but he was unable to shake off his adherence to a 'well-earned' theory of prejudice or to change his hostile attitudes in the light of the persecution of the Jews. To summarize: while Hitler and Rumbold shared certain perceptions about Jews, the latter believed that actual persecution was unnecessary and revealed the inferiority and potential barbarity of the foreigner. Ultimately Rumbold adhered to a liberal ideology — he did not believe that *all* Jews should be excluded from society.

Winston Churchill's views follow a similar pattern. Visiting Hitler's friend Hanfstaengl in the summer of 1932 Churchill asked 'why is your chief so violent about the Jews? I can quite understand being angry with Jews who have done wrong or are against the country, and I understand resisting them if they try to monopolize power in any walk of life; but what is the sense of being against a man simply because of his birth? How can any man help how he is born?' Churchill, who had voiced his own concerns about world Jewish power in the early 1920s was now rejecting the obsessive and irrational anti-Semitism of Hitler.[31]

Churchill, Rumbold and individuals such as Harold Nicolson (who had seen the rise of Nazism as a Counsellor of the British Embassy in Berlin from 1927 to 1929)[32] were in the small minority of people in Britain, including sections of the Anglo-Jewish community, who recognized from the start the potential of Nazi anti-Semitism. However, if they were in advance of public opinion in this way, it does not follow that the vast majority of the British people did not share all three statesmen's revulsion at Nazi anti-Semitism. The violence and humiliation associated with the Nazi boycott of Jewish shops in April 1933, the attacks on Austrian Jewry during the Anschluss and, more than anything else, the sheer butchery of the Kristallnacht pogrom in November 1938 brought vocal and widespread denunciations from the British public. To illustrate this point, the case of David Lindsay, Earl of Crawford and a man with strong antipathy to Jews, is revealing. In June 1939 Lindsay remarked that the *Protocols* [of the Elders of Zion] whether Jewish in origin or not, at least provide a definite programme for Jewry today' yet six months before he stated that 'the [Kristallnacht] pogrom now in progress makes me ill'.[33] The sincerity of this widespread British disgust is not in question. Nevertheless it is important to analyse the *nature* of this revulsion and particularly to examine its impact in the long term.

Andrew Sharf has commented with regard to Kristallnacht that 'it can never be emphasized too often that the dominant note struck by the British Press in the presence of Nazi anti-Semitism was one of genuine moral outrage' — murder was murder and could not be condoned.[34] Moreover the press and public were profoundly shocked by the pogrom. Only those, such as Blanche Dugdale, a leading non-Jewish Zionist in Britain, who intimately followed the plight of the Jews, were not surprised by the intensity of the violence.[35] For the vast majority of the British population the reaction was one of shock, compounded with a total failure to comprehend *why* the pogrom had occurred. It has been suggested that the press desperately sought a rational motive — 'somewhere, somehow, there had to be a more reasonable explanation than the deliberate decision of a Government to abandon civilized behaviour'.[36] But the events of Kristallnacht, with the destruction of synagogues, Jewish property, the mass arrest of at least 30,000 Jews and the loss of many lives would, by necessity, thwart such explanations. The net result was incredulity. David Lindsay wrote after the pogrom that there was 'so little cause for it whereas if anything of the kind took place here one would know that the Jews contribute much too high a proportion of the criminal classes'. To 'Chips' Channon MP 'The Jewish persecutions carried to such a fiendish degree are short-sighted, cruel and unnecessary'.[37] The significant word in this context is *unnecessary*.

Channon and Lindsay were social anti-Semites (or, in their own terms, hostile to negative Jewish traits or influences) who did not need to resort to violence. Nazi anti-Semitism remained a mystery to many in Britain because it *could not* be justified in terms of a response to Jewish behaviour. Social ostracism and 'polite' discrimination were acceptable but mass murder could not be rationalized.

Even those who admired the Nazi regime and worked desperately for friendship with Hitler — the loose grouping which Richard Griffiths has dubbed 'the Fellow Travellors of the Right' — encountered difficulties with the movement's anti-Semitism. Ernest Tennant, a merchant banker with strong connections in Germany, formed the Anglo-German Fellow-ship in 1935. His desire for co-operation with the Nazis persisted as late as July 1939 but he was still critical of the movement's persecution of the Jews.[38] Tennant, as did so many others in Britain, adhered to the liberal 'emancipation contract' with the Jews. In his journal in the early days of the Nazi régime Tennant remarked that 'over the Jewish question it is not fair to lay the entire blame on Herr Hitler. A section of the Jews are also to blame'. Like Rumbold, Tennant largely blamed the Galician and Polish Jews who 'would create a Jewish problem wherever they go'.[39] In 1934 Tennant noted that Hitler's 'handling of the Jewish question has . . . been his greatest mistake. That he was justified in reducing the Jewish control in certain trades and professions even the best Jews in Germany themselves admit, but it should have been done in a very different way. There was not need to insult the whole Jewish race which is what he has done.'[40] Tennant articulated the classic liberal ideology on the Jews, writing to the Chairman of the Fellowship, Lord Mount Temple: 'the tragedy of the Jew in Germany is that he will not be assimilated'. In Tennant's view this created a real Jewish problem but it did not excuse the 'deplorable . . . cruel and vulgar anti-Jewish campaign' of Streicher and others.[41] Similarly, Lord Dawson of Penn, the King's physician, admired much of what he saw in Nazi Germany and, according to his biographer, accepted that the Jews had obtained a 'stranglehold' on defeated Germany, but he also believed in his own words that the Nazis 'could displace the excessive power of the Jews without cruelty, they could make their regulations prospective and not turn to ruin people in established positions because they cannot show a long "aryan" ancestry'.[42]

Thus a range of opinion, from those who were generally sympathetic to Jews to those who were hostile to Jewish 'influence' could not understand the *need* for violent Nazi anti-Semitism. The treatment meted out to the Jews quite simply did not fit into the dominant liberal discourse in Britain. It was for this reason I will suggest that the impact of events such as Kristallnacht was so shallow and why they passed so quickly from the public's conscience. Richard Griffiths has pointed out the contrast between the initial shock in Britain after the November 1938 pogrom and the 'particularly striking . . . speed with which the first impressions appear to have faded'. An observer writing in the early part of 1939 confirms this anaysis: 'indignation towards German [anti-Semitic] methods had cooled off considerably'.[43] Within what one might call the liberal response in Britain there was a clear conflict between how Jews should have been treated and the reality of the situation in Germany. As a result of this discordance, and the unshakable belief in the assimilationist solution, few had comprehended the significance of the persecution of the Jews. Moreover an even smaller minority would connect their personal hostility to Jews to events such as the pogrom. The *persecution* of the Jews was unnecessary, thus it was unnecessary to dwell on why it had happened. By 1939, as will emerge later, the British public had returned to blaming the Jews for their own misfortune — as if Kristallnacht had not occurred.

The dominant British reaction was therefore determined by a liberal critique that some Jews, specifically *alien* Jews, were responsible for post-war German anti-Semitism. This anti-Semitism had been exploited by the Nazis in a violent and therefore totally unjustified way. Yet this liberal interpretation did not go unchallenged. To some in Britain, *all* Jews in Germany and elsewhere *were*, by *nature*, an alien race, and the Nazis were simply recognizing this 'fact'. Writing *before* the Nuremburg anti-Semitic decrees of September 1935, an ex-War Office official, Colonel Meinertzhargen, wrote 'my own view is that the German has a perfect right to treat the Jew as an alien and deny him German citizenship. He even has a right to expel him from Germany, but it must be done decently and with justice'. He stressed the Jewish irritant in German society, but his solution was Zionism — Meinertzhargen being a strong proponent of a Jewish national home in Palestine.[44] Others more extreme in their political views shared Hitler's solution to the 'Jewish problem' and advocated the extermination of the Jewish race.[45] Their numbers and influence in Britain must not be exaggerated. Nevertheless Mass Observation surveys in the war indicate a small but significant section of the population who, at least in private, advocated the literal removal of Jews from society.[46]

For the majority of those following a 'conservative' analysis (that the Jews were and always would be an alien race), the problem was how to justify Hitler's techniques. The 'Fellow Travellers of the Right' generally adopted a dual strategy. First, the severity of the 'Jewish problem' in Germany was persistently stressed.[47] British Fascists were particularly prone to this theory but they had no monopoly of it.[48] We have seen how Rumbold and others emphasized post-war Jewish activities but some, like the statesman Lord Londonderry and the journalist G. Ward Price (who has been described as 'the outstanding special correspondent of the 1930s'), went much further. They emphasized that Germany's Jewish problem was of such a profound nature that the Nazis were forced to deal with it.[49] As Richard Griffiths concludes: 'In a sense, most of those who felt that Germany was a "special case" were attempting to temper one form or other of antisemitism with a justification, for the British public, of what was happening.'[50]

Certainly 'legal' anti-Semitism could be justified in this manner by the Fellow Travellers, but they still faced a problem with any attempts to 'sanitize' Nazi violence towards Jews. The second aspect of their strategy was thus brought into play — the denial of Nazi atrocities, or attempts to claim that they were exaggerated by Britain's 'Jewish' dominated press.[51] The numbers who absolutely denied that the Jews were suffering atrocities, as with support for the physical persecution of the Jews, must be kept in perspective. Equally, however, its existence must not be ignored. One can trace a tradition pre-dating even the Nazi rise to power that doubted that the Jews ever had been subject to mass murder. A senior Foreign Office official wrote in 1940 in response to an account of the suffering of the Jews in Poland 'as a general rule Jews are inclined to magnify their persecutions. I remember the exaggerated stories of Jewish pogroms in Poland after the last war which, when fully examined, were found to have little substance'.[52] In the early days of Nazism this tendency was also apparent.

G.E.O. Knight, literary editor of *Books and Authors*, wrote in 1933 that he saw 'no murder of Jews' in Germany and the persecutions had been exaggerated. He concluded in his popular *In Defence of Germany* 'mountains had been made out of molehills'. The following year Ernest Tennant wrote in his journal of the 'abominable lies about Germany some spread by refugees'. Tennant believed that Jews, who were interfering with the British press, along with Jewish politicians, were 'able to keep our Cabinet Ministers continually supplied with anti-German propaganda'. Tennant was, however, by 1935, aware of the extremism of Nazi anti-Semitism, although he was anxious to avoid confronting it himself in his trips to Germany.[53] Others were more persistent in their disbelief. Beverly Nichols, a popular journalist, could write in September 1936 that 'the excesses have been wildly exaggerated' and the next year Ward Price referred to 'gross and reckless accusations'.[54] Knight, Tennant Nichols and Ward Price were all firmly in the appeasement camp, but it must not be assumed that all those who doubted the atrocity stories belonged to this category. Douglas Reed, *The Times* correspondent in Berlin until 1938, was one of the leading anti-appeasement journalists in pre-war Britain. In 1938 Reed shot to fame with his best-selling book *Insanity Fair* which predicted the Anschluss. Nevertheless Reed, described by one historian as an 'anti Nazi antisemite', adhered to a conspiracy theory which emphasized the 'Jewish problem' in Germany but denied that the Nazis were active in combatting it — their anti-Semitism was 'a hollow bluff'. By the middle of the War itself Reed's obsession about the Jews had overtaken all other considerations and he denied all the stories of the destruction of the Jews, claimed Hitler was controlled by the Jews and his anti-Semitism was a total sham.[55] Perhaps surprisingly, social surveys in the war and after found that Reed's early version of the holocaust denial had not been without influence, one of his readers being convinced of 'the Jewish menace' and fed up of hearing 'about supposed atrocities committed by Germans on Jews'.[56]

It has been noted that up to 1939 no aspect of Nazi anti-Semitism remained hidden from the world's view and that the British press had a remarkably good record of reporting the various stages of persecution up to and after the outbreak of war.[57] The pogrom of Kristallnacht was no exception. Lionel Kochan has pointed out that 'The Nazis made very little attempt to conceal any evidence of the pogrom' and the British press was thorough in its denunciation of this night of terror. Nevertheless Kochan over-generalizes when he states that 'nobody, of course, defended the pogrom'. As Griffiths reminds us, Britain had people who did.[58] This response came not so much in the form of defending the violence, but more in denying its very existence. The Southend Secretary of the pro-Nazi German friendship group, The Link, believed that the reports had been 'exaggerated' while the British Union of Fascists' popular paper *Action* reminded its readers of 'such blatantly untrue stories as that of the corpse factory during the [First World] War'. *Action* concluded that the false stories were part of 'World Jewry's War Plots', aiming to get public support for an anti-Nazi war. Similar comments could be found in *Peace News* as late as July and August 1939.[59] In short, by 1939 Britain had the basis for a burgeoning holocaust denial industry which would develop during the War and expand after it. It is thus neither a new phenomenon, nor has it been without influence.

Therefore, despite the efforts of the British press, to quote Richard Griffiths, 'the events of November 1938 had soon waned from people's minds. To some, the reports had been exaggerated. For others, there had been some justification for the German actions'.[60] Surveys carried out by Mass Observation soon after Kristallnacht, in early 1939, confirm Griffiths' analysis. The majority of those interviewed reverted to blaming the Jews for their own misfortune. A schoolmaster from Keswick remarked that Jewish sufferings were 'the bird coming home to roost'. Jews, he added, should 'cure themselves [of their exclusivity] first before they ask for sympathy'.[61] A survey of 11–12-year-olds in Southampton included responses such as 'Most countries are persicuting [sic] them because they always own important places such as theatres and hotels' or British Jews were *not* being persecuted, unlike the German Jews, 'because they have not done wrong'.[62] Nevertheless only two out of 30 17-year-olds in a London survey agreed with Hitler's *treatment* of the Jews, although many were distrustful of the Jews in general.[63] Disgust at Nazi techniques did not stop a continued consensus, post-Kristallnacht, that as 'a very ordinary' reply to Mass Observation put it 'the Jews really bring it all on themselves'.[64]

Late in 1942 a Polish Major, Jan Karski, brought to the West the news of the fate of European Jewry, including the liquidation of the ghettos and the existence of gas chambers in the death camps. H.G. Wells was one recipient of this information. Wells coldly responded to Karski by posing 'why antisemitism emerges in every country the Jews reside in'. Wells, along with George Bernard Shaw, was exceptional in his unemotional reaction to the destruction of European Jewry. It must be suggested, however, that his theory of well-earned anti-Semitism — that Jewish exclusivity led on to persecution — and his failure to comprehend the horror of the holocaust was typical of large sections of the British population.[65]

Popular reactions to Nazi anti-Semitism were thus marked by indifference, disbelief or claims of exaggeration, attempts to justify and, last, horrified shock qualified by a failure to ask *why* the persecution was occurring. Only a small minority perceived the irrationality of the Nazis' Jewish obsession and from this its full potential. George Orwell was aware of the common assumption in Britain that anti-Semitism was rational and thus felt it was the reason why talk of the persecution of the Jews made so little impact.[66] The overall outcome was that the suffering of the Jews was not a matter that generated much concern. The Mass Observer who, when reminded about the plight of the Jews, responded 'Must you? One had almost forgotten them' spoke for many.[67] Individuals like Harold Nicolson, Eleanor Rathbone MP and the Christian scholar James Parkes, who were both physically sickened by Nazi violence *and* kept the plight of the Jews constantly in mind, were comparatively rare.[68] Why then were people like Parkes so isolated? This paper has attempted to illustrate that *it is* possible to unravel the strands which at first sight appear bewildering but represent the complex set of British reactions to the first six years of Nazi persecution of Jews. Through a combination of 'assimilationist' and 'exclusionist' attitudes which cut across class divisions, the British public was inhibited in its understanding of the real nature of the cause of Nazi anti-Semitism. Thus, rather than investigating the irrationality of the Nazis' obsession, contemporary literature in Britain during the 1930s focused on the Jewish role in provoking anti-Semitism. A series of pamphlets produced by the Board of Deputies of British Jews and the Anglo-Jewish Association illustrate this point. Tables of statistics were produced indicating the limited Jewish role in all aspects of German society — the press, government, industry, cinema and so on. Much attention was paid to the East European post-war Jewish immigrants and attempts made to play down their numbers. In other words the pamphlets were designed to counter both Nazis' allegations as well as those of apologists such as Ernest Tennant. In this process the very use of statistics to disprove accusations added to the dehumanizing process — the tragic situation of German Jewry became obscured in the numbers, as did, by the attempt to minimize Jewish 'influence', the tremendous loss to German society that persecution brought with it.[69] Thus the centre of the debate was not why were the Germans, a 'civilized' country, resorting to barbarism, but was, or was not, Nazi anti-Semitism justified.[70] A liberal discourse was employed to explain an illiberal phenomenon. This led unsurprisingly to a failure of comprehension.

Such an analysis, while it might explain the continuing British reluctance to be interested in the holocaust, could appear to be of only limited significance. This, however, is by no means the case. The last part of the paper will analyse briefly its impact on three related areas — British refugee policy in the 1930s (and the Government's reactions to Nazi anti-Semitism), popular and state responses to the Jewish refugees actually in Britain and, last, the effect on British attitudes to Jews.

To examine first of all British refugee policy; it has been described as 'comparatively compassionate, even generous', yet this is hardly accurate. As Michael Marrus has pointed out, it 'is more a reflection on the international rejection of refugees than a comment on British benevolence'.[71] An analysis based purely on numbers admitted (and here Britain only *appears* generous because of the large number who entered as transmigrants in the last year before war) disguises the complexity of British immigration policy. British immigration policy, at least until 1938, was to continue the restrictive philosophy of the 1919 Aliens Act. Numbers would be limited and only certain selected groups or individuals would be allowed entry.[72] There is here a close parallel to the analysis of German anti-Semitism followed by Rumbold and others. Nazi Germany, it was assumed, had its share of *bad* Jews, aliens who were carriers of crime and socialism and 'would', to quote Tennant again, 'create a Jewish problem wherever they go'. To counter this possibility British refugee policy in the 1930s was determined by refusing entry to what one of the leading refugee organization leaders referred to as 'the wrong type' of refugee.[73] Much of the press in Britain embraced this philosophy and warned the Government that any influx of Jews of the wrong sort would create serious anti-Semitism. As Andrew Sharf concludes, the press believed that 'the Jew carried the seeds of his condition with him'. To admit any large number was 'to risk spreading the infection'. The introduction of foreign Jews was simply seen as a problem. To the labour movement and middle-class professional organizations in Britain, refugees were perceived as a threat to employment, wage levels and conditions of work. To the upper classes, foreign Jews were a potential threat to the stability of society through the introduction of subversion and crime. Nevertheless 'there was a fairly general agreement during this period to welcome, and to persuade the government to welcome, what was thought of as "the desirable Jewish refugee"'.[74]

British immigration policy in the 1930s was thus not totally exclusionary — the Government continued its policy of allowing in the right type of Jew or alien, a policy which had been instituted with the 1919 Act. The Government, although it wished to appease any anti-Semitic sentiment in Britain, did not carry out the demands for total restriction made by the British Union of Fascists.[75] Its policy was modelled more on the liberal philosophy of allowing the Jew who could assimilate best the chance to escape. It thus emerges that there *was* an *ideological* basis to British refugee policy, one that needs to be worked out in detail before any meaningful attempt at evaluation or international comparison is made.[76]

If British immigration policy remained largely unchanged throughout the 1930s, the same inflexibility is evident with regard to the Government's response to Nazi persecution. The persecution was regarded as Germany's own internal matter, and it certainly was not an issue, even post-Kristallnacht, that should stand in the way of Anglo–German understanding. A liberal democratic government was thus unable to confront the existence of anti-Semitism. In terms of government policy, the Jews were not a priority and thus, as Kochan concludes, 'Humanitarian sympathies yielded to *raison d'etat*'.[77]

The second area we must consider is the response to refugees actually in Britain; A.J.P. Taylor has suggested that the refugees 'received a warm welcome in England' and that 'every refugee was walking propaganda against the Nazis'. Taylor's analysis is not without foundation and many were treated with considerable kindness, especially by religious groups such as the Quakers and Christadelphians who offered their homes and sympathy to both child and adult refugees.[78] Nevertheless this was not the only response and there were many like the Hallgarten family who faced the frustrating question 'What have you really done that you had to leave your country?' Freda Hallgarten adds that 'many people were absolutely without understanding'.[79] A pamphlet produced by the Central Office for Refugees emphasizes this point, stressing that the refugees '*through no fault of their own* [my emphasis], have been placed in the most embarrassing of all circumstances'. It again illustrates how common was the assumption that anti-Semitism was the result of bad Jewish behaviour — 'what criminal act have you done?' — rather than the result of Gentile prejudice.[80] The experience of the 20,000 Jewish women who escaped Nazi Europe to become domestic servants in Britain confirms this analysis, as my other contribution to this volume indicates. Although some were treated with respect and understanding, the vast majority were treated simply as foreign labour, there to be exploited. Few managed to explain to their employers why they were forced to take such work. Pre-war life for the refugees in Britain was thus uneasy and insecure. Asylum had often been granted on a temporary basis, work was either unsuitable or impossible to get and the reception cold and unsympathetic.[81]

The essential failure to grasp the plight of the refugees was fully exposed in the spring of 1940. British public and large sections of the state united to enforce the mass internment of thousands of Jewish refugees from central Europe. German and Austrian Jews were now no longer 'refugees', they were 'enemy aliens'. In many cases the fact that they were Jewish made them doubly suspect (or, with some women, triply so). The long-standing hostility of the Beaverbrook, Rothermere and Kemsley press empires against the refugees came to a climax as Britain, in a military, political and economic crisis, faced invasion. Internment and the removal of thousands of refugees to the colonies was thus not a minor blot or 'May Madness', but represented the success of exclusionist hostility to foreign Jews in Britain. At a time of crisis it could lead to widespread deportation which could be carried out without any public opposition.[82] The generosity which Taylor refers to therefore needs to be severely qualified.

Lastly, what was the impact of Nazi anti-Semitism on British attitudes to Jews? This study clearly illustrates the *tenacity* of British anti-Semitism and the ability of individuals to separate their own hostility to Jews from events in Europe. No one was to express this more succinctly than Harold Nicolson in a diary entry written at the time of the liberation of the concentration camps in 1945: 'although I loathe anti-semitism I do dislike Jews'.[83] Nicolson was not being self-consciously hypocritical. He was simply drawing the line between justified and unjustified antipathy to Jews. To be 'naturally' opposed to a Jewish irritant in society was one thing, to persecute Jews was another. Indeed the surveys of Mass Observation in 1939, 1940, 1943 and even 1946 indicate how little hostile or ambivalent British attitudes to Jews had changed during and immediately after the holocaust. The message of these surveys was clear: 'it was up to the Jews themselves to combat antisemitism', and anti-Semitism, because of his failure and refusal to assimilate, his power in society or, more rarely, for racial reasons, was the fault of the Jew.[84]

To conclude, although there was widespread revulsion at the violence associated with Nazi anti-Semitism, few in Britain appreciated the enormity of the Jewish plight. The reasons for this are not straight-forward, but an awareness of the *nature* of British anti-Semitism is vital in any attempt to understand the complex reactions in the 1930s. It is true that pure gutter anti-Semitism of the Mosleyite variety was only a small and not necessarily important factor in this process (although the Government's timid refugee policy reflected a fear of organized racism much as the policies of the 1970s with the National Front).[85] In this sense Richard Griffiths is right to suggest that 'anti-Semitism of a political and active kind was . . . a minority interest in Great Britain'. But he is oversimplifying when he argues that 'for all except the most ingrained extremists, anti-Semitism was an attitude rather than a spur to political action'.[86] This is a rather narrow interpretation of 'political', confining it only to party structures. Within British culture was a more subtle form of hostility which in both its assimilationist and exclusionist form rejected the Jew as a Jew and blamed the Jew for his own misfortune. Such anti-Semitism was *not* unthinking but was based on ideological considerations which affected not only government policy towards refugees, but also the treatment by public and state of those who had managed to escape Nazi terror.

Ironically, Nazi persecution of Jews was viewed as essentially un-English, but it was native forms of anti-Semitism that led to Britain's failure to come to terms with the first stages of the 'Final Solution'. As George Orwell put it, the stories of atrocities committed against Jews 'bounce[d] off [English] consciousness like peas off a steel helmet'.[87] Orwell was convinced that anti-Semitism in this country was responsible for the inability of British society to conceive of the horrors of the holocaust during the Nazi era. Perhaps this is also true of today.[88] As the late Primo Levi has written: 'Uprooting a prejudice is as painful as extracting a nerve'.[89]

TONY KUSHNER
University of Southampton

NOTES

1. A.J.P. Taylor, *English History 1914–1945* (Oxford, 1965) pp.419–20.
2. See for example J. Gross 'Is anti-Semitism dying out?', *20th Century*, vol.172 (Spring 1963) pp.20–21; E. Hobsbawn, 'Are We Entering a New Era of Anti-Semitism?', *New Society*, 11 Dec. 1980; but for a more critical analysis C. Holmes, *John Bull's Island*: *Immigration and British Society, 1871–1971* (London, 1988) p.245.
3. J. Sarna, 'Anti-Semitism and American History', *Commentary*, vol.71 (March 1981), p.46.
4. B. Williams, 'The Anti-Semitism of Tolerance' in A. Kidd and K. Roberts (eds.), *City, Class and Culture* (Manchester, 1985) pp.74–102; C. Holmes, *Anti-Semitism in British Society, 1876–1939* (London, 1979); G. Lebzelter, *Political Anti-Semitism in England* (London, 1978).
5. G. Field, 'Anti-Semitism with the Boots Off', *Wiener Library Bulletin*, Special Issue (1982) pp.25–46; L. Gartner, 'Eastern European Jewish Immigrants in England', *Jewish Historical Studies*, vol.XXIX (1982–1986) pp.305–6 and T. Endelman, 'The Englishness of Jewish Modernity in England' in J. Katz (ed.). *Toward Modernity*: *The European Jewish Model* (New Brunswick, 1987) p.237.
6. Field, op. cit; pp.28, 34, 37; C. Holmes, *John Bull's Island*, p.145: Endelman, op. cit. and also his 'Anti-Semitism in War-Time Britain', *Michael*, vol.X (1986) pp.75–83.
7. Williams, op. cit; D. Cesarani, 'Anti-Alienism in England After the First World War', *Immigrants and Minorities*, vol.6 no.1 (March 1987), pp.5–29; B. Cheyette, 'An Overwhelming Question: Jewish Stereotyping in English Fiction and Society 1875–1914' (PhD, Sheffield University, 1986).
8. B. Cheyette, 'H.G. Wells and the Jews: Socialist Anti-Semitism and English Culture', *Patterns of Prejudice*, vol.28 no.3 (1988) pp.22–35.
9. See T. Kushner, *The Persistence of Prejudice: Antisemitism in British Society During the Second World War* (Manchester, 1989).
10. For the 'Chesterbelloc' see K. Lunn, 'The Marconi Scandal and Related Aspects of British Anti-Semitism, 1911–1914 (PhD, Sheffield University, 1978) and C. Holmes, *Anti-Semitism*, ch.11 for Mosley. For the need to put this organized hostility in the context of popular attitudes see T. Kushner, 'The Paradox of Prejudice: Organized Antisemitism in an Anti-Nazi War' in T. Kushner and K. Lunn (eds.), *Traditions of Intolerance: Historical Perspectives on Fascism and Race Discourse in British Society* (Manchester, 1989), ch.4.
11. See for example, Mass-Observation Archive (M-O A): DR June 1939, Oct. 1940 and Mar. 1943.
12. For fear of Jewish power see Kushner, *The Persistence of Prejudice*, pp.79–82, 85–7, 111–4.
13. B. Kosmin, 'Exclusion and Opportunity' in S. Wallman (ed.), *Ethnicity at Work* (London, 1977) pp.37–70 on discrimination and A. Sherman, *Island Refuge: Britain and Refugees from the Third Reich 1933–1939* (London, 1973) p.90 on the types of Jewish refugees the Foreign Office excluded. Louise London's thesis on 'British refugee policy, 1933–1951' (University of London) will shed further light on the way

this differentiation worked in practice.

14. T. Kushner, 'The Impact of British Antisemitism, 1918–1945' in D. Cesarani (ed.), *The Making of Modern Anglo-Jewry: New Essays in Anglo-Jewish History* (Oxford, forthcoming).

15. Holmes, *Anti-Semitism*, p.104 comments on such assimilationism. For an alternative account see Endelman, 'The Englishness of Jewish Modernity in England', pp.241–2.

16. For Wells see Cheyette, op. cit., and L. Kochan, 'H.G. Wells and the Jews' *Jewish Monthly*, vol.4 no.6 (September 1950) pp.361–9. His influence is indicated in Kushner, *The Persistence of Prejudice*, pp.93, 145.

17. R. Kee, *The World We Left Behind: A Chronicle of the Year 1939* (London, 1984) p.248 attempts to relate attitudes to Jews at home and persecuted Jews abroad but does not develop this theme.

18. R. Griffiths, *Fellow Travellers of the Right: British Enthusiasts for Nazi Germany 1933–39* (Oxford, 1983) ch.6 'Diverse Individuals' illustrates the limitations of this approach in what is otherwise a fine introduction to a neglected area.

19. M. Gilbert, *The Roots of Appeasement* (London, 1966) p.162. See also L. London, 'British Responses to the Nazi Seizure of Power and the Refugee Crisis in Germany' (unpublished ts) p.16.

20. For his xenophobia and anti-Semitism see M. Gilbert, *Sir Horace Rumbold: Portrait of a Diplomat 1869–1941* (London, 1973) pp.xiii, 34, 47, 49, 51, 127–8, 183, 185, 319.

21. Ibid., pp.418, 319 for Berlin.

22. Ibid., p.379.

23. E. Woodward and R. Butler (eds.), *Documents on British Foreign Policy 1919–1939*, vol.5 (London, 1956) p.4.

24. Ibid., pp.5–6 and despatch no.378, 13 Apr. 1983 in loc. cit., pp.38–41.

25. Ibid., pp.40, 44.

26. The phrase is Rumbold's — in despatch of 28 Mar. 1933 in ibid., p.5.

27. 13 Apr. 1933 despatch in ibid., p.41. M. Gilbert, op. cit., pp.377–8, 381, 396 indicates the importance of *Mein Kampf* to Rumbold as a true pointer to Hitler's behaviour.

28. Rumbold stated in his despatch of 13 Apr. 1933 that 'It may be as well to refer here to a misconception widely held abroad . . . that this hostility to the Jews is directed against the Hebrew faith. This is not the case. Hitler'[s] . . . objection to the Jews is racial'. In Woodward and Butler, op. cit., pp.43–4.

29. Ibid., p.44 and Gilbert., op. cit., p.xiii.

30. Quoted by Gilbert, op. cit., p.379.

31. W. Churchill, *The Second World War*, vol.I, *The Gathering Storm* (London, 1948), p.65. For his earlier views see M. Cohen, *Churchill and the Jews* (London, 1985) ch.2.

32. N. Nicolson (ed.), *Harold Nicolson: Diaries and Letters 1930–1939* (London, 1966) pp.347–8.

33. J. Vincent (ed.), *The Crawford Papers: The Journals of David Lindsay* (Manchester, 1984), pp.591, 596.

34. A. Sharf, *The British Press and Jews Under Nazi Rule* (London, 1964), p.58. See also F. Gannon, *The British Press and Germany 1936–1939* (Oxford, 1971) p.226.

35. N. Rose (ed.), *Baffy: The Diaries of Blanche Dugdale 1936–1947* (London, 1973), p.115. G. Beardmore, *Civilians at War: Journals 1938–1946* (London, 1984) pp.21, 23, gives the sympathetic reaction of a left-wing author.

36. Sharf, op. cit., p.7.

37. For details see L. Kochan, *Pogrom: 10 November 1938*, (London, 1957). Vincent, op. cit., p.591 for Lindsay; R. James, *Chips: The Diaries of Sir Henry Channon* (London, 1967) p.178.

38. For his career see Griffiths, op. cit., pp.116–8 and Tennant's autobiography *True Account*, (London, 1957). For his continued belief in appeasement in the summer of 1939 see J. Douglas-Hamilton, 'Ribbentrop and War', *Journal of Contemporary History*, vol.5 no.4 (1970) p.62.

39. W.W. Ashley papers, University of Southampton archive, file BR 81, Tennant journals, memorandum May 1933, and journal entry 29 Jan. 1932.

40. Ibid., journal entry 5 Sept. 1934.

41. Tennant to Mount-Temple, 24 Sept. 1935 in Ashley papers BR 81.
42. F. Watson, *Dawson of Penn* (London, 1950) p.292.
43. Griffiths, op. cit., p.342; P. Harlow, *The Shortest Way With the Jews* (London, 1939) p.238.
44. Colonel R. Meinertzhagen, *Middle East Diary 1917 to 1956*, (London, 1959) p.158 and passim.
45. Most infamous was the racist Arnold Leese. For his advocation of a 'lethal chamber' for Jews see *The Fascist*, no.69 (Feb. 1935).
46. See M–O A: DR 2535, 1145, 2402 Oct. 1940 and DR 2090, 2265, 2829, 2485 Mar. 1943; National Council for Civil Liberties file 311; *Tribune*, 19 May 1944.
47. See Griffiths, op. cit., pp.71–5.
48. For British Fascists' responses to Nazi anti-Semitism see the *British Union Quarterly*, vol.3 no.1 (Jan.–Apr. 1939) editorial 'Redressing the Balance' or *Action*, no.145 (26 Nov. 1938).
49. Lord Londonderry, *Ourselves and Germany* (London, 1938) pp.169–71 and G. Ward Price, *I Know These Dictators* (London, 1937). For the positive assessment of Ward Price see Gannon, op. cit., p.34. His continued distrust of German Jews is made clear in the *Daily Mail*, 9 Oct. 1939 and 20 Apr. 1940. A. Bryant, *Unfinished Victory* (London, 1940) pp.14, 103–6, 139–45 was one of the last 'mainstream' attempts to 'excuse' Nazi anti-Semitism through the behaviour of Jews.
50. Griffiths, op. cit., p.75.
51. For claims that the 'Jewish' press was responsible for atrocity stories see *Action*, no.144 (19 Nov. 1938) or Tennant's journal entry, 5 Sept. 1934 in Ashley papers.
52. R. Leeper minute, 21 Apr. 1940 in P.R.O. FO 371/24472 C5471.
53. G. Knight, *In Defence of Germany* (London, 1933) pp.9–13 quoted by Griffiths, op. cit., p.77. For Tennant see his journal comments of 5 Sept. 1934 and letter to von Ribbentrop, 7 Sept. 1935.
54. Nichols in *Manchester Sunday Chronicle*, 13 Sept. 1936 quoted by Sharf, op. cit., p.79 and Ward Price, op. cit., pp.119–21 quoted by Griffiths, op. cit., p.167.
55. D. Reed, *Insanity Fair* (London, 1938) ch.17. For his denial of the persecution of the Jews see pp.152–5 and his later conspiracy theories *Lest We Regret* (London, 1943) p.239. R. Thurlow, 'Anti-Nazi Antisemite; The Case of Douglas Reed', *Patterns of Prejudice*, vol.18 no.1 (1984) pp.23–34 and Kushner, *The Persistence of Prejudice*, pp.99–101 cover Reed's career in detail.
56. M–O A: DR 2804, 3293 and 2485 Mar. 1943 and DR July 1946, BAT 5 and WAS 1.
57. By Sharf, op. cit., p.193.
58. Kochan, op. cit., pp.11, 126–7; Griffiths, op. cit., p.340.
59. *Anglo-German Review*, Dec. 1938. J.S. Wiggins 'The Link' (MA Thesis, St Andrews University, 1985), p.35 for comment; *Action*, no.144 and 145 (19 Nov. 1938 and 26 Nov. 1938). See E. Mannin's comments in *Peace News*, July-Aug. 1939 for a non-Fascist version of the same theory.
60. Griffiths, op. cit., p.346.
61. M–O A: TC Anti-Semitism Box 1 File D.
62. M–O A: TC Anti-Semitism Box 1 File C.
63. Ibid.
64. M–O A: FR A12 (carried out in Feb. 1939).
65. Wells quoted in 'Messenger from Poland', Channel 4, 25 May 1987. For Shaw see D. Lawrence (ed.), *Bernard Shaw; Collected Letters* (London, 1988) pp.522–3, 752. Popular responses and Wells' influence are clear in M–O A: DR Mar. 1943 and July 1946.
66. G. Orwell in *Tribune*, 11 Feb. 1944.
67. M–O A: DR 1206 Oct. 1940.
68. All three were involved in the National Council for Rescue from Nazi Terror which aimed to pressurize the British government into changing its restrictive policy towards allowing Jewish refugees to enter Britain. See its minutes, 1943–46 in the Parkes papers, University of Southampton archive.
69. See for example the Joint Foreign Committee of the Board of Deputies· and the

Anglo-Jewish Association's *The Persecution of the Jews in Germany* (London, 1933) which appeared in three editions and the Board's *Germany and the Jews*, (London, 1937, revised edition Feb. 1939). Israel Cohen, *The Jews in Germany* (London, 1933) pursued a different line indicating the *contribution* of Jews to German society.

70.   See for example the correspondence between James Parkes and the Board of Deputies and Ernest Tennant over whether the Board's figures on Jewish 'involvement' understated the Jewish 'role'. In the Parkes papers, University of Southampton, 16/706.

71.   The analysis is by Sherman, op. cit., p.267; M. Marrus, *The Unwanted: European Refugees in the Twentieth Century* (Oxford, 1985) p.154.

72.   See for example the comments of the Home Secretary, Joynson-Hicks, on immigration and naturalization policy, differentiating good 'assimilationist' Jews from those who came to Britain and remained apart. See the *Jewish Chronicle*, 2 Apr. 1926 quoted by Cesarani, op. cit., p.28 (n.108). P.R.O. FO 372/3284, T 7056, 27 Apr. 1938 quoted by Sherman, op. cit., p.90 makes it clear that such a policy intensified in the 1930s.

73.   The quote is from Otto Schiff, with regard to Home Office refugee policy at a meeting of refugee organizations, 23 Apr. 1939 in the Barash papers, Manchester Central Reference Library, M533.

74.   Sharf, op. cit., p.170. For the labour movement's response to the Jewish refugee crisis see Kushner, *The Persistence of Prejudice*, pp.88–90.

75.   Humbert Wolfe of the Ministry of Labour stated in a minute of 5 Mar. 1935 that 'up to the present . . . the British policy has been not to vary the aliens administration in favour of or against the refugees'. In P.R.O. LAB 8/78. BUF demands for total restriction can be found in *Action*, no.145 (26 Nov. 1938).

76.   I have benefited from discussion with Louise London over the details of British refugee policy in the 1930s.

77.   See Kochan, op. cit., pp.141–5. Von Dirksen, the British Ambassador in Britain, believed public opinion had moved against Germany by the events of Kristallnacht and that this would create a barrier between the two countries. See E. Woodward and R. Butler, *Documents on British Foreign Policy 1919–1939*, vol.IV (London, 1950) pp.333–4, 360. An opinion poll in Britain after the pogrom showed that 73 per cent of the British population thought that Nazi anti-Semitism *was* an obstacle to good understanding between Britain and German — H. Cantril (ed.), *Public Opinion 1935–1946* (Princeton, 1951) p.382. The British government, however, did not appear to view this as a problem in terms of international diplomacy.

78.   Taylor, op. cit., p.419. For the Christian response see for example Z. Josephs, *Survivors: Jewish Refugees in Birmingham 1933–1945* (Birmingham, 1988) ch.5.

79.   Imperial War Museum (IWM) refugee tapes nos.4494 and 3967. See also tape no.4645 and 'A German Jewish Scientist', *Why I Left Germany* (London, 1934) p.1.

80.   Central Office for Refugees, 'Entertaining Our Refugee Guests' (London, 1939) p.7; IWM refugee tape no.3867.

81.   T. Kushner, 'Asylum or Servitude? Refugee Domestics in Britain', *Bulletin of the Society for the Study of Labour History* vol.53, No.3 (1988) pp.19–27.

82.   Kushner, *The Persistence of Prejudice*, pp.141–150.

83.   N. Nicolson (ed.), *Harold Nicolson: Diaries and Letters, vol.2: 1939–1945* (London, 1967) p.469.

84.   M-O A: FR 1669L, April 1943 'The Means of Overcoming Antisemitism'.

85.   See Sir Samuel Hoare, the Home Secretary's comments suggesting that a more generous refugee policy would create problems as 'there is the making of a definite anti-Jewish movement' in Britain — in *Hansard* HC, vol.341 col. 1468, 21 Nov. 1938.

86.   Griffiths, op. cit., pp.11, 360.

87.   G. Orwell in *Tribune*, 11 Feb. 1944.

88.   See G. Steiner's comments that the holocaust is 'Not our [Britain's] patch' in his review of Primo Levi's *The Drowned and the Saved — The Sunday Times*, 10 Apr. 1988.

89.   P. Levi, *If Not Now, When?* (London, 1987) p.111.

The British State and Immigration, 1945–51: New Light on the Empire Windrush

In many of the standard texts on the history of race relations in modern Britain, the arrival of the Empire Windrush *in 1948 is seen as a symbol of the escalation of West Indian immigration and of 'race problems'. However, by detailed analysis of official records and local studies, it can be shown that the process whereby 'race' became a major political issue was a more uneven and complex one than the standard historiography often suggests. There was an ambiguity of attitudes, national and local, not strong enough to challenge the mainstream of racism, but sufficient to create a far more involved debate about the ultimate significance of the* Empire Windrush's *voyage.*

Most historians of post-war immigration and 'race relations' begin with some reference to the landing in June 1948 at Tilbury Docks of 492 Jamaicans from the *Empire Windrush*. This 'symbolic starting point for the postwar emigration from the Caribbean'[1] is seen as introducing the 'problems' of race relations now familiar in British social and political life.[2] However, until very recently, few writers have actually devoted much attention to the period immediately after the War. The history of 'race' in Britain generally moves from detailed consideration of the war years on to 1958 with its 'race riots' and the involvement of Fascists in those disturbances. A more detailed survey of the circumstances of 1948 and the ramifications for both government policy-making and for black–white relations in Britain show a very complex series of social and political circumstances which only resolve themselves into the 'symbolism' of the *Empire Windrush* after a period of ambivalence and often rather covert debate. If the major concern is to identify the processes whereby 'race' became politicized, then attention needs to be paid not only to debates within Parliament, the Civil Service and the national media but also within the local context. Too often, an inexorable drive towards antagonism and institutionalized prejudice has been assumed. This may be the fundamental outcome of 'race relations' in the post-war years but what lies behind that eventuality is a series of contradictory pressures and attitudes, all of which played some part in shaping the future of 'race relations'. It is the complexity and ambiguity which is important to identify, for it offers a rather more thorough-going evaluation of the process of the politicization of 'race' in British society.

There is, within the mass of existing literature, a divergence of opinion on the importance of the *Windrush* episode. Writers such as Hiro point out that '. . . to the British authorities' relief, this shipload of the West Indians did not prove to be the first wave of "an unarmed invasion"'[3] and note that only limited migration from the West Indies to Britain occurred while the more inviting prospect of the USA was available. Only the McCarran–Walter Act of 1952, which imposed a virtual ban on such migration to the USA, produced a greater concentration on the 'mother country'.[4] More recently, Layton-Henry has suggested that no one in Britain fully realized that the *Empire Windrush* and the *Orbita,* which arrived in Liverpool in October, pointed the way to 'largely spontaneous' migration.[5] Robert Miles and Annie Phizacklea stress that official recruitment schemes for European Volunteer Workers, former members of the Polish armed forces and other continental European labour were the main concern of the Government in filling labour shortages at the end of the Second World War. 'Thus little attention was paid to the arrival in 1948 of some 400 people from the West Indies on the *SS Empire Windrush,* all of whom came in search of work, although the Colonial Office did monitor the repercussions'.[6] They also note that the *Windrush*'s arrival produced 'little political interest'.[7] Thus while Miles and Phizacklea are concerned to identify the process whereby 'race/immigration' was constructed as a 'problem' within British politics by 1962, they concentrate on the 1950s as the crucial years in this development.

By way of contrast, Joshi and Carter have produced an analysis of the 1945–51 Labour governments' attitudes towards West Indian immigration which challenges the emphasis on the 1950s as the formative years: 'contrary to the commonly held view, . . . "race" as a "problem" had already been essentially structured by 1951'.[8] In their assessment, debates within the Government and the ranks of the Civil Service, made more immediate by the news of the *Windrush*'s impending arrival, clearly rehearse the more public pronouncements of the 1950s which other commentators have focused upon.

There is, of course, a sense in which historians write with hindsight and tend to compress chronology, transferring a significance to 1948 which can only be seen with the advantage of a longer-term view of 'race relations' in Britain. Despite the newsreel and press coverage of the *Windrush*'s arrival, it does seem, as Miles and Phizacklea suggest, that the ship's passengers were news for only a short period and that there was little popular concern at the time about the beginnings of a large-scale migration from the Caribbean. What discussion there was took place in an unpublicized and often very reticent manner; exchanges of memos and departmental Civil Service committees were the main sources of debate. The questions raised were concerned with the broad issues of labour shortages in Britain and how to respond to immigration from the colonies which might fill those shortages but which, in the eyes of officials and some politicians, would add to the racial tensions already apparent in some parts of the country. There was the added problem, however, of how to limit that immigration. This was a particularly difficult problem for a Labour government, committed at least on paper to the creation of a more just and equitable society through the introduction of the 'Welfare State', and anxious to avoid any charge of racism, whether in its attempts to control immigration or in its dealings with its black citizens at home. The Labour government sought, after the war, to formulate a new relationship within the Commonwealth, one which moved away from the old imperial dominance of the 'mother country'. Any limitation on the movement of peoples within this new creation, particularly one which smacked of a 'colour bar', would tarnish this new image. As will be seen, it was a desire to avoid this impression which dominated much of the 'official mind' in the immediate post-war years.

Yet the outcome of the deliberations appeared non-existent. No formal policy was invoked by the Labour governments with regard to West Indian immigration and it is easy to see why historians have suggested that these years had no significance in the formulation of 'race policy'. However, Joshi and Carter are surely correct to identify the processes whereby a defining of attitudes took place during this period. Undoubtedly, the shaping of policy did take place through these informal exchanges. It may be somewhat of an exaggeration to see this particular period as crucial in the identification of 'race' as a 'problem' since the inter-war period, and particularly in response to the black populations in the seaport towns, may have been even more important in this context.[9] What did change was the circumstances of the post-war years: whatever the popular conception, the arrival of the *Windrush* did offer a glimpse of a new relationship between Britain and the Commonwealth, one in which labour migration was to play an increasingly significant role and provide a new set of political questions for the British state.

To examine this view in more detail, consideration can be given to what is an influential perspective on the history of 'race' in Britain after the Second World War. According to this analysis, the immediate post-war period saw 'a steady but very slow deterioration in public attitudes towards and treatment of people with dark skins'.[10] Blame for this state of affairs, at least in a negative sense, is attributed to politicians. Given that before the 1960s the feelings of British people towards blacks were 'hesitant, ambiguous and confused'[11] with different sets of conflicting responses, what emerged in the later years was a much more consistently hostile set of attitudes. In part, politicians were to blame because of 'their total indifference to, or unawareness of, the potential dangers inherent in the entry, among a people brought up on the traditions of imperialism, into which the myth of racial superiority had been tightly woven, of those of African and Asian descent'.[12] Such a perspective is understandable but in need of reconsideration. Politicians and Civil Servants were, on the evidence of official records, only too aware of the 'dangers' of black settlement in an imperialist white Britain. What they could not see was any real means of combatting these dangers. The notion of legislation against racial discrimination was one which found little sympathy with politicians and their civil servants. As Thomas has pointed out, it was a Private Member's Bill in the House of Lords which marked the first 'official attempts to deal with the problem of legislating against racial discrimination'.[13] This was in 1949 and legal opinion on the three specific clauses directed at areas of behaviour was that all three were either unenforceable or covered by existing legislation. The fear was that any attempt at legislation would only enhance the resistance of white racists and would be both difficult to administer and ultimately counter-productive. Some civil servants expressed the view that offering 'unfair advantage' to Commonwealth citizens would create a hostile backlash among the white population. The question of controlling the entry of West Indians into Britain also raised difficulties. Any system of limitation or exclusion which would affect blacks would create the impression of a colour bar. It was felt that a system of informal controls was more effective: discussions with colonial governments on ways of limiting emigration through passport controls or persuasion about the realities of life in Britain were preferred. In this way, negative views about the 'Mother Country' and its attitudes to its colonies would be kept to a minimum. Although Cabinet discussions in 1950 and 1951 had eventually produced some suggestions for controlling the entry of British subjects from colonial territories into the United Kingdom, these were rejected, largely for the reasons outlined above.[14]

Thus, there was created a contrast between the public image and the private concerns. As Pilkington writes, 'The Attlee Government appeared unruffled by the influx of West Indians and Ministers made no public comment on the matter. Indeed there seemed no reason why they should. The West Indians came of their own free will, paid their own passage, found their own accommodation and jobs, and went about their business like anybody else'.[15] The reality was that the concerns were present but, for a variety of reasons, nothing, in terms of concrete policy, was decided or executed. As Paul Rich has noted, the rejection of legislation meant that successive governments in the 1950s followed a policy of 'benign neglect and a shifting of responsibility for the immigrants' reception and eventual "assimilation" into British society onto the voluntary sector and local authorities'.[16] This period of relative torpor was broken by the 1958 disturbances in Nottingham and Notting Hill (although throughout the 1950s there had been a growing voice urging immigration controls) and culminated in the 1962 Commonwealth Immigrants Act.

A more detailed study of the arrival of the *Empire Windrush* and the reactions of all those involved, politicians, those on board the ship and the communities who 'received' them, helps to broaden the perspective on post-war 'race' problems and allows an assessment of the dilemmas facing many of the parties involved.

From official sources, it appears that the Colonial Office was aware of the impending arrival of the *Windrush* from the beginning of June 1948.[17] Its major concern seems to have been finding accommodation for those arrivals who had no fixed arrangements — both the Ministry of Health and then the Ministry of Labour were contacted with regard to temporary shelter.[18] However, earlier discussions in the Colonial Office had already noted the 'problems' of coloured immigration, the tensions it would inevitably create and the need to avoid incidents and to maintain at least the appearance of an 'open door' policy.[19] As Lord Listowel, Minister of State at the Colonial Office, wrote to Ness Edwards, Parliamentary Secretary to the Minister of Labour: 'I appreciate the difficulties in dealing with such an unsponsored contingent of men . . . We must therefore see that the smoothest possible arrangements are made to minimise the risk of any undesirable incidents or complaints that the Mother Country does not bother to look after coloured Colonial British subjects'.[20] This was to remain the publicly expressed image of much of the preparation for the *Windrush*'s arrival, which involved many branches of government agencies, including the Ministry of Labour, Ministry of Health, Colonial Office, Ministry of Trade, Assistance Board and the Treasury.[21]

There was some hostility expressed when news of the impending arrival became public. Some newspapers reacted with what was to become a standard line of 'Send Them Back' but this was not easily sustained in a post-war situation, where black colonial citizens had made considerable contributions to the war effort. The Minister of Labour, George Isaacs, was also not encouraging in his initial House of Commons reply to questions about the *Windrush*. His view was that the arrivals could be given no assurances about employment and he publicly expressed his hope that 'no encouragement will be given to others to follow their example'.[22] On 22 June, some Labour backbenchers wrote to Prime Minister Attlee, voicing fears over the Government's provision of support for the Windrushers and the possibility that the country would become an 'open reception centre' for colonial immigration 'regardless of whether assimilation was possible or not'.[23] Attlee's reply, after the ship had arrived, stressed the need to support colonial citizens but offered the qualification of saying that there might be cause to revise the open door policy if 'a great influx of undesirables' occurred.[24]

Statements to the press, however, were designed to allay fears of discrimination: Isaacs' House of Commons comments had provoked unease in the Caribbean and Attlee took steps to indicate his own direct involvement in the preparations by way of reassurance. The Ministry of Labour also issued a press statement claiming there was no colour bar facing the arrivals.[25] Clearly, the public image conflicted with the bureaucratic view of the likely reception: uppermost in many officials' minds was the need for dispersal. This reflected a notion that concentration of blacks, such as existed in Stepney, Manchester and Liverpool, would lead to hostile responses. If there was a fairly rapid dispersal from the *Windrush*, then there would be no 'problem' to which public attention could be drawn.[26] there was, however, particularly in the Colonial Office under Arthur Creech-Jones, a desire to challenge racism. This idealism does stand out in the otherwise rather uninspiring 'official mind' on questions of race in this period. In 1946, the Welfare Department of the CO had raised the question of confronting the attitudes of the British public by introducing anti-discriminatory legislation[27] and Creech-Jones himself had stressed that race prejudice was 'the one unforgiveable sin' for Colonial Office officials.[28] Thus, there were idealistic views within the Civil Service but they became subsumed by the pragmatism of other concerns and issues, as will be shown below.

The *Windrush*'s arrival was greeted with what appeared to be a clear-cut set of plans. Officials boarded the ship when it docked and collated information on the skills and requirements of its passengers. Arrangements were made for potential service recruits or rejoiners, for those with accommodation already arranged (free travel permits were issued to the destinations) and those without any clear-cut plans were allocated space in the Deep Shelter at Clapham, used during the war for air-raids and later to house prisoners-of-war.[29] The official verdict was that the plans worked very well. Others were less certain. Baron Baker, a Jamaican who joined the RAF during the war and who was active in voluntary work within the black community after 1945, offers a rather different view.

> At the time I was the only link between our people and the Colonial Office. I was told about the 'Windrush' by Major John Keith and so I went to see him. I asked him what preparations the Colonial Office was going to make for those people and he said none. So I suggested he use the Clapham Common Deep Shelter . . . We had a long discussion about the Deep Air Raid Shelter, and finally I told Major Keith (on 22nd June 1948) that I was going on board the 'Windrush' that night and if a telegram wasn't sent to me to say the shelter was open, then I would tell the passengers on the ship that not one person should disembark until I got that assurance.
>
> I went onto the ship late that night, and about half an hour afterwards I received the telegram. So it was not until the last moment that a decision was made to open the shelter.[30]

Whatever the internal difficulties, the final report on the operation issued by the Colonial Office in July 1948 was couched in self-congratulatory tones. It noted that the shelter had been 'evacuated' on 12 July, less than the three weeks' period granted by the War Office.[31] The manager and staff at the shelter had been pleased by the lack of incident and by the behaviour of the men placed there: by that time, only 17, it was claimed, had not been found employment. The conclusion was of a job well done. 'I think it can be said that a situation which contained complex social and other difficulties has been in the main resolved satisfactorily'.[32]

However, it is possible to take a more pessimistic view of the outcome of the 'operation', both in the short-term sense of its success in placing the West Indians in work and accommodation and in the more general implications for race and immigration policy in those years. First, more detailed reading of the Ministry of Labour records indicates the fragility of the employment situation. The initial division of the 492 was into three groups — volunteers for the armed services, those who had (or claimed to have) work and/or accommodation and those who were arriving without any definite plans. According to the initial screening of the complement, these categories numbered 52, 204 and 236 respectively. The first category were taken to London for interview, the second given travel warrants and arranged transport and the third taken to Clapham. It was only groups one and three who could be traced with any certainty. Of the initial 52 volunteers for the forces, it seems that only 18 were finally accepted for the RAF; as the final report puts it, a smaller number than was anticipated. Of the 236 housed at Clapham, there is evidence that many of those initially placed in jobs were soon to find difficulties. Much was made of the wide geographical and employment spread of the men from Clapham. Scotland, Wales, the Midlands, the West Country as well as the Home Counties featured in their relocation: jobs ranged from foundry work, agriculture, railways, building, painting and tailoring. The interim report, published at the end of June, was pleased with the response from regional offices of the Ministry of Labour: '. . . there are a number of really good employers in this country who are without prejudice and are prepared to give this colonial labour a trial'.[33] But a slightly longer-term perspective reveals a rather different situation. Those 15 sent to work on the land in Hampshire were 'useless and unwilling', according to the Ministry of Labour, and left after a very short period.[34] Bolton, whose immigrant community was frequently held up as an impressive example of integration, also experienced some difficulties. Six Jamaicans sent to work in a textile firm there found little satisfaction. Four left very soon after arrival and the other two the employer was said to be anxious to lose.[35] No concrete reasons are offered by the Ministry: from other sources, it seems that many of the Windrushers felt they had been misinformed (or not informed at all) about conditions of work, rates of pay, tax and insurance and on the cost of living. This caused discontent and some unemployment as more satisfactory jobs were sought. Twelve Windrushers sent to iron foundries in the Midlands left because they could not stand the heat of the furnaces, according to the local Ministry office.[36] Of the 15 sent to work in the Baglow Bay Tin Plate Works, near Neath, only five were left by September.[37] Again, no official explanation was offered for this particular occurrence but the Ministry files provide plenty of evidence of racism displayed by employers, unions and workers which led to blacks being refused work or leaving jobs after a short period of time.[38]

Of those who claimed independent sources of living and employment on arrival, eventually 237,[39] little or nothing definite is known. It was assumed that they settled into existing black communities or homes but the fear was that many had, in so doing, added to the 'colour problems' of places like Liverpool and Manchester. One ominous note was sounded by the Cardiff office of the Ministry of Labour: of 35 Jamaicans interviewed, none was found suitable for work in the iron and steel industry, the one sector of the local economy with suitable vacancies.[40] Overall, the final verdict on the success of the *Windrush* operation seems rather misplaced.

Indeed, a recently-published commemorative pamphlet, dealing with the feelings and attitudes of the Windrushers, gives a rather different perspective on the whole venture. 'Official' records tell us very little of their experiences or backgrounds and tend to assume that the overwhelming attractions of British society, the 'pull factor', were the dominant influence for each of the migrants.[41] The responses of the Windrushers to their treatment on arrival has been largely ignored. It seems that expressions of hostility in Parliament and in the press reached them en route.

> As we got closer to England there was great apprehension on the boat because we knew the authorities did not want us to land. I got two ex-RAF wireless operators to play dominoes outside the radio room on the ship so we could keep informed of the messages coming in.
>
> We heard on BBC News that if there was any disturbance on the immigrant ship, HMS Sheffield would be sent out to turn us back . . . We heard there was consternation in Parliament and that newspapers like the Daily Graphic and the Express were saying we should be turned back . . .
>
> On the boat there was sadness about this and there was a move by some activists to protest. But others of us said whatever happens we must show peace and love, nothing should be allowed to go wrong and nothing did go wrong.[42]

The attractions of Britain may not have been quite so overwhelming as is sometimes suggested. For some, Britain was originally intended as a transit point for moving on to the USA. Winston Findlater had worked on a farm there previously and intended moving with his wife, Lynette, to Connecticut 'but the children arrived and my wife fell ill, so we're still here'.[43] Perhaps there was not the naive vision of the 'Mother Country' as the perfect solution to problems at home and thus the experiences in Britain were less of a surprise than has been indicated.

Whatever the success or otherwise of the *Windrush* operation in the short term, there were also implications for future policy and attitudes towards blacks in British society. Despite the public statements about positive support for West Indian immigrants, the inter-departmental wrangling over the arrival of the *Windrush* and the responsibility for providing for its passengers revealed not only questions of Civil Service demarcation but also the negative responses towards migration on any significant scale. As Ness Edwards made clear: 'An important point to bear in mind in this connection is that we do not want to take any action with this shipload of Jamaicans which will encourage others to follow them'.[44]

This desire not to provide a welcome which would encourage others dominated many aspects of the official response to the Windrushers. In fact, a mythology about the success of the operation and its attraction for other West Indians became established. Thus, when news of the *Orbita*'s impending arrival was known, the explanation offered was that the previous landing 'has apparently encouraged others to try their luck in this country'.[45] And in December, when a further ship, the *Reina del Pacifico,* was due to dock in Liverpool from Jamaica, officials at the Ministry of Labour were anxious to change the pattern of previous support. While concerned to get the arrivals out of Liverpool, thus not adding to the 'problem' in the city, there was an interesting exchange of views about the merits or otherwise of issuing free travel warrants, as had been done with the *Windrush* and the *Orbita*. Initial plans for those from the *Reina del Pacifico* saw this as a vital part of the process.[46] A subsequent teleprinter message to Regional Office in Manchester from London said that the circumstances did not merit free travel. 'To do so in such a case would logically lead to giving free travelling facilities to every individual who might arrive'.[47] Although the original decision to provide free travel within Britain was eventually implemented, a note of caution (and an indication of policy formulation) was sounded: '. . . we cannot go on indefinitely giving these free travel facilities and unless there are special circumstances such facilities will not be granted in future'.[48]

Given the degree of pessimism expressed within official circles, it is interesting to look at the initial response at a local level to the arrival of the Windrushers. For the 200 or so who came to the Clapham Deep Shelter, there seems to have been little reaction. There were some welcoming ceremonies with local dignatories and sympathetic MPs but, since their stay was relatively short-lived, little else is recorded. There was a black presence in the area before the Windrushers arrived; complaints from West Indians about the raising of rents and over-crowding of rooms were heard at Southwark rent tribunal in June 1948[49] and there was a black community organization with voluntary workers who aided the settlement of the new arrivals.[50] However, coverage in the local press of the *Windrush* episode after the docking of the ship seems to have been minimal, certainly compared with later years,[51] and was not presented as the beginnings of large-scale migration and its possible problems. No doubt the relatively small numbers and the success of the government agencies in the fairly rapid dispersal of the men contributed to this. In addition, however, it may be relevant to consider the remarks of Nicholas Deakin in his study of 'race' in Stepney.

During these immediate post-war years, Stepney had a significant black community, which did lead to complaints from white groups in the area. In 1946, a Ministry of Health report noted the increasing number of black seamen in the locality and the dearth of hostel provision. The following year, there was a deputation to the local council about conditions in Cable Street, particularly with regard to allegations of inferior housing and prostitution.[52] Yet, as Deakin notes, although race relations was a 'constant feature of council agendas and debate in the columns of the local press', the 'context in which race relations were discussed was that of anti-Semitism'.[53] He offers several factors in explanation of this concentration: Jewish involvement in the powerful local post-war Communist Party, allegations of anti-Semitism in the local Labour Party and the 'tentative revival of prewar fascism'.[54] It was a conception of local race relations still defined very largely by the debates of the 1930s. This is not to say that there was no political discussion of the black presence, either in Stepney or elsewhere. The disturbances in Liverpool in 1948 and Deptford the following year produced significant comment.[55] However, the situation in Stepney offers an illustration of the need for more careful local studies. Tensions in Liverpool had a long history and it should not be automatically assumed that a 'modern' version of race was immediately imposed on the 'new' immigration. As with much of the post-1945 society, it owed a great deal to the pre-war years.

A similar situation appears to have been the case in South London. As already noted, the arrival of the Windrushers at Clapham received very little coverage in the local papers. The *South London Press* seems to have been the only journal to offer even factual coverage of the arrival and local reception.[56] What did take up much of the space on 'race' issues was the Union Movement and its local activities. Launched in February 1948, the organization had, by May, produced Home Office bans on political processions within much of London. Despite this, meetings and street demonstrations continued throughout the summer of 1948 and these produced a good deal of local confrontation. Organizations such as the Association of Jewish Ex-Servicemen (AJEX) and the 43 group confronted the Fascists on the streets and in public meetings. At Kennington Town Hall in January 1949, during a Union Movement meeting, tear gas was thrown into an audience of some 700 by anti-Fascists. Only in the municipal elections later in 1949, when 15 Union Movement candidates standing in various London constituencies polled less than 2,000 votes in total, did it seem that the threat of a Fascist revival was flagging. In fact, there is a lack of any significant study of the Union Movement during this period.[57] In South London, there was a good deal of street confrontation during June and July of 1948[58] in and around Lambeth and there were Union Movement candidates in the autumn local elections in the area.[59] There was organized political opposition and extensive debates and exchanges of letters in the local press.[60] Thus, it does seem that, at least in the initial evaluation of migration from the West Indies, potential opposition was muted by the concentration on Fascism and anti-Semitism. As Thurlow notes, it was not until 1951 that the Union Movement attacked the 'coloured invasion'.[61] Undoubtedly, prejudice and discrimination continued as they had done for many years. The findings of writers like Little, Richmond and Banton make this very clear.[62] Robert Kee's *Picture Post* article in 1949 on the 'Colour Bar' provides further evidence.[63] However, with some very obvious exceptions, the late 1940s did not see a major policization of the issue of West Indian immigration and settlement in Britain.

There is, of course, one sense in which the state did engage directly with the question of black immigration and labour. By promoting employment schemes for white European workers to fill existing labour shortages and by choosing to discourage, albeit in an informal manner, black workers from the Commonwealth, a clear set of preferences were displayed. Race may not have been the only issue here — limited contracts and strict conditions of employment could be used for European workers; no such limits could be placed on citizens from the Commonwealth. Even allowing for these differences, it is clear that a covert policy towards West Indian immigration was emerging. However, the politicization of those attitudes, in the sense of making them the object of open political debate,[64] was a longer and more laborious process. Other themes occupied more centrally the political stage.

Gupta has quite clearly indicated that the Labour governments of 1945–51, and the labour movement in general, were ambivalent in their approach to imperial commitments. 'A large body of opinion inside the movement was representative of "Little Englanders", who were preoccupied with social transformation at home and anxious to avoid military and political entanglements abroad'.[65] Similarly, he suggests that the electorate which had returned a Labour government in 1945 was concerned not with the colonies but with 'the creation of a welfare state: the maintenance of full employment, stable prices and social security'.[66] Kenneth Morgan, although perhaps more sympathetic to the achievements of the governments during these years, also notes the lack of priority towards colonial and Commonwealth affairs.[67] The summer of 1948 was a particularly busy one in terms of legislation and major political issues: May saw the ending of the British mandate in Palestine and an escalation of the conflict there; the beginnings of the London dock strike which led to the evocation of the Emergency Powers Act of 1920 — the first time since the General Strike of 1926. In July, there were two major challenges, the inauguration of the social security system, including the National Health Service, and the escalation of the Soviet blockade of Berlin.[68] The absence of any major discussion or analysis of the implications of the *Windrush*'s arrival, as noted above, is reflected in the almost non-existence of references in the autobiographies and biographies of the leading political figures of the day. Most standard texts on the period have little or no reference to the events of 1948.[69]

The explanation for this absence has, in part, been offered. To quote Michael Banton, writing in 1955, the government would not offer 'a facile solution to a complex problem'.[70] In addition, the political pressures and priorities lay elsewhere. The 'Little England' approach, a concentration on domestic change and a political outlook still conditioned by the pre-war years, must also be recognized. As Morgan has noted, 'the Attlee government does not emerge, on the whole, as a body of committed or instinctive radicals'.[71] Even the British Nationality Act of 1948, which is sometimes seen as a major turning point in the politicization of immigration and the methods of control, was essentially a confirmatory measure, re-stating the rights of colonial citizens. Decisions on immigration control were to come rather later.[72]

What emerges, ultimately, from an analysis of the *Windrush* episode, is a series of ambivalent positions. Above all, there was an official conviction, as Smith has shown, that any additional West Indian immigration would add to race 'problems' in British society.[73] On the other hand, there could be no public admission of this view, for fear of destroying Commonwealth relationships. There was no commitment to anti-discrimination legislation because received opinion was that it would be ineffective. Internal debate made it clear that control of immigration was, in the absence of a more thorough and complex policy, the only way to avoid difficulties. Publicly, this view could not be stated. Thus, immigration policy operated rather like nineteenth century imperialism. Wherever possible, and for as long as possible, informal control was the solution. When this failed, as it did by the 1950s, a more formal system was put into operation. The 'moral panics' of the 1950s ensured that this was the case. Thus, control of immigration was avoided in the *Windrush* years, at least in a overtly political fashion, but its basis was being constructed. What is still required is a more detailed study of the process of politicization. We know about the 'official mind'. Less clear is how a modern concept of 'race', one which now saw black immigration as the real 'problem', came to be the source of political expression, such as can be seen in Lambeth in 1951.[74] Until we have this more detailed knowledge, the generalizations about these early post-war years and the compression of the chronology will continue to dominate the standard works. Without such an analysis, we will remain unclear about the essential processes which led to the policization of 'race' in modern Britain.

KENNETH LUNN
Portsmouth Polytechnic

NOTES

I would like to thank Tony Kushner and Sybil Lunn for their constructive comments on an earlier draft of this article.

1. C. Holmes, *John Bull's Island: Immigration and British Society, 1871–1971* (London, 1988) p.220.
2. See, for example, A. Richmond, *Migration and Race Relations in an English City: A Study in Bristol* (London, 1973) p.27, which concentrates on the mid-1950s as the period in which 'concern' was expressed about West Indians in Britain.
3. D. Hiro, *Black British White British* (London, 1971) p.8.
4. Ibid., pp.9–10. See also N. Deakin, *Colour, Citizenship and British Society* (London, 1970) pp.44–5.
5. Z. Layton-Henry, *The Politics of Race in Britain* (London, 1984) p.20.
6. R. Miles and A Phizacklea, *White Man's Country* (London, 1984) pp.23–4.
7. Ibid., p.25.
8. S. Joshi and B. Carter, 'The role of Labour in the creation of a racist Britain', *Race and Class*, vol.XXV, no.3 (1984) pp.69–70.
9. See, for example, N. Evans, 'Regulating the Reserve Army: Arabs, Blacks and the Local State in Cardiff, 1919–45' in K. Lunn (ed.), *Race and Labour in Twentieth-Century Britain* (London, 1985) pp.68–115.
10. M. and A. Dummett, 'The role of Government in Britain's racial crisis' in C. Husband (ed.), *'Race' in Britain: Continuity and Change* (London, 1982) p.99.
11. Ibid.

12. Ibid.
13. A. Thomas, 'Racial discrimination and the Attlee government', *New Community*, vol.X (1982) p.273.
14. Ibid., pp.276–7.
15. E. Pilkington, *Beyond the Mother Country: West Indians and the Notting Hill White Riots* (London, 1988) p.33.
16. P. Rich, 'Blacks in Britain: Response + Reaction, 1945–1962', *History Today*, (January 1986) p.15. The most useful general accounts of 'official' discussions initiated by the *Windrush* are P. Rich, *Race and Empire in British Politics* (Cambridge, 1981); Pilkington, op. cit.; Joshi and Carter, op. cit.; D.W. Dean, 'Coping with colonial immigration, the Cold War and colonial policy: the Labour government and black communities in Great Britain, 1945–51', *Immigrants and Minorities*, vol.6, no.3 (November 1987), pp.305–33. M. Smith, 'The Ministry of Labour and National Service's Response to West Indian Immigration to Great Britain 1945–51', undergraduate dissertation (BA Hons), University of Southampton, 1989, is an impressive handling of these particular sources and offers some challenging views of racial attitudes in these years.
17. See internal memo, 5 June 1948, LAB 26/218 (Public Record Office).
18. Ibid.
19. See Joshi and Carter, op. cit., pp.58–60 for a summary of the discussions.
20. 5 June 1948, LAB 26/218.
21. See minutes of meeting at Ministry of Health, 15 June 1948, LAB 26/218.
22. Cited in Pilkington, op. cit., p.19.
23. Letter cited in Dean, op. cit., p.320.
24. 5 July 1948, cited in ibid., p.317.
25. *Evening News*, 17 June 1948.
26. Ministry of Labour circular to Regional Controllers, 19 June 1948, LAB 26/218.
27. See Dean, op. cit., pp.324–5.
28. See P.S. Gupta, *Imperialism and the British Labour Movement, 1914–1964* (London, 1975) p.311.
29. For details, see Joshi and Carter, op. cit., Dean, op. cit.,
30. 'Baron Baker: The Man Who Discovered Brixton' in Lambeth Council, *Forty Winters On* (1988) pp.17–18. Note, however, that War Office permission for Clapham appears to have been granted rather earlier (see minutes of meeting at Ministry of Health, 17 June 1948, LAB 26/218, which offered up to 350 places for three weeks).
31. Final Colonial Office report, 22 July 1948, LAB 26/218.
32. Ibid.
33. 30 June 1948, LAB 26/218.
34. Meeting of the Colonial Office Working Party on the Recruitment of West Indians for United Kingdom Industries, 27 Oct. 1948, LAB 26/226.
35. Report from North West Region, Ministry of Labour, 4 Nov. 1948, LAB 26/226.
36. Ministry of Labour regional conference re placing of 'Colonial Negroes', 20 Jan. 1949, Midlands report, LAB 26/226.
37. Report of Cardiff Office, Ministry of Labour, 29 Sept. 1948, LAB 8/1516.
38. For details, see Smith, op. cit., pp.9–15.
39. Memo from F. Hawkins, Regional Welfare Officer, 28 June 1948, LAB 8/1516.
40. See n.37.
41. For a summary of 'push' and 'pull' factors, see Holmes, op. cit., pp.220–1.
42. 'Sam King', in *Forty Winters On*, op. cit., p.8. The reference to 'activists' appears confirmed by a *Daily Worker* report that local Communist Party members had met the Windrushers and found a number of them to be socialists, members of Norman Manley's People's National Party (see Walter Holmes, 'Workers Notebook', *Daily Worker*, 29 June 1948).
43. 'Winston and Lynette Findlater', in *Forty Winters On*, op. cit., p.14.
44. Ness Edwards to Lord Listowel, 9 June 1948, LAB 26/218.
45. W. Hardman to F. Tarrant, North West Regional Office, 24 Sept. 1948, LAB 8/1516.
46. Memo to North West Regional Office, 16 Dec. 1948, LAB 8/1516.

47. W. Hardman to North West Regional Office, 16 Dec. 1948, LAB 8/1516.

48. Memo, 17 Dec. 1948, LAB 8/1516.

49. See *South London Observer*, 11 June 1948.

50. See 'Baron Baker', op. cit., pp.17–19.

51. See, for example, Jeffrey Green, *Leslie Thompson: An Autobiography* (Crawley, 1985) p.118.

52. N. Deakin, 'The Vitality of a Tradition', in C. Holmes (ed.), *Immigrants and Minorities in British Society* (London, 1978) pp.173–4.

53. Ibid., p.172.

54. Ibid., pp.172–3.

55. See, for example, the responses to the 1948 disturbances in Liverpool, as cited in P. Fryer, *Staying Power: The History of Black People in Britain* (London, 1984) pp.367–71.

56. See *South London Press*, 25 June 1948.

57. Brief details of Union Movement activities can be found in M. Walker, *The National Front* (London, 1977); R. Thurlow, *Fascism in Britain: A History, 1918–85* (Oxford, 1987); D.S. Lewis, *Illusions of Grandeur: Mosley, Fascism and British Society, 1931–81* (Manchester, 1987).

58. For details, see *South London Observer*, *South London Press* and *Battersea Boro' News* for these months. The *Daily Worker* also provides much information on the Union Movement and anti-Fascist activity in 1948.

59. *South London Observer*, 10 Sept. 1948.

60. See, for example, *South London Observer*, 11, 18 June 1948.

61. Thurlow, op. cit., p.246.

62. K. Little, *Negroes in Britain* (London, 1948); A. Richmond, *The Colour Problem — A Study of Racial Relations* (Harmondsworth, 1955); M. Banton, *The Coloured Quarter* (London, 1955).

63. *Picture Post*, 2 July 1949.

64. See Miles and Phizacklea, op. cit., pp.20–21.

65. Gupta, op. cit., p.346.

66. Ibid., p.283.

67. K. Morgan, *Labour in Power, 1945–51* (Oxford, 1984), p.231.

68. For details, see K. Harris, *Attlee* (London, 1982), pp.398, 422–3.

69. For example, neither H. Pelling, *The Labour Governments, 1945–51* (London, 1984) or K. Laybourn, *The Rise of Labour: The British Labour Party 1890–1979* (London, 1988) have any discussion of these issues.

70. Banton, op. cit., p.239.

71. Morgan, op. cit., p.56. This page contains the only reference in the volume to race and immigration in what is probably the major survey of the Labour governments in these years.

72. See N. Deakin, 'The British Nationality Act of 1948: A Brief Study of the Mythology of Race Relations', *Race*, vol.XI (1969), pp.77–83.

73. Smith, op. cit.

74. Banton, op. cit., pp.72–3, 239–40.

Race, the New Right and
State Policy in Britain

*Much has been written about the 'New Right' and 'new' racism.
However, it is apparent that the content of current emphases
ignores both the complexities of 'New Right' ideology and its
use of perspectives and attitudes from earlier periods. Indeed,
it appears that 'race' is not, at least in practical terms, a leading
feature of Thatcherite government and policy, despite certain
well-publicized instances and the rhetoric of critics of the 'New
Right'. Where there has been a clash of ideologies, it has been
more at the level of the local state, particularly in the area of
anti-racist strategies. It is argued that opposition to certain
of these strategies is aided by their inappropriateness for the
nature of British society in the late 1980s.*

Introduction

This article will attempt to do three things. In the first place, it will consider
whether or not the 1970s and 1980s have witnessed the emergence of a
distinctive form of New Right racist discourse in Britain. This issue is
complicated by the fact that the ideology of the 'New Right' is not itself
coherent but is a contradictory and unstable amalgam of ideas drawn from
the different traditions of social authoritarianism and market liberalism.
In the various discussions of the so-called new racism that have been
advanced in recent years, what is most striking is that only the ideas of
the social authoritarians have been used to demonstrate the centrality of
racism within New Right ideology. Any suggestions that there is some
kind of straightforward ideological 'fit' between the New Right and the
new racism is thus open to serious doubt. Further, the key elements of
social authoritarianism that are said to provide the foundations for the
new racism are not in themselves new but have had considerable currency
in the past. This is particularly true in the case of the elision of 'race',
'culture' and 'nation' that is usually identified as the cornerstone of new
racist discourse. It is therefore important to be more precise over exactly
what it is that is new about the new racism. The first section of this paper
concludes with an attempt to show that the specificity of the new racism
lies in its populist appeal and in the emphasis it gives to ideas of 'cultural
difference' and 'ethnic diversity'.

Second, the paper will examine the contention that the last two decades
have witnessed the progressive 'racialization' of British politics as race has
become a 'leading issue' within the ideology of Thatcherism. The problem
with this thesis is that it focuses only on the language and discourse of race
and thus fails to come to terms with the fact that, as with other strands of

Thatcherism, there is a gap between New Right rhetoric and the reality of New Right practice. In discussing the issue of race policy the article will identify two areas where the new racism has had a concrete impact, namely in the spheres of immigration policy and law and order/policing policy. More generally however the Government's responses to 'race problems' have been much more pragmatic in nature, as evidenced by the fact that the 'race relations industry' has continued to grow since 1979, much of it sponsored directly or indirectly by central government.

Third, the paper will argue that an adequate grasp of race policy must recognize that there are alternative sources of policy initiative within the state, apart from those originating from central government. In recent years there has been a growth both of professional anti-racism and of municipal anti-racism and the paper will illustrate these by drawing on examples from the spheres of education and social work. However, the popularization of the new racism via the media, together with the successful 'anti-anti-racism' campaigns mounted by some sections of the popular press, have served to undermine the legitimacy of such initiatives. In this sense therefore the impact of New Right ideology on race policy has been more negative than positive, since it has served more to curtail and undermine anti-racism than to foster the development of a distinctive set of New Right race policies. However, the paper will conclude by pointing towards some of the inherent weaknesses in the anti-racist initiatives themselves and will argue that the failure to secure a wider legitimacy for these initiatives cannot be laid wholly at the door of the New Right.

New Right? New Racism?

It has been argued that the last 20 years have witnessed the emergence of a distinctive form of New Right racist discourse in Britain.[1] However, the various discussions of the new racism have focused mainly on neo-conservative ideas to demonstrate the alleged centrality of racism within New Right ideology. Such race thinking represents only one of the two contradictory strands of thought within the New Right, which we will designate as social authoritarianism and market liberalism. The arguments of the market liberals are strikingly different from the racist chain of reasoning offered by the neo-conservative social authoritarians. However, in contrast to the situation in the United States, libertarian arguments have so far failed to make much of an impact in this country. Instead they have been submerged beneath a hotch-potch of neo-conservative ideas, most of which are not new but have had considerable currency in the past. This tendency is epitomized by key New Right race thinkers like Enoch Powell and Sir Alfred Sherman, who are on the liberal wing with respect to economic affairs while at the same time articulating neo-conservative views on race. Both have made important contributions to the melange of ideas said to constitute a 'new racism', which is notable more for its traditionalist conservatism and xenophobic nationalism than for any attempt to approach the race issue from the point of view either of the maintenance of individual liberty or of the expansion of the free market. In effect, these 'libertarians' become 'authoritarians' on matters of race.

Consequently it is to the writings of the authoritarian New Right that social scientists have turned in trying to piece together the discursive elements of the new racism. Three key sources are usually singled out as the primary definers of New Right thinking on race and racism. First, and most important, there are the speeches and writings of Enoch Powell who by common consent is identified as the founding father of the new racism and is its single most important political representative in the period since 1968. Second, there is the output of those writers associated with *The Salisbury Review*, the journal launched in 1982 by the so-called Peterhouse Group.[2] In the race field this group is best known for the work of individuals like Roger Scruton, Sir Alfred Sherman, John Casey, Peregrine Worsthorne, T.E. Utley and Charles Moore. To this mixed bunch of academics and journalists should be added the name of Ray Honeyford, the controversial Bradford headteacher whose sacking in the wake of his contributions to *The Salisbury Review* became a national *cause celebre*.

Third, there is a growing body of journalistic writing which in the 1980s has disseminated more widely New Right thinking within both the quality and tabloid sections of the British press. Increasingly, neo-conservative intellectuals have been invited to express their racial views within the columns of the press while at the same time newspaper columnists and editors have taken every opportunity to advance more and more strident opinions on race matters.[3]

It is noticeable that the speeches and writings of Mrs Thatcher and the members of her governments are quoted far less frequently by those concerned to identify the component parts of the new racism. It is also strikingly evident that relatively little attention has been given so far to the alternative neo-liberal arguments on race. Arguably this is because, to date, libertarian ideas have not been brought to bear on race issues in any kind of extended or systematic fashion. However, a limited number of contributions from within the liberal New Right tradition do offer some important points of comparison with the more authoritarian aspects of the new racism.[4] In considering these market-liberal contributions to contemporary New Right race discourse, it will be possible to identify their points of similarity and difference with the ideas of the social authoritarians.

The most obvious area of agreement between the two competing New Right perspectives lies in their mutual hostility to any attempt to outlaw prejudice and discrimination or indeed any form of benevolent state intervention designed to remedy racial inequality. However a different logic lies behind the involvement of each camp in a common front against 'the race relations industry'. For instance neo-conservative new racism resorts to instinctivist theories to explain why such state intervention cannot work. In a coded language which eschews supremacist propositions and deliberately avoids too much overt reference to race, the new racism intimates that native British people, like any other group, are naturally hostile to outsiders who do not share their way of life or their instinctive allegiance to the nation. Little can be done — other than by limiting or reducing the numbers of 'aliens in our midst' — to ease racial conflict, and abortive efforts to do so only further victimize native whites who suffer most from the harmful effects of multi-racialism. Neo-liberals add to this theme by suggesting that any attempt to outlaw racial discrimination through the use of coercive legislation, or indeed any form of anti-racist state intervention, will only cause further racial friction and thus worsen race relations.[5] However it is important to note that their neo-liberal convictions make some writers hostile not only to race relations legislation and other forms of state intervention against discrimination but also to the immigration laws. Nothing could be more profoundly anti-Powellite than Stephen Davies' contention that 'the immigration laws are racist both in concept and operation and violate personal liberty'.[6] So, while Powell and the new race conservatives focus in a mystical way on the need to preserve the cultural identity of the British nation, 'extreme' neo-liberalism denounces the very idea of treating individuals differently according to the group to which they belong. For this reason, market liberals are opposed to all forms of discrimination, whether this be expressed in the irrational form of individual prejudice against groups or through state-sponsored affirmative action programmes.

There is also some common ground between the contending New Right positions with respect to the emphasis each gives to the importance of cultural differences in the analysis of race issues. For Powellite new racism, cultural differences are profound and fundamental and cannot be eradicated through legal or administrative processes such as those entailed in the issuing of a British passport. It is claimed that black people can never be an authentic part of the British nation because of their lack of cultural roots in this country and their alien ways of life. Multi-culturalism is to be discouraged since it will inevitably lead to friction and conflict. Echoing in part these arguments, some neo-liberals take the view that it is indeed a basic truth that 'like prefers to be with like' and that people should therefore have the right to choose freely which cultural groups they wish to identify and associate with.[7] However neo-liberals tend to reject the idea that the cultural characteristics of ethnic groups are immutable since, given the opportunity and incentive, groups are capable of adapting their behaviour and attitudes. This argument has been advanced most notably by the black American social scientists, Thomas Sowell and Walter Williams, who both maintain that market processes are the most effective means of removing irrational discrimination and enabling disadvantaged ethnic groups to climb the economic ladder of success.[8] Sowell and Williams assume that it is the cultural traits of ethnic groups that account both for the level of their economic performance and the nature of the discrimination that they are likely to encounter. According to these writers, poverty among certain ethnic minorities is not a product of 'pure discrimination' but of cultural characteristics.[9]

They claim that ethnic groups — for example the Jews and the Chinese — with appropriate characteristics like entrepreneurship, hard work and thrift, have achieved economic success in the United States despite discrimination and racial hostility. Other groups, like the Irish, who were once culturally unsuited to the American urban environment, have managed to adapt and change to achieve integration. More important, they suggest that, if allowed to operate freely, market mechanisms are likely over time to reduce any 'incorrect' ethnic stereotyping by economic agents. Employers who make inappropriate assessments of a group's economic worth will lose out in the market to those employers who know better and are willing to buy their cheap labour; but as other employers become more aware of the true merits of a group its economic rewards will increase. Conversely a group that is unwilling or unable to adapt its cultural characteristics will continue to be poorly rewarded. Sowell and Williams argue that any state intervention in this process tends to be counter-productive since it undermines the capacity of market competition to determine whether ethnic stereotypes are 'correct' or not. Consequently, government interference in the shape of minimum wage legislation and affirmative action measures are deemed highly inappropriate since they remove exactly the kind of opportunities impoverished ethnic groups need in order to prove their economic worth.

Proper consideration of the neglected neo-liberal perspective on race thus suggests that any similarities between the two competing themes in New Right ideology are more apparent than real. On closer examination there appear to be at least three major differences between the social authoritarian and market liberal analyses of race. First, there is a major tension between the neo-conservative form of spiritual belief in a transcendent and exclusive form of British nationhood and the commitment of neo-liberalism to individual liberty irrespective of racial identity. Thus, while the law and order rhetoric of conservative nationalism has looked to 'strong state' remedies to deal with the problems presented by a riotous and disorderly black population, libertarian arguments have warned against mobilizing the coercive power of the state against racial minorities in an over-oppressive manner.[10] Second, there is a world of difference between the alacrity with which the social authoritarians impose the brutal choice of either 'repatriation' or 'compulsory incorporation' on minority black groups and the anxiety of neo-liberals to expand choice and freedom within a socially and culturally diverse society.[11] Such an ideological opposition has been particularly evident in recent controversies about the education of the black child, where outright rejection by the social authoritarians of multi-cultural education in favour of assimilationist schooling contrasts strongly with a neo-liberal advocacy of the education voucher scheme as a means of ensuring the responsiveness of schools to the wishes of ethnic minority parents.[12] Third, the neo-conservatives can be distinguished from their neo-liberal counterparts in terms of the authoritarian-populist nature of their racial discourse. An important hallmark of the new racism has undoubtedly been its readiness to mobilize public opinion by appealing to the 'common sense' and to the 'genuine fears' of the British people; above all, it is an ideological discourse which claims to represent the concerns and aspirations of white British society and culture. In contrast to the populist rhetoric of the neo-conservatives, neo-liberals have been more concerned to advocate the use of market forces to purge those irrational forms of economic discrimination and racial prejudice which may well be popular in society at large.

Given the lack of ideological fit between the two contradictory strands within New Right race thinking, there would seem to be a convincing case for rejecting the very idea of a coherent and distinctive form of New Right race discourse. All told, there can be few grounds for associating the much-discussed new racism with anything other than 'born again' conservatism of a rather old-fashioned, virulently authoritarian variety where national unity and social order are the paramount values. Furthermore, although the neo-liberal faith in the market as the panacea for curing racial ills may be misguided, their principled opposition to racism suggests that it is the market liberals who should be seen as more properly representing New Right thinking.[13] In contrast, the latter-day cultural nationalists appear to share much more in common with conservatives of an Old Right political persuasion. Nevertheless it has been the authoritarian conservatives who have made much of the recent running in policy debates about race. For the most part it has been 'their support for the compulsory incorporation of black people into the "British way or life", tougher "law and order" measures and, in the most extreme cases, "generous arrangements for repatriation"'[14] that seems to have captured the popular imagination, the attention of social scientists and the sympathetic ears of Mrs Thatcher and her ministers. However this should not be taken to imply that neo-liberalism can be dismissed on the grounds that it has played little or no role in contemporary race policy debates. Neither is there much evidence to suggest that these racist sentiments have been translated into a radically new Conservative race programme by the Thatcher governments.

Thatcherism and the Politics of Race

In recent years a number of commentators have presented race as a leading issue in the ideology of Thatcherism and the New Right. The rise of Thatcherism is seen to be inextricably bound up with the 'racialization' of British politics and with the successful promulgation of a popular ideological discourse whose core themes of national culture and identity are invariably linked to the language of race.[15] A major problem with this thesis is that it focuses too much on the language of race and nation and how they are articulated together in contemporary race politics. It has thus failed to come to terms with the fact that, as with other strands of Thatcherism, there is a gap between New Right rhetoric and the reality of New Right practice. An examination of the broad spectrum of the state's intervention on race in the 1980s suggests that to date a rational and coherent package of policies and practices with a clear Thatcherite imprint has yet to emerge. There has been no radical break with the past. Many of the actions taken since 1979 represent either a development and refinement of earlier policies or a pragmatic response to immediate problems and pressures rather than the implementation of a well-defined new Tory race strategy.

We insist, therefore, that the main dimensions of the state's current response to race-related problems and issues were already established when the Thatcher government took office. It is important to remember, of course, that throughout the 1960s and 1970s there had been a significant and steady shift to the right in British race politics. The populist New Right had scored its first major political success with Powell's repeated interventions on the race issue and the impact of these was such that by 1979 Powellite race thinking had become deeply embedded in key areas of state policy and practice (particularly in the areas of immigration control and the policing of black communities). Nevertheless, there are important areas of state activity which have not been penetrated in the same way by Powell's 'new racism'. Indeed, many of these areas have become the object of much vitriolic abuse and sustained opposition from Powell and his New Right allies, who have mounted a sustained attack on the Race Relations Acts, race Quangos like the Commission for Racial Equality and the local Community Relations Councils, the various local authority race initiatives that have developed in the last decade and also the new forms of multi-cultural and anti-racist professional practice that have evolved in education and social work. Since 1968 Powell's racial message has preached a pessimistic fatalism which has been wholly negative over the prospects for easing racial friction and eliminating racial discrimination. However, this antagonism towards strategies designed to achieve racial equality has, perhaps surprisingly, failed to surface so far in any serious attempt by the Thatcher government to dismantle or roll back the liberal integrationist side of the state's interventions on race. On the contrary, there is evidence that the much-criticized 'race relations industry' has continued to grow since 1979, much of it sponsored directly or indirectly by central government. For example, various central-government-financed special programmes inherited by the Thatcher administration (including the Urban Programme, a variety of Manpower Services Commission initiatives and s.11 of the Local Government Act, 1966) have not only been retained but have been increasingly used by some local authorities to fund special posts for work with ethnic minorities. Rather than rolling back race-related spending programmes like s.11, the Conservative governments have marginally increased its impact by widening the geographical areas and types of posts that can be funded under this provision.[16] In this way the Thatcher government has actually facilitated the creation by local authorities of the race relations advisers and special units so vehemently criticized by New Right intellectuals and the popular press.

The Tory government's pragmatic retention of established integration policies and race relations machinery can, in part, be explained by the problems and pressures it has faced on the race front. Like previous governments, its strategy has been significantly conditioned by the threat of racial conflict and disorder and there seems little doubt that the 1981 street uprisings played an important part in structuring the Government's response to the 'race problem'. While a tough law and order response and unconditional support for the police unquestionably prevailed in the aftermath of the riots, Scarmanite arguments and political pressure also made it extremely difficult to run down the 'race relations industry' or to oppose mainstream social policy aimed at securing 'good race relations' and racial harmony. In this context it has been impossible for the Government to translate anti-integrationist rhetoric into a concrete policy stance radically different from that established by previous administrations.

Instead the 1980s have been characterized by a sharper development of the two previously established dimensions of the state's response to race issues. On the one hand, the dominant strategy of the containment and control of Britain's black population has been dramatically extended and fashioned in new ways. On the other hand the decade of Thatcherism has witnessed a growth in integrationist policies and an upsurge of struggles for racial equality. It would be wrong, however, to counterpose these simply as opposed and competing strategies for dealing with 'race problems', since from the 1960s onwards liberal-reformist policies have been developed in part as a response to perceived problems of order and control. Inner-city policy and, more recently, multi-cultural education are good cases in point where the concern of policy makers has to some extent been to control and diffuse the resistance and dissent among black youth.

Nevertheless, it is important to realize that an adequate grasp of race policy must recognize that there are alternative sources of policy initiatives within the state apart from those originating from central government. In recent years important initiatives at the level of the local state have challenged the established patterns of state management in the area of race and in so doing have provoked a storm of right-wing opposition. It seems to us that together these initiatives form an important part of an overall pattern of continuity and change in race policy since the 1980s.

Continuity and Change in Race Policy and Provision

Since the early 1960s the dominant feature of state race policy has been the development by successive governments of tougher, racially discriminatory immigration controls. This institutionalization of racism in immigration law and practice has been increasingly accompanied by the deployment of formidable legal and administrative resources to monitor and control the daily lives of black people. In particular, the coercive policing of black communities now constitutes the cornerstone of the intensified state surveillance and control of Britain's black population. Like its predecessors, the Thatcher government has set the tone for its handling of race by intensifying still further the system of immigration controls. Beyond this, it has failed to provide any distinctive political direction in the area of race policy. Certainly there has been no real attempt to impose a radically different set of race policies from above. While various agencies of the state such as the police and the immigration authorities have been involved in a series of 'tightening-up' exercises in the area of race, this has not in the main been as a consequence of any centrally co-ordinated 'top down' racist strategy. One effect of such political non-decision making is that lower-level state agencies like the police have had considerable scope for the development of discretionary policy and practice in their own professional fields. The policing of black communities presents a spectacular example of this process with the development of police thinking on race and black crime being translated into new policing strategies and techniques in the main quite independently of any external political controls.

The Thatcher administration has to an important extent worked within the established conventional policy paradigm on race. This has always been marked by a distinct lack of any strong central political direction and control in the formulation and implementation of race policy in key areas of provision. One recurrent feature of this has been the loose, non-directive character of the limited central policy initiatives that have been produced.[17] In particular, much has been deliberately left to the discretion of local authorities, who must decide whether and in what ways to avail themselves of the possible opportunities made by central government provision. For example, s.71 of the 1976 Race Relations Act requires local authorities to pursue an equal opportunities programme and s.37 makes it possible for local organizations to take positive action to compensate for racial inequalities. However, the degree of autonomy given to local authorities in shaping their responses to such legislation has led to the development of significant variations between local authorities and even between departments within the same authority.[18]

Another important feature of central government policy initiatives has been the 'deracialized' way in which these have been presented and implemented. There has been a long-running concern to avoid policies that specifically address the problem of disadvantage or that may be seen to be of benefit to ethnic minorities. This has most obviously been the case with inner-city policies, which have traditionally avoided offering particular benefits exclusively to black communities living in areas of 'special need'. Instead, these communities are only able to benefit in a limited and indirect way from the allocation of resources to their urban area as a whole. This, too, subordinates ethnic minority interests to the discretionary power of local authorities who are able to decide the way in which central government grants are actually used.[19]

Thus, although race now has a higher profile in British politics — and certainly in the popular press — it has continued to occupy a marginal position on the central government policy-making agenda. It appears that some elements remain of the 'nervous neglect' of race, characteristic of all previous post-war British governments. Nevertheless, important changes in state policy and practice have taken place. In the main, these changes have come from two distinct but overlapping sources. First, various professional groups such as teachers, social workers and police officers working within the state system have been important agents of innovation. One notable feature of this process has been the degree of discretion and collective autonomy they have had in shaping their own professional practice in race-related matters. As a result, deep-rooted professional values that had encouraged the adoption of colour-blind, universalist approaches to working with black 'clients' have been challenged from inside the professions themselves by more racially explicit professional beliefs and practices. However, the resulting expansion of professionally-initiated, multi-cultural and anti-racist strategies has opened up the state professions to an intensified level of political scrutiny and ideological opposition.[20] Second, we need to take account of those local authority race initiatives which have, in the main, emerged since Thatcher took office. There are a number of reasons underlying the initiation of new race policies and programmes by local authorities. First, the riots of 1981 catapulted the issue of anti-racism onto the local political agenda, especially in urban areas with relatively large black populations. In particular the riots and to some extent the subsequent Scarman Report pushed a number of the new Labour local authorities, elected in 1981, towards an examination of their own institutional structures and organizational practices. Second, the size and voting strength of their black electorates prompted some local authorities — not always those in 'safe' Labour areas or with left-wing sympathies — into new initiatives.[21] Third, political shifts within the Labour Party have been important in stimulating change. Certain sections of the 'new urban left' in the Labour Party have come to identify ethnic minorities as a natural part of Labour's new constituency while, more importantly, black councillors have entered local government via the Labour Party in increasing numbers. Finally, growing pressure from local black activists and community organizations has also been important in drawing attention to the racist nature both of the local political process and of service provision in the black community.

In its response to these pressures, municipal anti-racism has proved to be highly controversial and, to date, its concrete effects have been confined to a limited number of local authorities.[22] The content of municipal anti-racism has also varied between local authorities. However, it should be pointed out that many councils have, in effect, taken up and exploited opportunities provided by existing race relations legislation and central government funding. Most versions of municipal anti-racism have involved some combination of the following: an equal opportunities policy for staff within the local authority together with a positive action programme for its implementation; anti-racist or racism awareness training for staff; the appointment of special race advisers;

race relations committees of elected councillors; racial monitoring and ethnic record-keeping procedures; consultative arrangements with local black community groups; grant-aid to ethnic groups and self-help organizations; and advertising campaigns and publicity programmes such as the GLC's anti-racist campaign in 1984.[23]

Where it has developed, municipal anti-racism has been designed to affect the professional practice of local state employees. However, in our view it would be inaccurate to link municipal anti-racism too closely with the various new forms of racially-explicit professional practice. For one thing, the ideas that inform professionals' practices are disseminated more widely on a national basis within their own professional communities. This has meant that race initiatives in teaching and social work have not been confined to those local authorities that have pioneered municipal anti-racism. Perhaps more important, the racially explicit modes of professional practice in question pre-date municipal anti-racism and have included multi-culturalist as well as anti-racist philosophies. Although there is a tendency in New Right quarters to collapse together these two professional orientations to race work, it is important to recognize that often in reality they are opposed and different. Multi-cultural approaches tend to emphasize the importance of the self-identity, ethnic culture and family background of the client or pupil. Anti-racists focus more sharply on racism itself and its institutional forms. Anti-racists, therefore, support policies designed to change institutions rather than pupils or clients.[24] Professional anti-racism seeks to root out racist ideas and practices within professional organizations themselves and to change the content and method of professional work.

However, professional anti-racism of this kind is by no means typical within the caring professions. In fact, both teachers and social workers have in the past subscribed strongly to colour-blind, assimilationist ideologies and still today within both fields these ideologies are mobilized to justify inaction on race-related issues. Nevertheless, policy debates and changed practices have emerged within both areas. For social work, the development of new policies for working with ethnic minorities emerged slowly and after 'a long period of inertia'.[25] Furthermore, new 'racially-aware' social work practice has over-emphasized culturally-based explanations of behaviour which can sometimes be infected with insidious racist overtones. Although this cultural emphasis has been challenged within social services departments and social work education, the issue of ethnic culture remains central to contemporary policy debates in social work.

In large measure, the effective politicization of this issue within the social work profession since 1983 has resulted from the interventions of organized black social workers. It was the Association of Black Social Workers and Allied Professionals (ABSWAP) that made the running in the most highly-publicized areas of social work policy debate in recent times, the issue of 'transracial' adoption and fostering. The controversial case put by ABSWAP insists that black children must be placed exclusively with black families in order to avoid the pitfalls of identity confusion and poor self-concept suffered by black children fostered or adopted by white families. This stress on the primary importance of building a positive cultural and racial identity in clients replicates the multiculturalist approach in education, with its emphasis on the importance of incorporating elements of ethnic culture into the school curriculum in order to give the black child a more positive self-image. It should be noted that this approach to the education of the black child has also been subjected to much criticism and political opposition, not only from right-wing sources but also from within the black communities and from black academics.[26] We do not intend to go into this debate here. Instead we wish to make the point that, within the various debates and struggles over the formulation, initiation and implementation of anti-racist policies and practices in the areas of education and social work, the issue of ethnic cultures and their role in 'good race practice' is crucial and far from settled.

We have no doubt that local political struggles and internal professional conflict over which policy best represents 'black interests' have been the most important sources of change in race policy in the 1980s. They have gone some way to redress the long-standing 'underdevelopment of British race-related policies' in a period when central government has broadly favoured a policy stance of relative inaction and inexplicitness on race.[27] In this sense, local state initiatives have created a partial 'racialization' of policy.[28] Far more Social Services Departments and LEAs now take an overt stance on race and more local authority provision is targeted at the specific needs of black communities. At the same time considerable resistance and opposition has been expressed towards such race initiatives, most notably in the popular press, which has mounted a strident campaign against all forms of anti-racism and multi-culturalism. It is through this effective populist onslaught against anti-racism that the ideology of the New Right can be seen to be making an impact in the contemporary politics of race.

The New Right Offensive Against Anti-Racism

The ideological campaign mounted by the populist right in the area of race has taken a distinctively new turn in the 1980s. One vital change has been the widespread dissemination of new right race-thinking within both the quality and tabloid sections of the British press.[29] New Right intellectuals have increasingly been invited to express their views within the columns of the press while at the same time race reporting in the post-1981 period has become more infected by the concerns and preoccupations of the new racism. This amplification and popularization of Powellite themes has affected race policy in at least two significant ways. First, media coverage of the 1981 and 1985 riots, in conjunction with the sensationalist coverage of 'street crime', has helped to set the agenda for subsequent policy debates over the policing of black communities.[30] In its reporting of riots and inner-city crime problems, the press has had an important effect on policing policy, particularly in terms of 'normalizing' the new styles of policing and legitimating paramilitarism as a justifiable response to the exceptional problems presented by disorderly black populations. Second, the new right popular press onslaught against anti-racism has worked to undermine the legitimacy of these anti-racist initiatives themselves by presenting them as being at one and the same time both ridiculous and menacing.

The growth of explicit anti-racist policy has sparked off a spiralling press counter-offensive which has been paralleled in recent contributions from New Right intellectuals.[31] Taking these different interlocking sources together, we believe that the ideological assault on anti-racism has three features that are critically attuned to the rhetoric of the new racism. First, it is the anti-racists who are said to be the real racists while the white majority are presented as the oppressed victims of these anti-racist policies. The claim that white pupils were being seriously disadvantaged at school was of crucial significance in the Honeyford affair which did so much to advance New Right arguments in the educational debate over multiculturalism and anti-racism. However, as such this is not a new argument. Rather it is one that is fundamentally compatible with the long-standing Powellite distaste with the idea of according any special treatment to 'immigrant minorities'. Indeed it can be said to play on a well-established official nervousness about white resentment towards initiatives that are specifically directed towards the needs of ethnic minorities.[32] Second, the 'anti-anti-racism' campaign has presented anti-racists as intolerant extremists and 'race fanatics', hell-bent on undermining the British way of life. Honeyford's tolerant reasonableness was counterposed to the totalitarian impulse that lay behind his personal 'multi-ethnic nightmare of intolerance'.[33] The implication here is that anti-racist 'witch-hunts' are alien to the British tradition of tolerance and moderacy. Third, the new right counter-attack on anti-racism has typically been expressed not in overt racial terms but in the familiar and more 'acceptable' language of national identity and cultural difference. The destructive effects of the dilution of British culture has been the clarion call in the fight against multiculturalism and anti-racism and contained within this has been a renewed attack on black culture and the pathology of black family life.[34]

The ideological project of the New Right offensive has clearly been to roll back even those tentative and limited advances that have been made in the development of anti-racist policy and practice. More expediently, the issue has been identified as a potential vote winner for the Tory Party as anti-racism is fast becoming 'by definition an ideological neurosis of the extreme "loony left"'.[35] In the face of this situation the leadership of the Labour Party has shown that it is unwilling to nail its anti-racist colours to the mast. Instead Labour's new realism is likely at best to favour the least offensive and most traditional forms of multicultural policy. As a result it is now increasingly likely that anti-racism will be shuffled to the bottom of the political agenda in the majority of local authorities, whether Labour or Conservative controlled. In its place, such race initiatives that surface are likely to be formulated, implemented and legitimated in 'culturalist' terms.

Conclusion

An adequate assessment of the recent history of anti-racism in Britain must recognize that the reversals and set-backs that have occurred are not entirely due to the political and ideological potency of the new right. The discussion has emphasized the ways in which 'populist racism' has been successful in mobilizing sections of the population against anti-racism through an appeal to a sense of 'belongingness' and 'nationhood'. Yet this should not blind us to some of the problems inherent in many of the anti-racist strategies themselves and we shall conclude with a brief consideration of four key problems that in our view must be confronted before it will possible to make further advances on the anti-racist front.[36]

First, it must be recognized that it is easier to be anti-racist in theory than it is in practice. Translating a broad set of anti-racist principles into detailed anti-racist policies and practices is a complicated process and there are many areas of genuine uncertainty where it is often difficult to 'know' in particular cases what anti-racism actually means.

Second, we must recognize that both professional and municipal anti-racism have tended to adopt an elitist 'top-down' approach on the assumption that 'you *will* take your medicine because *we* know what is best for you'. However the New Right have shown how important it is to mobilize public opinion in the prosecution of a cause and, though it would be naive to underestimate the problems involved, especially given the hostility of the popular press, nevertheless in their different ways Rock Against Racism and the GLC have shown that anti-racism can be fun! More important, these populist forms of anti-racist activity can help to create a wider legitimacy within which the 'serious' work of equal opportunities or anti-racist education can flourish.

Third, it is necessary to engage in a root-and-branch rethink over the question of the place of culture within anti-racist programmes. In the past it seems to us that there has been a tendency to treat the category of culture in an unproblematic and ahistorical way. As a result, cultures have appeared to be frozen in time rather than living and changing entities. It is also necessary — discomforting — to recognize that in many respects those who call for anti-racist policies and programmes based upon forms of ethnic/cultural absolutism are mirroring precisely the cultural determinism of their New Right opponents.[37]

Fourth, and following from the previous point, it is important to recognize that within black communities there are a diverse range of interests that may not necessarily be in agreement over what the priorities of an anti-racist strategy ought to be. The emergence in recent years of an independent black feminist movement for example, or the steady expansion of the Asian business class, are developments that must be reflected in political debate and discussion if anti-racist strategies are to command the broad support of those whose needs they are designed to meet.

MARK MITCHELL and
DAVE RUSSELL
Portsmouth Polytechnic

NOTES

1. See for example: M. Barker, *The New Racism* (London, 1981); Centre for Contemporary Cultural Studies, *The Empire Strikes Back* (London, 1982); P. Gordon and F. Klug, *New Right, New Racism* (London, 1986).
2. The Peterhouse Group derives its name from the fact that its members are associated in one way or another with Peterhouse College, Cambridge.
3. A discussion of this trend is given in N. Murray, 'Anti-Racists and Other Demons: The Press and Ideology in Thatcher's Britain', *Race and Class*, vol.XXVII (1986) pp.1–19.
4. In Britain, these contributions are to be found mainly in the publications of the libertarian Institute of Economic Affairs, especially in its journal *Economic Affairs*. A brief discussion of the market-liberal view of racial inequality is to be found in A. Seldon (ed), *The 'New Right' Enlightenment* (Sevenoaks, 1985) and in D. Graham and P. Clarke, *The New Enlightment: The Rebirth of Liberalism* (London, 1986) which accompanied the Channel Four television series of the same name.
5. See for example M. Daljord, 'American Second–Generation Immigrant' in Seldon, op. cit., p.218.
6. S. Davies, 'Sources and Origins', in Seldon, op. cit., p.29.
7. See Daljord, op. cit.
8. See T. Sowell, *Markets and Minorities* (Oxford, 1981); W. Williams, *The State Against Blacks* (New York, 1982). A brief summary of the arguments of Sowell and Williams is given in J. Majewski, 'The Economics of Race and Discrimination', *Economic Affairs* (Feb./Mar. 1988) pp.23–9.
9. Economically this theoretical approach distinguishes between two types of discrimination. Pure discrimination involves the straightforward expression of likes and dislikes. However, since markets make people pay for expressing such preferences, the higher the cost of pure discrimination, the less it will be practiced. Perceptual discrimination involves stereotyping ethnic groups on the basis of certain perceived cultural characteristics which employers may well use as a cost-effective means of searching for suitable workers. See Majewski, op. cit.
10. This point is made explicitly by N. Ashford, 'The Bankruptcy of Collectivism', in Seldon, op. cit., pp.33–4.
11. Peregrine Worsthorne has advocated that the 'immigrant population' that remains in Britain should be subjected to a process of 'compulsory incorporation'. See Gordon and Klug, op. cit., pp.32–3.
12. This case is argued strongly by R. Homan, 'Ethnic Minorities Reject the Remote State', *Economic Affairs* (April/May 1986) pp.26–9.
13. This point has been made to us in private correspondence by Peter Saunders.
14. Gordon and Klug, op. cit., p.43.
15. This argument is most cogently made in P. Gilroy, *There Ain't No Black in the Union Jack* (London, 1987), pp.44–59. See also Centre for Contemporary Cultural Studies, op. cit., pp.15–36; and Barker, op. cit., pp.12–47.
16. See G. Ben-Tovim, J. Gabriel, I. Law and K. Stredder, *The Local Politics of Race* (London, 1986).
17. Ibid.
18. Ibid., p.143.

19. Ibid. See also C. Husband, 'Racism, Prejudice and Social Policy' in V. Coombe and A. Little (eds.), *Race and Social Work* (London, 1986) pp.3–13 and K. Young, 'Ethnic Pluralism and the Policy Agenda in Britain' in N. Glazer and K. Young (eds.), *Ethnic Pluralism and Public Policy* (London, 1983) pp.287–300.
20. This process has gone much further in the teaching profession than elsewhere.
21. See B. Troyna and J. Williams, *Racism, Education and the State* (London, 1986) and H. Ouseley, 'Local Authority Race Initiatives' in M. Boddy and C. Fudge (eds.) *Local Socialism?* (London, 1984) pp.133–56.
22. The term municipal anti-racism is taken from Gilroy, op. cit. pp.136–48.
23. See Ouseley, op. cit. for a discussion of these municipal anti-racist initiatives.
24. The implications of this distinction between multiculturalism and anti-racism are discussed in Troyna and Williams, op. cit.
25. Husband, op. cit. p.11.
26. See for example M. Stone, *The Education of the Black Child* (London, 1981); H. Carby, 'Schooling in Babylon' in Centre for Contemporary Cultural Studies, op. cit. pp.183–211; and F. Dhondy, B. Beese and L. Hassan, *The Black Explosion in British Schools* (London, 1982).
27. Young, op. cit., p.296.
28. Troyna and Williams, op. cit.
29. See Murray, op. cit.
30. G. Murdock, 'Reporting the Riots: Images and Impact' in J. Benyon, *Scarman and After* (London, 1983), pp.73–95.
31. See in particular the essays in F. Palmer (ed.), *Anti-Racism: an Assault on Education and Value* (London, 1986).
32. See Husband, op. cit.
33. The quotation is taken from the headline of an article by Honeyford, published in *The Guardian*, 21 June 1985, p.18.
34. The terms 'multiculturalism' and 'anti-racism' tend to be used interchangably in New Right discourse.
35. Husband, op. cit. p.12.
36. A more detailed critique of the anti-racist strategies pursued by some sections of the new urban left is developed in M. Mitchell and D. Russell, 'Race and Racism' in P. Brown and R. Sparks, (eds.), *Beyond Thatcherism* (Milton Keynes, 1989) pp.62–77.
37. This argument is advanced by Gilroy, op. cit., pp.64–8.

INDEX